it is ...
... the 6 teachers & to leave 25 co...
... as reque... ... Mrs Cheney &
... The former ... Infant Asylu...
... of the Corp... ... expressly ...
take any office in it) now Mrs Cheney
one of the directors. I said I did not
acquaintance with the subject, or exp...
said none had; we were to learn
I thought it was better not to have
... She said the Institution w...
Roxbury; they were now treating for
... They hoped the Roxbury ladies
... in it. They did not mean to c...
Directors at present, but only some ...
felt sure. They have asked Mrs Sar...
... Ellis from Roxbury, Lilian Clarke, ...
... Hooper Brookline. Mrs Cheney is ...
... reason did not consent to be a ...
... will help by advice &c. I still declin...
... been thinking since whether I ought
... it to be so near us where I could ...
... It is a sort of thing I dread ...
many nice moral & prudential que...
... women whose babies are taken in ...
... I to shrink from taking my sha...
...culties! We shall make blunders
blamed for it, but we must buy our ex...

PITY *for* EVIL

MONICA KLEM &
MADELEINE MCDOWELL

PITY *for* EVIL

SUFFRAGE, ABORTION & WOMEN'S EMPOWERMENT IN RECONSTRUCTION AMERICA

ENCOUNTER BOOKS NEW YORK · LONDON

First American edition published in 2023 by Encounter Books, an activity of Encounter for Culture and Education, Inc., a nonprofit, tax-exempt corporation.
Encounter Books website address: www.encounterbooks.com

Manufactured in the United States and printed on acid-free paper. The paper used in this publication meets the minimum requirements of ANSI/NISO Z39.48–1992 (R 1997) (*Permanence of Paper*).

FIRST AMERICAN EDITION

LIBRARY OF CONGRESS CATALOGING-IN-PUBLICATION DATA IS AVAILABLE

Names: Klem, Monica, 1987- author. | McDowell, Madeleine, 1990- author.
Title: Pity for evil : suffrage, abortion, and women's empowerment in reconstruction america / Monica Klem & Madeleine McDowell.
Description: First Edition. | New York : Encounter Books, 2023
Includes bibliographical references and index.
Identifiers: LCCN 2023029097 (print) | LCCN 2023029098 (ebook)
ISBN 9781641773393 (hardcover) | ISBN 9781641773409 (ebook)
Subjects: LCSH: Women's rights—United States—History.
Abortion—United States—History.
Classification: LCC HQ1236.5.U6 K565 2023 (print) | LCC HQ1236.5.U6 (ebook) | DDC 323.3/40973--dc23/eng/20230814
LC record available at https://lccn.loc.gov/2023029097
LC ebook record available at https://lccn.loc.gov/2023029098.

The women described in this book were not,
by and large, widely known personalities even during
their own lifetimes—yet they quietly devoted their lives
to supporting vulnerable women and their children.
To the women doing the same in our own time,
this book is dedicated.

CONTENTS

THE MEDICALIZATION OF WOMEN'S REPRODUCTIVE LIVES

The modern American woman can determine whether she is pregnant within about two weeks of ovulation with a simple hCG test. She can chart her pregnancy with any number of mobile apps. Her health, and that of her child, is carefully monitored by a bevy of medical professionals. Even should she decide to give birth outside of a hospital, modern medicine and technology will inform her pregnancy and birth experience. Meanwhile, technologies of the state match the technologies of medicine. Births and miscarriages (after twenty weeks gestation) are registered, statistics collected, doctors licensed, and medical centers subjected to inspection. In the nineteenth century, however, these technologies were either in their infancy or did not exist. Statistics related to childbearing were incomplete and inconsistently collected and maintained. Relatively few women saw a licensed doctor about their pregnancy, and if they did, that doctor could tell them little to nothing before the second trimester.

Lack of professional medical involvement similarly figured heavily into debates about the legal dealings surrounding abortions. Although undoubtedly some licensed doctors performed abortions, the profession's public stance was vehemently opposed.

Early anti-abortion legislation allowed medical societies the right to revoke the licenses of doctors involved in abortions that were not medically necessary and to discredit as quacks nonprofessionals who performed abortions. Precisely this distance, however, between professional medicine and abortion could make abortions challenging to prosecute.

Convictions of mothers for abortion and infanticide were incredibly rare in the English-speaking world, even when the evidence was quite strong. When a conviction was secured, women frequently received minimal sentences or clemency. Some scholars have suggested that this systematic leniency came out of an approval of infanticide as a means of family limitation. However, legal tolerance for infanticide had less to do with moral ambiguity than it did with the difficulty of doing justice within the legal system. Some did believe that one was less culpable for killing an infant or a fetus than an adult, either because such young victims were less capable of physical pain than adults or because they would not suffer from any awareness of being killed. Still others believed that the death of an infant had a small social cost compared to that of an adult who played a role in either the family or market economy. At the same time, late-term abortions were very frequently considered morally equivalent to infanticide. Indeed, popular discourse understood abortion, infanticide, and abandonment as fundamentally similar acts—they were all attempts to rid oneself of an unwanted child.[1] Accordingly, society evaluated them with similar sets of assumptions about guilt and causation. The advent of children's rights discourses condemned all of them.[2]

Although the law distinguished between abortion and infanticide, the latter being the worse crime, there was sometimes no reliable way to distinguish between late-term induced abortion and infanticide. Without medical involvement, definitive evidence was hard to come by. Many abortions, even late-term abortions performed "with instruments," worked by causing a woman to go into premature labor and did not necessarily involve directly killing the fetus in utero. Therefore, the body of the woman, not just that of the fetus, might have to be examined for proof of an abortion. More sophisticated methods of abortion existed, but their use was largely restricted to trained doctors. To complicate matters further, as the anti-abortion campaigner Dr. Horatio Storer pointed out, one might mistake injuries from an abortion for scars from a difficult birth that involved, for instance, the use of forceps. Even if a woman's body provided clear evidence of an abortion, the likelihood that an examination for the purposes of gathering evidence would be made was slim, unless she was dead or dying.[3] This, in turn, reinforced an image of women as victims of abortion rather than its perpetrators. A doctor might be called to attend a woman suffering complications from an abortion, but the scandal attendant on revealing an abortion no doubt limited even those cases. All these factors worked to create a situation in which one of the only ways to secure a conviction of an abortionist was with the testimony of the woman. If a woman's testimony, and therefore her cooperation, were needed, she was unlikely to face prosecution.

Similarly, attempting to prosecute infanticide ran up against the problem that there was often no sure way to distinguish a stillbirth from natural causes, a premature delivery that a child did not long survive, accidental death of an infant, some other natural death of an infant, and neonaticide.[4] Women accused of infanticide were very rarely women for whom doctors played any role in their pregnancy or labor. A great many were poor women who gave birth alone.[5] The lack of witnesses, let alone a witness with professional standing, made it incredibly difficult to determine what happened. Legal changes in the late eighteenth and early nineteenth centuries in many places required prosecutors to prove that an infant had been born alive and intentionally killed in order to secure an infanticide conviction. It is not surprising that juries were frequently unwilling to convict women. There was too much reasonable doubt.

Ambiguity about whether abortion or infanticide occurred toward the end of a pregnancy was matched by even greater ambiguity about events early in pregnancy. Historians believe that far more abortions were attempted early in pregnancy, and until the later decades of the nineteenth century, common law rarely considered abortion previous to "quickening" a crime. Quickening referred to the moment when a mother could feel the movement of the fetus, usually occurring around the fourth or fifth month of pregnancy. While some traditions associated that movement with ensoulment, by the mid-nineteenth century, scientific, if not common, knowledge concluded that quickening had no medical significance. It signified not the start of human life, which scientific advances by then had shown to begin at the fusion of egg and sperm, but simply the subjective feeling of the mother. However, previous to quickening, there was no certain way to know that a woman was pregnant unless a doctor looked for a fetal heartbeat. But even a heartbeat would have been difficult to detect with a stethoscope before the second trimester.

A woman in the early months of pregnancy might have very substantial reasons to suspect that she was pregnant, but amenorrhea alone was not proof. Consider this bit of correspondence from 1864:

> Now, Mother I want to talk privately. How soon shall I know for certain? Do you really think it all means baby?

> When will he begin to let me know that he is there? Everything is just as still as a mouse. I sometimes have a slight nausea or a little dizzy turn—but that is about all that looks suspicious—except of course the non-appearance of a certain periodical event. Do you feel certain that you are to be a Grandmother? That's what I want to know. Burn this sheet.[6]

If a woman took some substance purported to be an abortifacient and her amenorrhea ceased, that was not definitive evidence that whatever she took caused an abortion. Scientists now estimate that around 15 percent of pregnancies in women under thirty-five end in miscarriage and these most often happen early in pregnancy. The most frequent cause is chromosomal abnormalities. Therefore, even if a woman miscarried after having taken a purported abortifacient, that would not necessarily prove that the miscarriage was artificially induced. In short, previous to quickening, it would be quite challenging to prove that a woman had been pregnant, had known that she was pregnant, and had caused the end of her pregnancy.

Modern medicine has made women's reproductive lives legible to the law. Pregnancies, whether they end in birth, miscarriage, or abortion, are now usually heavily medicalized. Should some aspect come before the court, modern medicine has made it far more likely that the facts of the case could be established beyond a reasonable doubt. On the one hand, this legibility means that the state can exercise far more control over reproduction if it so chooses. On the other hand, that knowledge also makes women's bodies far more legible to themselves as well.

'INVESTIGATORS OF WOMEN'S DUTIES'

In the years immediately following the American Civil War, women all over the United States gained the right to own and manage property and began slowly to acquire other legal rights. In 1868, despite the burgeoning split in the women's movement over the passage of the Fourteenth Amendment, women in New York and Boston created the first major women's clubs in the United States. Susan B. Anthony founded both *The Revolution* and the New York Workingwomen's Association. Caroline Dall published *The College, the Market, and the Court.* Nearly two hundred New Jersey women cast ballots in a statewide election. Anthony told Anna Dickinson that to "agitate our demand" of women's rights was "the great need now."[1]

Only seven years earlier, at the outset of the Civil War, Anthony had described slavery as "the question of all questions that is now agitating our entire country."[2] She, like nearly all of the major leaders of the early women's rights movement, had been a Garrisonian abolitionist.[3] For these radical abolitionists, a revolution in public sentiment was a prerequisite for substantive social change, especially in law and policy.[4] Agitating—and educating—public sentiment was a key means of accomplishing this shift.[5] "We do not look to prohibitory laws to do the work" of doing away with "war, violence, crime, intemperance, the gallows, our present system of prisons and punishment," Elizabeth Cady Stanton wrote.[6] The early women's rights advocates understood, with Lincoln, that "he who moulds [sic] public sentiment, goes deeper than he who enacts statutes or pronounces decisions. He makes statutes and decisions possible or impossible to be executed."[7] Like other nineteenth-century activists, both the early anti-abortion movement and the early women's rights campaign "relied as much on moral suasion and public education as they did on coercion and law enforcement."[8]

The agitation of early women's rights advocates had taken place on lecture stages and in the pages of women's publications, in small towns and big cities, at times across the United States although often centered in the Northeast. Amelia Bloomer founded *The Lily* in 1849, and Paulina Wright Davis started *The Una* in 1853. In the years leading up to the Civil War, Caroline Dall, Elizabeth Oaks Smith, Ernestine Potowski Rose, Susan B. Anthony, Antoinette Brown, Lucy Stone, and Elizabeth Cady Stanton were "exemplary and capable advocates of Women's Rights and exposers of her immeasurable Legal Wrongs," as they lectured in towns across the Northeast.[9]

The anti-abortion movement's efforts also had begun before the Civil War. In 1857, the Suffolk County Medical Society published a *Report of the Committee on Criminal Abortion.* Authored by Dr. Horatio R. Storer, Dr. Henry I. Bowditch, and Dr. Calvin Ellis, the report insisted that existing Massachusetts law on abortion was "fundamentally wrong," because "it utterly ignores the existence of the living child, though the child is really alive from the very moment of its conception, and from that very moment is, and should be considered, a distinct being."

That same year, the American Medical Association published Dr. Meredith Reese's *Report on Infant Mortality in Large Cities*, which identified abortion as a significant contributor to the increasing infant death rates it discussed. By 1868, anti-abortion advocacy was seeking to shift public opinion on the question of abortion. Storer, founder of the "doctors' crusade" against abortion, published three books and numerous articles on abortion—including two aimed at popular, nonmedical audiences—and declared that his efforts on that topic had culminated "in an agitation which is now shaking society, throughout our country, to its very centre."[10]

Because abortion became a topic of public controversy, the early women's rights activists were forced to respond to it. While they and Storer approached the subject differently in their choices of emphasis, their analyses converged and complemented each other. Storer repeatedly cited Thomas Percival's 1803 *Medical Ethics*, saying "to extinguish the first spark of life is a crime of the same nature, both against our Maker and society, as to destroy an infant, a child, or a man." Similarly, Dr. Anna Densmore told the women's club Sorosis that "The living principle is there from the first moment of fecundation, and should be fostered and nourished and brought into the world in every instance that conception takes place."[11] While Storer argued that situations in which a woman who sought an abortion was "under duress, by threat of other personal violence from her husband or seducer" were "so rare, that in a general statement they may be assumed not to exist," he also termed any other individuals involved in obtaining that abortion as "more criminal," since "for whatever excuse the latter [i.e., women undergoing abortions] may suppose themselves to possess, the former can have none."[12] Similarly, the *Women's Journal* argued that both the woman who sought an abortion and the man who had "betrayed" her should be understood "at least, as equal partners in guilt, although often the man is the greater sinner."[13]

This book examines the narrow moment in time when women's rights advocates and anti-abortion campaigners worked in tandem to improve the conditions of society for women and to save the lives of unborn children by decreasing the prevalence of abortion. It was a moment of extraordinary diversity in the women's rights movement, and yet a moment of extraordinary unity in the agreement among sociomedical investigators, women involved in charity, and women's rights advocates on the social factors driving abortion and the structural causes to which its incidence could be ascribed.

Women's rights advocates agreed with anti-abortion campaigners, but not merely as a matter of course or because they belonged to the same segment of society. Rather, they contributed distinctively to the national conversation about abortion by beginning their analyses by considering women first and foremost as moral beings. A woman was a person and a citizen whose moral nature gave her—simply as a human being—an obligation to be morally upright, for her own sake and for that of the small and large societies to which she belonged. Her capacity for moral action allowed her to contribute wisely to the upkeep of a republican society. Her choices also shaped her own character. Consequently, the early women's rights activists were interested in what factors in family life and society tended to encourage women to act virtuously, and what pushed them toward immoral acts. They were interested not only in discovering what women's rights and duties were, but also in what aspects of societies made it harder or easier for women to fulfill their duties and use their rights well. Seeking the vote for women meant seeking recognition of women's citizenship—the right to act as an independent moral being in the public square.

Early women's rights advocates sought to make it easier for women to make virtuous choices, and they believed that such efforts were in the public interest. This was what differentiated the women's rights activists from other anti-abortion activists. They focused on structural causes of abortion not because they saw women who sought abortions as a sociomedical phenomenon, but because they wanted to offer individual women the possibility of choosing a better way, of rising above what they saw as the degradation of a woman led to choose an abortion. And yet they saw women who sought abortions as more than victims and more than sinners in need of reformation. They chose to look instead at the fundamental dignity of all women as moral beings, and with sympathy and pity, to call each to more.

Reconstruction, Revolution, *and Republicanism*

The Revolution newspaper, owned by Susan B. Anthony and edited by Elizabeth Cady Stanton and Parker Pillsbury, demonstrated how early women's rights advocates connected their belief that women were moral beings deserving of rights to their condemnation of abortion. When *The Revolution* made its debut on January 8, 1868, its "Salutatory" announced that the newspaper would "effect changes through abolitions, reconstructions and restorations." *The Revolution*'s first issue appeared two months after the close of the American Equal Rights Association's failed campaign for referenda on black and female suffrage in Kansas. Its editors explained that "the enfranchisement of woman is one of the leading ideas that calls this journal into existence."[14] While many at the time, "in the name of democracy, republicanism and patriotism," were "rushing the dismembered fragments of our nationality on to a still deeper ruin," the staff of *The Revolution* argued that they aimed to strengthen the country's foundations. Only when women realized and asserted their full moral, intellectual, and political equality could Americans "build a genuine republic that will stand forever."[15]

In January 1870, Anthony changed the first part of the newspaper's motto to "The True Republic."[16] The proximate cause of the update was financial; the change came some six months before funding difficulties that would force Anthony to transfer ownership of the paper to Laura Curtis Bullard and was prompted by negotiations with Harriet Beecher Stowe and her sister, the more radical women's rights advocate Isabella Beecher Hooker. They had agreed to be corresponding editors for the paper for a year "on the *condition* that you will change the name of the paper to the *True Republic* or some name equally satisfactory to us."[17] While reluctant, Anthony was willing to consider their proposal, but Stanton vehemently vetoed changing the name. Anthony, however, remained convinced that the addition of the Beecher sisters to the paper's staff would provide *The Revolution* with "a tremendous lift into popular favor." She suggested adding "A New Era—The True Republic" to the paper's masthead instead.[18]

This change signified more than a concession to the Beecher sisters. That women's suffrage would lead to a "true republic" in the United States was a frequent refrain by women's rights leaders that hearkened back to the abolitionist roots of the suffrage movement and the principles of the American Revolution. Participants in the 1864 Anniversary of the Women's National Loyal League—the first women's political organization with a national reach, formed by Elizabeth Cady Stanton and Susan B.

Anthony to promote a constitutional amendment to abolish slavery—had resolved, "That until the old union with slavery be broken, and the Constitution so amended as to secure the elective franchise to all citizens who bear arms, or are taxed to support the Government, we have no foundations on which to build a true republic."[19] A speaker at the inaugural Annual Meeting of the American Equal Rights Association in 1867 explained that "after the troublesome war we have just passed through, we are called upon not only to reconstruct the ten unrepresented States of the nation, but to purify the republicanism of our government in the Northern States and make it more consistent with our professions."[20] The first issue of *The Revolution* contained coverage of a lecture given by Massachusetts abolitionist and women's rights advocate Lucy Stone, in which she insisted that "the claim [that women had the right to vote] was by no means a new one, but was at least as old as the Declaration of Independence"—though, as of yet, the American woman "was, in fact, governed without her consent."[21] In 1881, the just-released first volume of the *History of Woman Suffrage*, written and edited by Stanton, Anthony, and Matilda Joslyn Gage, lamented that "the woman suffrage movement has not yet been accepted as the legitimate outgrowth of American ideas—a component part of the history of our republic."[22] In short, suffragists insisted that true republicanism required that women vote.

How did the early women's rights advocates arrive at this claim? The American Revolution had been fought to establish a republic, but few had believed that end required female suffrage. A truly representative, self-governing republic, rather, required a virtuous (male) citizenry, some fraction of whom could vote. Ties of affection should lead them to shun narrow interests and embrace the common good. Civically engaged, they ought to uphold not just good government, but a good society. In the post-revolutionary era, women were supposed to be wisely self-governing—capable of prudently choosing a spouse, or if they did not marry, of remaining independent with their "virtue" intact. Wives were to be competent helpmeets to their husbands and form them into virtuous citizens.[23] Marriage, in this model, was supposed to be "the republic in miniature; it was chaste, disinterested, and free from the exercise of arbitrary power."[24] If, on the one hand, this elevated vision of marriage served women well, it also made their progress dependent on their husband's susceptibility to their influence.

A shift of focus to woman as mother, rather than as wife, occurred around 1830. As Jan Lewis argues, this shift allowed for greater female power because children were more malleable than their fathers. Additionally, the ideology of "republican motherhood" gave women a political role "through the raising of a patriotic child."[25] And that role could be expanded, as it was late in the nineteenth century and early in the twentieth, to claim that women had a particular political role to play in matters of public health and education.[26] The recasting of women's education in the 1820s and 1830s promoted a broader understanding of women's role in society. Women, in Lucy Stone's words, "learned to stand and speak."[27] They entered civic life through participation in clubs and associations, teaching and administering schools, leading reform movements, and bringing education and religion to frontiers domestic and foreign. Unsurprisingly, women sought to redefine the "boundaries of the domain within which [they] ought to meet obligations to the larger social good."[28]

Women's rights advocates, without rejecting the importance of motherhood, sought an even broader role in the republican project. Participants in the 1854 Woman's Rights Convention in Albany, New York, had resolved that "women are human beings whose rights correspond with their duties; that they are endowed with conscience, reason, affection and energy, for the use of which they are individually responsible."[29] Like the pioneering women's educators Zilpah Polly Grant Banister and Mary Lyon, they saw no distinction of gender in the personal obligation to "disinterested benevolence." Women's rights advocates believed that women's direct participation in political society was critical to the nation's future, and claimed that both individual families and society at large would benefit from women's gains.[30] Lucy Stone wrote to her friend and sister-in-law Antoinette Brown Blackwell that "we are all getting to be women's rights advocates or rather investigators of women's duties."[31] Educated women who were active citizens pursued their own elevation and that of the nation—and elevating the public meant educating the public, not just one's husband and children. Extending the vote to women would prevent the United States' being "lost by faithlessness to [its] idea."[32]

"Centuries of degradation"

Yet Susan B. Anthony spoke for many when she conceded that many women were as yet unprepared for the demands of liberty. "Not even amended constitutions and laws can revolutionize the practical relations of men and women. . . . Constitutional equality only gives to all the aid and protection of the law, while they educate and develop themselves, while they grow into the full stature of freemen."[33] The moral analyses and rhetorical strategies of abolitionism undergirded the early women's rights movement's analyses of social issues and moral questions.[34] Prior to the Civil War, *The Una* made the comparison between the degradation of the slave and of American women explicit: "The parallel holds throughout.—Women and negroes, in marriage and singleness, in slavery and in nominal freedom, stand on the same platform and hold the *same* position in the laws, customs, and conduct of business in the freest government of the earth!"[35]

In the early women's rights advocates' telling, the American legal system had repressed women by suspending their legal existence during marriage and severely restricting their civic participation outside of it. Public opinion taught that women were unintelligent, irrational, and dependent creatures, and relatively few women rebelled against such expectations; as Kathryn Kish Sklar writes, "many believed that women could not perform their duties as moral beings, under the current state of public sentiments."[36] Legal structures and public opinion had degraded women at both the personal and societal level. Elizabeth Cady Stanton and other contributors to *The Revolution* argued that this state of affairs led wealthy women to aspire to becoming "namby-pamby, doll-faced, wishy-washy, milk-and-water feminine bundles," afflicted with "mental, moral and material weakness," who found their "chief delight" in believing "themselves born to cling to whatever is nearest, in a droopy, like the ivy-to-the-oak way, and to be viney, and twiney, and whiney throughout."[37] Middle-income and poor women suffered in more immediate ways, as custom and law made it difficult for a woman to support herself or dependents through honorable means and, consequently, endangered her life and the lives of her children.

Stanton rather apocalyptically characterized the position of women in American society: "We have no women. The mass are monstrosities... fitly described by the prophet Ezekiel as mothers who devour their own children and sell the souls of men for bread."[38] Many American women had lost their humanity—or rather had their humanity denied them. And inasmuch as these women and their children suffered individually from this state of affairs, society at large suffered, too. Parker Pillsbury explained that infanticide and intemperance were proof that slavery had "degraded, brutalized . . . yea, beastialized [sic] myriads" of the members of the communities of freed slaves he visited in 1869.[39] *The Revolution*'s editors applied the same analysis, evidence, and conclusions to middle-class and impoverished white women when the subject of abortion in their ranks was broached in its pages—only substituting women's subjugation in law, marriage, fields of work, and so on, for slavery. An article on infanticide in the newspaper's first issue insisted that "with centuries of degradation, we have so little of true womanhood, that the world has but the faintest glimmering of what a woman is or should be."[40]

In 1856, Stanton had asked the National Woman's Rights Convention, "What mean these asylums all over the land for the deaf and dumb, the maim[ed] and blind, the idiot and the raving maniac? What all these advertisements in our public prints, these family guides, these female medicines, these Madame Restells?"[41] Hereditary disease and illicit means of family limitation—particularly abortion—were, in her telling, evidence of women's degradation. The early women rights activists' analyses of these complex moral issues were animated by the understanding that rights and duties were inextricably linked. When she became a mother, a woman acquired significant obligations of care toward her child: "Happy mothers know what tides of the most strong and innocent love flow into their souls with the advent of each helpless child, making the little one's care a natural instinct as well as a most reasonable duty."[42] The early women's rights advocates understood that, because this duty began with pregnancy, women should have the right to determine whether and when she might become a mother, through the practice of voluntary motherhood—essentially, woman-instigated abstinence. This understanding also meant that a woman who sought an abortion or committed infanticide was abandoning her duties as a mother. Thus, the *Women's Journal* could term infanticide "such an unnatural crime,"[43] and *The Revolution* could describe abortions as "revolting outrages against the laws of nature and our common humanity."[44]

However, the early women's rights advocates did not believe that any woman would commit these filicidal crimes lightly. The early women's rights advocates decried the "false public sentiment" that barred women from most professions, prevented them from earning wages equal with those earned by men, understood their working to earn their living as shameful, characterized those found guilty of sexual sin as "ruined," and in so many other ways crippled women. Caroline Dall wrote that "the standard of womanly education does not lead where it should, because controlled by a public opinion which demands too little."[45] This state of affairs was understood as a form of moral violence against women; the woman who obtained an abortion demonstrated that "either by education or circumstances she has been greatly wronged," even as she wronged another human being by that act.[46]

The early women's rights advocates' moral vision was vast and complex. Prior to the abolition of slavery, Ernestine Rose wrote that "while I deprecate slavery... yet I can have pity and commiseration for the Slaveholder, knowing as I well do know, that he too suffers from the evils of slavery. For it is an eternal law of humanity, that the wrong doer shall suffer from the evils he perpetrates on others."[47] While similarly acknowledging abortion and infanticide as inherently wrong, the early women's rights advocates had great pity and compassion for women who had committed these wrongs.

Achieving Women's Elevation

In many early women's rights advocates' view, the greatest obstacle to women's elevation—older than the fight for suffrage and of greater concern to a greater number of American women—was the problem of the "sexual double standard." This was the social consensus that women who fell into sexual sin—most often those whose bodies presented positive proof thereof, unlike those of their male partners—were to be "trodden under foot, and spurned from society and driven from a parent's roof," while "common consent allows the male to habituate himself to this vice, and treats him as not guilty."[48] As Linda Kerber has argued, "Issues of sexual asymmetry dominated public discourse to an unprecedented extent as people tried to define a place for women."[49] Tales of seduction, ruin, and abandonment—or seduction and abortion—were rife, and the woman who was "ruined" or killed was often judged more harshly than the man who seduced her and abandoned her or led her to obtain an abortion.

Many of the early women's rights advocates, united in their belief in the fundamental moral equality of men and women, directly attacked the sexual double standard. Denying the common idea that women were inherently more moral than men, they argued that there was as little excuse for men's immorality as there was for women's, and that one moral code should apply to both sexes.[50] If public sentiment repudiated the sexual double standard, men would be less likely to sexually abuse women with impunity, and women would have less fear of being "ruined," which would in turn decrease some of the pressures that led women to seek abortions.

In fighting the sexual double standard, the early women's rights advocates also worked with the ideology of "passionless" women, accepting what they found useful and rejecting what they found harmful. The ideology of passionlessness, which arose out of eighteenth-century evangelical religion, flipped the traditional image of women as hypersexual on its head, asserting that women were "*less* carnal and lustful than men." By the mid-nineteenth century, this line of thought and its corresponding belief in women as agents of moral reform had primarily permeated the religious middle class, not the working class or the highest elites.[51] Nonetheless, passionlessness offered women social power, self-respect, a higher moral status, and the justification for a more intellectual education. While many early women's rights advocates questioned the resultant prudery that left women ignorant about their bodies, rendering them more vulnerable to seduction or sexual violence, they embraced other aspects of passionlessness; they fought against women's "sexual vulnerability and dependence" and advocated for equality in marriage.[52]

The ideology of passionlessness contributed to the reorientation of popular understandings of marriage from an essentially hierarchical relationship to one in which "women were complimentary, and piously influential, marriage partners."[53] It provided the basis of the prevalent argument for voluntary motherhood—that women had the right to refuse sex to their husbands when they did not want to become pregnant.[54] It supported increasing resistance to marital rape. It cast women as the victims, not the perpetrators, of sexual immorality. Finally, passionlessness downplayed "altogether [women's] sexual characterization, which was the cause of their exclusion from significant 'human' (i.e., male) pursuits."[55] The early women's rights advocates believed wholeheartedly in women's moral agency and insisted that women's power increased when they were freed from an essentially sexual definition.

Beyond critiquing the sexual double standard, women's rights advocates also offered a host of suggestions for women's elevation in the pages of *The Revolution*. Martha Brinkerhoff, a women's rights lecturer and *Revolution* correspondent, wrote that her audiences were becoming convinced that "there is no other hope for the country but the education and enfranchisement of her women."[56] Both were necessary for women to become the equals of men in terms of intellect, strength, and morals. Other contributors suggested women's increased interest in politics and religion, their improved physical strength, and the opening of new avenues of employment. In the end, they circled back, again and again, to the vote.

In *The Revolution*'s telling, the extra-political benefits of gaining the vote would prepare women to assume the duties of suffrage responsibly. Suffrage would demonstrate the fundamental equality of men and women and provide women with self-respect and a sense of public and private responsibility not previously held. Suffrage would symbolize women's increased ability to shape public opinion through their full participation in public and political life: "Remove woman's shackles and she will soon create a public opinion that will declare it a disgrace for a man to outrage the woman he has sworn to protect."[57] It would make it easier for American women to become good mothers and good citizens, engaged in public and political life. Women's elevation—effected and demonstrated by suffrage—would bolster personal and familial—and, therefore, civic—virtue.

Suffrage was simultaneously the symbol par excellence of

women's essential equality and a necessary precondition to the elevation of women in many aspects of life. This goal required that women themselves work toward their own development. Another contributor to *The Revolution* wrote: "Woman has most of the work of her elevation to do herself. She must throw aside, or give a second place to many of the trifles that now absorb her."[58] Women needed to claim not only political and civil rights but also the right to self-improvement and self-respect. They needed to claim and express their full dignity.

En Fin

The apparent increase in nonnatural infant mortality roughly coincident with the resurgence of women's rights activity following the Civil War gave some suffrage opponents leeway to argue that the women's rights movement promoted filicide. In 1869, Susan B. Anthony took part in a debate of sorts with the Rev. Justin Dewey Fulton, the pastor of Boston's Union Temple Baptist Church and a "zealous opponent of drink, the drama, women's suffrage and Roman Catholicism."[59] When Fulton, speaking against women's suffrage, stated that America needed "mothers, not murderers," Anthony responded that she "repel[led] the thought that the teachings of any of the advocates of Woman Suffrage tended in any such direction as hinted by Mr. Fulton."[60] Of course, there was no correlation between promoting suffrage and encouraging or condoning abortion or infanticide, Anthony insisted. Suffragists sought economic possibilities and security for vulnerable women, "that women be given an opportunity to work, to obtain means whereby homes may be secured and girls and women saved from the perils which certainly surround them in the world when without homes."[61] The early women's rights advocates sought to identify the structural injustices that led women to commit infanticide and abortion while mitigating their guilt. They also worked to develop concrete measures that could help individual women extricate themselves from these conditions.[62]

When women's rights advocates addressed infanticide and abortion, they were joining broader public conversations. They rewrote, or at least edited, popular narratives about women, children, sexuality, and economics. In the United States, the valence of these questions was profoundly shaped by the legacy of slavery and large-scale immigration. Particularly after the Civil War, concerns about urban and industrial life were often dealt with under the banner of Reconstruction. Women's rights advocates, like public-health reformers, understood increased abortion and infanticide as a result of the social structures created by urbanization and industrialization, and they framed their attitudes toward them accordingly. But they also folded those concerns into their older project of creating the "true republic." This combination created a distinctly feminist approach. In particular, many hoped to ameliorate these structural injustices with not only the vote, but also personal relationships and opportunities for "self-elevation."

This book circles back again and again to a powerful figure of the good citizen that appeared in the women's rights movement, the woman doctor. These women, some single, some married, some widowed, pursued a professional life long restricted to men. They both staked a claim for professional equality and sought to use their professional status to elevate their sisters. Their position allowed them to address, with propriety, many of the gravest consequences of the sexual double standard. They could preach the need for better education about women's health, on topics ranging from fashion to their reproductive lives. They could broaden the availability of medical care to marginalized women, whether those women were poor or had transgressed sexual mores or, as was often the case, both. They could inform their middle-class sisters of many of the actual needs of their less privileged sisters, helping to give shape and matter to the imagined solidarity of all women. While less at the forefront of the women's rights movement than names we know better, these women, through their professional lives and activisms, shaped how that movement understood and responded to issues such as abortion and infanticide.

The book begins with a look at the ways in which abortion and infanticide—issues which were cited by women in the suffrage movement as definitive evidence of women's degradation—were popularly understood. Chapter 2 situates the contributions of *The Revolution*'s authors to these major public discussions, highlighting how they reacted to and attempted to shape "public sentiment." Chapter 3 delves into some aspects of the relationship between increasingly professionalized medicine and its anti-abortion campaign and the project of women's elevation. The challenges posed in uniting middle-class activism, however well intentioned, and the attempt to help all women overcome the damage wrought by the sexual double standard, are elaborated in Chapter 4, with an examination of the relationship that two women doctors, Anna Densmore French and Charlotte Lozier, had with the New York women's club Sorosis. Chapter 5 considers the ways in which seeking women's elevation framed women's rights advocates' approach to the struggles of working-class women, including responses to the famous Hester Vaughan infanticide case. Chapter 6, on the Massachusetts Infant Asylum, shows a small but significant attempt to create an institution that reflected new insights about the struggles the sexual double standard entailed for poor women—an attempt, however limited, to move beyond the middle-class cult of domesticity as the answer to all. Chapter 7 considers the way in which the theory of women's elevation was worked out in the creation of the Society for Helping Destitute Mothers and Infants in Boston. Finally, Chapter 8 traces the shifting approaches to abortion in the popular press and law, and in the women's rights press, that took place in the early and mid-1870s.

Chapter One

ABORTION SHIFTS IN THE PUBLIC IMAGINATION

In early August 1857, newspapers from Illinois to Maryland reported on the death of Regnat Lawson, whose demise they labeled "one of the most shocking and infamous crimes ever perpetrated" in Chicago. Two men—James Temple, Lawson's twenty-years-older foster father and presumed seducer, and Dr. James Swansey, a prominent doctor—were purported to have brought her to Chicago against her will, declaring that she was insane and foiling her attempts to escape. They took Lawson to a hotel, where "an abortion [was] procured upon her against her will," and left her in the unwilling care of a midwife, who sought the attention of the coroner—thinking that he was a health officer—for advice about bringing her to a hospital. On the coroner's advice, two doctors examined Lawson and discovered that an abortion had been performed on her. They listened to her account of events and informed the coroner of her status and story. When Lawson died several days later, both Temple and Swansey were arrested and Temple was charged with murder in police court.[1]

The title of a *Chicago Daily News* article on the case—"Seduction, Abortion, and Death"—neatly summarizes much abortion coverage through the 1850s. The most commonly reported cases were those where the woman died, and popular press accounts overwhelmingly featured unmarried women portrayed as victims of seduction and medical malpractice. The press tended to portray a woman who had procured an abortion as guilty of trusting too much, but not of any general licentiousness. Coerced by her seducer, or out of a misguided desire to hide her shame, she fell victim to an abortionist who not only ended her pregnancy and her child's life, but often her own life as well. Women were viewed, not only popularly but also in court, as passive victims in cases of statutory rape, seduction, abortion, or sodomy.[2]

Because of the circumstances surrounding Lawson's death, an inquest was opened and held over the following six days. A team of doctors conducted a postmortem examination, during which they found part of a placenta and signs of infection, which suggested that an abortion had been performed. After the doctors presented their findings, the coroner's jury interviewed other witnesses, including Dr. Bevan, who had attended Lawson shortly before her death. The picture that emerged from the testimony gathered at this time was somewhat less sensational than what had been originally published. While it seemed less likely that Lawson was physically coerced into undergoing the abortion, Lawson's seduction by her adopted father, her abandonment by him and Swansey in Chicago after the procedure, and the physical and moral suffering she underwent during the whole saga came into higher relief. Additionally, Bevan related that Swansey had "admitted his participation in the crime" in conversation with him before Lawson's death.[3] On August 6, the coroner's jury returned a unanimous verdict finding that Lawson's cause of death was "peritonical inflamation [sic] in childbirth fever, caused by abortion . . . brought on and produced by a certain instrument . . . used by Dr. James Swanze and James H. Temple, in and upon the body of her . . . in a manner tending to destroy the life of her."[4] Two days later, the case was moved to recorder's court, which was responsible for handling most criminal cases in Cook County.[5] There, Swansey and Temple were informed that they were facing manslaughter charges, pending the grand jury's decision.[6]

In the mid-nineteenth century, abortion was prosecuted under the common law as an offense against the mother, who was not considered the guilty party. American criminal law at that time consistently and paternalistically portrayed women involved in sex-related crimes as victims.[7] Before 1867, Illinois abortion law only extended to medicinal abortions and did not mention other methods of abortion.[8] But Illinois law at the time defined involuntary manslaughter as "the killing of a human being without any intent to do so, in the commission of an unlawful act, or a lawful act, which probably might produce such a consequence, in an unlawful manner."[9] A manslaughter charge might reach an abortionist whose patient died as a result of an abortion by mechanical means. About a month after they were released on $10,000 bail, Swansey and Temple were indicted "for causing the death of a young woman named Regnet Lawson by producing an abortion."[10]

From the start, Swansey defended his own innocence, sometimes at the expense of Temple's reputation.[11] A few days after the indictment, Swansey returned to the recorder's court to request that he and Temple be tried separately, because he believed that he "could not have an impartial hearing if tried jointly with Temple."[12] The narrative of the case that Swansey spread before the trial—both in person and through sympathizers at the *Bureau County Democrat*—implicated Temple: "The unfortunate girl has been medically treated or drugged, before treated by Dr. S.; that she was put under his treatment after the abortion was produced, and, appearing to be out of danger, was removed to Chicago without any agency or request on his part, and was there neglected without his knowledge until too late."[13] The *Chicago Daily Tribune* reprinted this narrative with the explicit disclaimer that it directly contradicted the evidence gathered by the coroner's jury.

When Swansey's trial began on November 9, his defense team—which included a U.S. district attorney who would be relieved from his job the following spring—made a slightly different argument, which acknowledged a greater degree of involvement in Lawson's case: "The unfortunate girl, Regnet [sic] Lawson, had taken drugs, procured by herself, to produce an abortion," they proposed, and "when she came under Dr. Swanzy's care she was in such a condition as to render it absolutely necessary to remove the fetus."[14] In this telling, the one person who had committed a crime was the now deceased Lawson herself, in violating the law against medicinal abortions. Swansey likely suggested that there was little inherent danger to the woman in the operation he had undertaken, since the central question during his *habeas corpus* hearing was whether "abortion by mechanical means" was likely to cause the death of a woman undergoing the procedure.[15] That it would almost certainly cause the death of the fetus does not seem to have been discussed; it is likely that difficulties in establishing fetal causes of death dissuaded prosecutors from prosecuting a presumed abortionist for a fetus's death.

On November 13, without retiring to deliberate, the jury unanimously acquitted Swansey; the charges against Temple were subsequently dropped.[16] With his newly gained freedom, Swansey finally took it upon himself to revive Temple's reputation, by "relieving his character of the very unjust and unfounded imputations, based upon his connection with the deceased and unfortunate girl." In the affidavit he produced—which was created two days after his acquittal and witnessed by the police justice who had initially dealt with his booking—he offered a third version of the events that led to Lawson's death. Lawson's pregnancy, he said, was owing to "a young man who accompanied her home from a singing school," and she had on her own initiative begun "taking drugs to produce an abortion." Temple, who was "the kindest man she had ever seen," in Swansey's telling, was initially ignorant of the pregnancy and of Lawson's attempts to end it. Swansey now allowed that he had traveled to Chicago with Lawson and Temple, who paid Lawson's expenses "out of the mere regard which naturally grew out of his relations to her as an adopted child." They had used false names in the Chicago hotel "to conceal her real condition and protect her reputation and character." Once there, Swansey admitted, he had performed an operation which he deemed "necessary to the restoration of her health and perhaps her life," and which would have the added benefit of keeping "her character relatively safe from exposure."[17]

In the newspapers' early telling, the case had been emblematic of declining civic virtue if not out-and-out corruption. Temple had become Lawson's foster father when she was orphaned at the age of two, and was a wealthy farmer and "a church member in good standing." Swansey was "a native of England, a man of family, and possessing considerable influence in Bureau County."[18] Because they were "well known citizens of this state and men of wealth and education," their alleged crime was made "only the more dark and venal."[19] Newspaper reporting on the outcome of the cases was generally muted, though it was clear that not all believed justice had been meted out. The *Alton Weekly Courier* went beyond intimating corruption generally to suggest bribery, observing that "what agency [Temple's] money had in saving himself and the unprincipled physician from punishment we of course do not know."[20] After expressing its doubt as to the veracity of Swansey's ultimate tale, the newspaper gave a somber closing to its coverage of the story: "The poor girl is dead and in her grave, and those who are believed to have seduced her from the path of virtue, and then murdered her in cold blood to conceal the crime, have been turned loose unpunished, ready and perhaps anxious to commit other similar atrocities."[21]

A Medicolegal Campaigner and Two Sociomedical Investigators

The year of Regnet Lawson's death, Dr. Horatio Storer was appointed chairman of the American Medical Association's Special Committee on Criminal Abortion. This appointment was the culmination of an effort that Storer had begun more locally. A gynecologist and the son of the first professor of midwifery at Harvard, Storer had begun his campaign against abortion within the medical community in Boston shortly after the late-1856 closure of the Boston Lying-In Hospital. He began by canvassing medical colleagues across the country for information about abortion laws.[22] And in February 1857, at a meeting of the Suffolk County Medical Society, he proposed the creation of a committee to investigate the necessity of additional laws or any other means of suppressing "this abominable, unnatural and yet common crime" in Massachusetts. Storer, Calvin Ellis, and

Henry I. Bowditch comprised this committee, and they issued their report in May.[23] At the June meeting of the State Medical Society of Massachusetts, Storer presented a resolution on behalf of the Suffolk County Medical Society which asked the state-level society to request the Massachusetts Legislature for "a careful revision of the Statutes upon that crime."[24] In July, Storer received word that the American Medical Association (AMA) had appointed him chairman of its Special Committee on Criminal Abortion.

While Storer, Ellis, and Bowditch were presenting their findings to the Suffolk County Medical Society, Dr. David Meredith Reese was in Nashville, presenting his report on *Infant Mortality in Large Cities, The Sources of Its Increase, and Means for Its Diminution* to the AMA. The report warned that infant mortality had "attained gigantic proportions among us, and is increasing with amazing rapidity."[25] In most large mid-century cities, roughly half the deaths in any given year were of children under the age of five. In 1853, in New York, that percentage had risen to 57 percent—and the number of infant deaths recorded as stillbirths and due to premature birth in New York had risen 140 percent over the preceding decade. Reese was sure that this increase represented "the ghastly crime of abortionism." He was not alone in his conclusion that increased "criminal abortion" (as opposed to non-induced abortions, or miscarriages) significantly contributed to increased infant mortality. Contemporaries in France similarly attributed rising reported numbers of "stillbirths" to increased criminal abortion, and French law eventually required any delivery (no matter how early) to be reported in an attempt to limit abortions. Reese also acknowledged that increasing syphilis rates likely contributed to infant mortality and stillbirth rates.[26]

During the same year, William Wallace Sanger, the first resident physician at the New York state prison on Blackwell's Island (now Roosevelt Island), was hard at work on his 699-page *History of Prostitution: Its Extent, Causes, and Effects Throughout the World.* The book had been commissioned by New York City's almshouse.[27] For the section that dealt with New York City, Sanger had interviewed hundreds of women on Blackwell's Island who had been arrested for prostitution. He found that the infant mortality numbers for the children of the prostitutes he interviewed vastly exceeded the numbers Reese had given for New York City; in his estimation, the rate was four times higher. Taking for granted the popular association of prostitution (and illicit sex more broadly) with abortion, Sanger, like Reese, assumed that these numbers (including, as they did, reported stillbirths), counted some, but nowhere near all, abortions procured by prostitutes. The total number, he asserted, would be startling. So, he concluded, the "sacrifice of infant life, attribute it to what cause you may, is one of the most deplorable results of prostitution, and urgently demands active interference."[28]

At an American Academy of Arts and Sciences meeting in 1858, Storer estimated that "the frequency of abortions as compared with still births at the full time is at least 8 times as great in Massachusetts as in the worst statistics of the city of New York."[29] He ended his presentation expressing regret that the decline in population growth could not be ascribed to "greater abstinence and greater prudence in sexual matters."[30] Shortly after this meeting, Storer began publishing a series of articles, primarily in the *North American Medico-Chirurgical Review*, under the heading "Contributions to Obstetric Jurisprudence." Eight would appear before 1859 was out, all of which dealt with abortion: "Is Abortion Ever a Crime?," "Its Frequency and the Causes Thereof," "Its Victims," "Its Proofs," "Its Perpetrators," "Its Innocent Abettors," "Its Obstacles to Conviction," and "Can It Be at All Controlled by Law?"[31]

While Storer's crusade rallied the medical profession against abortion, Dr. Meredith Reese and Dr. William Sanger's reports on infant mortality and prostitution recast those issues, and abortion with them, as threats to public health and morals. The two "sociomedical investigators" sought out statistics in order to lay the groundwork for public-health reform.[32] Their work was cited in everything from the popular press to official reports justifying new government programs and institutions. The two men formed part of a new transnational movement framing health as a public problem to be solved. They emphasized the commercial, economic, and political systems behind these social problems rather than the guilt of individuals. Nonetheless, they shared the common nineteenth-century tendency to conflate physical and moral "natural laws," believing health and morals to be inextricably intertwined. Modern life, they feared, threatened both. In short, abortion and prostitution constituted part of what would eventually be referred to as the "social question"—the matrix of societal problems and debates created by modern, urban, and industrial life.[33]

Reese's contribution to abortion discourse was not limited to accounting for infant mortality rates. He also honed in on the new commercial face of abortion. Reese worried far more about abortion as an emerging industry than as the desperate act of an individual woman. More than the woman who sought an abortion, abortionists, the politically corrupt, and a greedy press were the guilty parties. In the mid-nineteenth century, private interest of any sort was seen as a threat to the public good, so abortion as a trade reeked of the worst sort of corruption, gorier than alcohol or vice. Unsurprisingly, then, abortion increasingly stood as a symbol and indicator of other kinds of moral and political corruption. Newspaper editors were keenly aware of the business side of the growing abortion trade, and yet a great many newspaper editors profited from running thinly veiled advertisements for abortifacients or abortionists, despite critiquing their competitors for the practice.[34]

Reese condemned the "murderous trade" "tolerated, connived at, and even protected by corrupt civil authorities" and promoted by a press willing to print "the advertisements of these male and female vampires, for a share in the enormous profits of this inhuman traffic in blood and life."[35] This commercial language, four years before the start of the American Civil War, undoubtedly also conjured up comparisons to critiques of American slavery, particularly as the symbolic use of abortion figured into slavery and Civil War debates. Demonstrating tensions between American and English abolitionists, William Lloyd Garrison's *Liberator* reported that at an English meeting, the African-American anti-slavery campaigner Sarah Parker Remond had been welcomed with an address that cited the American tendency to "child murder" as proof of the "fallen national character of the Americans."[36] Abortion was also used symbolically within American arguments over how to respond to slavery; the Ohio *Ashland Union* in 1864 would accuse an abolitionist meeting in New York of promoting "infidelity, free love, abortion, the right to sin in heaven, Abolitionism, the war, and Lincoln."[37] Like Reese, Sanger also blamed the print press, especially advertising, for social ills. He argued that the sale of pornography and advertisements for abortion should be legally restricted.[38]

Sanger's understanding of the motivations for women to become prostitutes and, accordingly, to obtain abortions at first appears to reflect popular understandings of women and sexuality. With the notable exception of cases of habitual intemperance, Sanger placed the responsibility for a woman becoming a prostitute on anyone other than herself. Prostitutes, like other women engaged in illicit sex, were victims. They were victims of economic necessity, they were victims of seducers, or they were victims of bad parents or bad husbands. They were the victims of an insufficiently Christian society that cast out fallen women. The extrapolated guilt for abortions lay on economic injustice, devious men, and family members who failed to fulfill their bounden duties. Thus, Sanger described prostitutes as having "suffered abortion."[39]

Storer, on the other hand, challenged the portrayal of women as passive victims of abortion, describing as nonsensical the common law treatment of abortion as a crime against the mother.[40] The law punished, he argued, "an attempt, which does not exist, upon the well-being or life of the mother." Rather, he believed, guilt for an abortion usually belonged first to the mother and then, in decreasing order, to "accomplices": friends and acquaintances who had urged her on, nurses, midwives and female physicians, husbands, druggists, and "worst of all, though fortunately extremely rare, physicians in regular standing."[41] For Storer, recognizing female agency meant prosecuting women who obtained criminal abortions.

Reese, too, acknowledged female agency in the incidence of abortion, but he distinguished between the "profligate, or even the unfortunate," who sought to hide their shame, and married women who wanted to delay the duties of caring for children.[42] His analysis placed abortion at the heart of a social problem—

the decline of marriage. Marriage was widely seen as under threat from liberalized divorce laws, drunkenness, prostitution, and so on. For those who believed that marriage existed, at least in part, for the sake of procreation, abortion within marriage was a far more worrying threat to the public than the occasional desperate act of an unmarried female victim of seduction.[43]

Yet the recasting of abortion as a threat to marriage had the perhaps unexpected consequence of leading reformers to fight abortion on the margins, where it was perhaps easier to reach. Reese, for instance, proposed the creation of both state-run foundling hospitals and lying-in asylums for expectant mothers, hoping they would "remove the temptations to the unnatural crime of abortionism" and "prevent the abandonment and cruel murder of unborn and newly-born infants" by providing an alternate means of "the concealment of the shame of unhallowed mothers."[44] Unmarried mothers should be aided even if that meant diminished societal judgment for illicit sex. William Sanger's *History of Prostitution* similarly called for more American foundling hospitals. He praised those of continental Europe and decried the "strong prejudice" against them among "Protestants" who believed that they encouraged "illicit intercourse."[45]

While Sanger's analysis cast women as victims, he did not consider them permanent or natural victims. And Storer, for his part, did not think that sending women to jail was the *best* way to fight abortion. He argued that the press and advertisers needed to be restrained from profiting off the abortion trade and that education was essential.[46] He also advocated professional reforms that, as many scholars have pointed out, were part and parcel of establishing the power and prestige of the (mostly male) medical profession. Sanger similarly argued that societies could effectively limit prostitution—a major contributor to abortion rates—by providing education, especially in physiology, and economic opportunities to women.[47] His analyses of prostitution in Great Britain (primarily London) and the United States (primarily New York) homed in on the question of women's employment, insisting upon the "intimate relation which poverty bears to prostitution."[48]

Abortion in the Public Imagination in the Late 1860s

The beginnings of anti-abortion agitation in the late 1850s was interrupted by the Civil War. Like many social issues, it came back into focus after 1865. Public references to abortion became more about abortion itself and increasingly reflected the outlook of the sociomedical investigators. The association of abortion with corruption remained intact, and in the post-bellum press, the wealthy abortionist Madame Restell and her New York mansion became the default image of the abortion business as part of the decadent Gilded Age. Because the only significant statistical claims about abortion rates came out of New York City and the state of Massachusetts, abortion was widely portrayed as a Northern and urban problem. As such, it was frequently used to illustrate the hypocrisy of "Yankee" claims to moral superiority.[49]

Abortion was also frequently offered as proof of Christian hypocrisy: missionaries raised funds to convert Hindus with tales of child sacrifice in the Ganges, while it appeared that many Protestant married women were seeking abortions.[50] Despite—or perhaps because of—such charges, the religious press weighed in on the topic. In March 1867, *The Northwestern Christian Advocate*, a weekly newspaper published by the Methodist Episcopal Church in Chicago, ran a lengthy essay on

"Foeticide." Editor Rev. Thomas M. Eddy's essay showcased new attitudes toward abortion, drawing on several scholarly works and popular tracts written by Horatio Storer. He echoed the concern that abortion, "a species of infanticide," was on the rise in the United States. He illustrated increased attention to fetal life by arguing that quickening was irrelevant to the morality of an abortion because the fetus, "at any age, [was] 'in being,'" and a "'reason*able* creature'—potentially endowed with reason." He sought to counter the older narrative by insisting that seduction or rape did not precede all abortions. Rather, "not only the ignorant but the instructed, not only the 'outsider' but the church member, and not only the pews but the pulpit bars...resorted to criminal abortion."[51] The Methodists were not alone. In 1867, *The Congregationalist and Boston Recorder* published a lengthy essay by Rev. John Todd entitled "Fashionable Murder." Reprinted in various other papers, it was also reworked into a book, *Serpents in the Dove's Nest*. Todd insisted that the "wilful [sic] killing of a human being at any stage of its existence, is murder."[52] Like Eddy, Todd cited Storer's work as part of his impetus for writing.

In the press, abortion was now widely considered the murder of an unborn child, not simply a crime against the mother. Diagnoses of what drove the apparently high abortion rate varied widely. Eddy embraced structural attributions of guilt. It belonged to the Protestant Church for its clerics' general silence on the topic. It belonged to the "newspaper whose satanic advertisements of quack nostrums and quack doctors further this fearful evil." It belonged to the "quack doctors, irregular practitioners and the whole race of vagrant female hyenas who will take foetal life for fifty dollars and gratuitously kill or ruin the credulous wife or 'unfortunate.'" And he agreed that the focus should be on the married. Ramping up prosecutions would unfairly put all the weight on "fallen women," a clear injustice given that at "present foeticide is practiced by the married to a far greater extent." Finally, Eddy acknowledged the importance of education, assessing that most women who procured abortions "know not what they do." Therefore, he argued, the "two mighty movers of moral reform, the pulpit and religious press, must at once come to the rescue." He called for "a small compact, inexpensive tract upon this topic [to] come from our presses, and be distributed by multiplied thousands for the instruction of our Methodist millions."[53] Todd, on the other hand, placed the blame squarely on women, whether unmarried women who sought to hide their shame or married women who "prefer to devastate with poison or with steel their wombs rather than bear the discomforts attached to the privilege of maternity, rather than forego [sic] the gaieties of a winter's balls, parties and plays, or the pleasure of a summer's trips and amusement."[54]

Weeks after the publication of Todd's "Fashionable Murder" article, women's rights advocate Isabella Beecher Hooker unsuccessfully tried to take to the pages of *The Congregationalist* to counter his assertions.[55] In her letter, which she circulated among her friends before publishing it independently seven years later, she accused Todd of injustice to women and having presented a shallow analysis of a weighty subject. "That some women have... been led into deadly sin and into the fearful suffering which inevitably follows the serious transgression of even physical law is true, perhaps even to the extent you have stated, and such need warning," she acknowledged.[56] But she blamed the incidence of abortion on "the widespread ignorance, which, like vice itself, is dragging down hundreds into immeasurable wretchedness."[57] Invoking the idea that women were "passionless," she argued that mothers should better instruct their children about the procreative nature of sex and the importance of communication in marriage—and, she implied, should therefore be better instructed themselves.[58] Raising children with these understandings would help them avoid sexual immorality and would foster happy, companionate marriages—which, she implied, would reduce the incidence of abortion outside of and within marriage.

More radically, *The Circular*, published by John Humphrey Noyes's Oneida Community, called for reform "on the subject of foeticide."[59] While agreeing with Todd that abortion was "the destruction of unborn children," the newspaper gave a radically different account of motivations. *The Circular* blamed marriage and the position of woman for compelling her "through wrong and subversive ways to strive toward the position of freedom that is before her." The lack of "a mode for controlling propagation," it argued, drove "wives and poor men" to "rude, coarse, barbarous, unscientific and wicked means."[60] Blame should be placed on "Society and its institutions," particularly "the columns of newspapers . . . crowded with vile advertisements addressed to special classes, and for special purposes, under the thin disguise of whose ambiguous language, an offer is made of the means of committing child murder."[61] It suggested "as the Spiritual remedy, true Religion; as the Social remedy, Communism; as the Physical remedy, Male Continence."[62]

While the public sphere now often condemned abortion as the murder of an unborn child, women still died at the hands of untrained abortionists, and those deaths continued to shape perceptions of abortion. A *New York Herald* article called for an abortionist to be hanged because he had "at least two murders on his hands"—meaning, two women on whom he had attempted abortions had died.[63]

Women were still largely seen as victims of abortion, and attempts to cast them primarily as the guilty parties, like Todd's, generated pushback. A letter to the editor in the *Boston Daily Globe* lamented that in "pulpit and press" women had been "tried as the criminal, and of course adjudged guilty... withholding those facts, known also to all experienced physicians, which would arraign man as her accomplice, and in many cases the instigator." The author pointed to "unwilling maternity, recklessly thrust upon the wife by a husband, who, in most cases, desired no offspring, and was ofttimes the first to suggest, and even compel to foeticide."[64]

While *married* women's guilt in abortion, we have seen, was increasingly emphasized, for the unmarried, the old narrative of seduction, with the abortionist as its "ally and abettor" held strong. A young seduced woman seeking an abortion could still easily be cast as "a poor, simple girl, whose lack of proper parental protection may well excuse all her sin, in the view of charitable neighbors."[65] In contrast, many assumed that consent to marriage was consent to "the maternal state" without qualification. This assumption was very much at odds with women's rights advocates and other radicals' insistence on "voluntary motherhood" and the right of a woman, even within marriage, to control access to her body.[66]

Married women's abortions wrought particular anxiety for two reasons. The first was the violent rejection of the all-important role of woman as mother in a society that was premised on marriage, understood in terms of separate spheres and the cult of domesticity. A second issue, however, as we have seen, is that many believed that abortions procured on married women would never be prosecuted, making their incidence a particularly insidious threat to society.

This hardening distinction between abortions procured by the married and by the unmarried was tied to worries about the decreasing native white birthrate. The *New-York Tribune* reported on the third annual meeting of the American Social Science Association, in October 1867, in which Dr. Nathan Allen argued that the "American-born" population of the state was decreasing due to "the ill-health of American women and the dreadful practice of procuring abortions."[67] The claim that only immigration was holding up the white birthrate clearly alarmed many Americans. Although the fear of what would later be termed "race suicide" did not *cause* disapproval of abortion, it added urgency. In this context, abortion frequently was linked to infanticide and high infant-mortality rates.

In addressing both abortion and infant mortality, reformers tended to focus on helping the unmarried. While they may have felt that married women presented the greater problem, unmarried women were easier to sympathize with and easier to help. This attitude manifested itself in an increasing desire to ensure that there were homes for illegitimate children. Arguments for the creation of "well-conducted foundling-hospitals" now overwhelmed concerns that such institutions might somehow promote illicit sex. They would at least "greatly diminish child-murder and abortion."[68]

In general, the press seems to have reflected an increasing belief that the state, and not just private charities, should provide for infants whose parents could or would not. If the state could not reach in to eliminate abortions within marriage, it could at least try to limit abortions on the margins by offering options to desperate women. Other legal remedies were also considered, most aimed at abortionists rather than at the women who used them. One was the restriction of advertisements, a mode adopted through the 1873 Comstock Act and various similar state acts. Another was increasing punishments for abortions, which did occur, though the difficulty of that tactic was early apparent. A movement to amend Nevada law to strengthen penalties for physicians performing abortions was withdrawn upon the argument that "it was very difficult to prove this crime, and a too stringent punishment might defeat the object desired to be secured," presumably by driving the crime further underground.[69]

Skepticism about the effectiveness of legal means meant that "public opinion" continued to hold its place as the best probable bulwark of morality. "It is quite time there were a more decided and effective public sentiment," the Massachusetts *Springfield Republican* opined, in an article about a young woman who died from an abortion.[70] But the Indianan *Marshall County Republican* was more optimistic: "We hope that those who believe in virtue and justice, and the peace and glory of a community with a good name will stand firm and hurl the lances of public sentiment at these criminals and their crimes, whatever course the law may take."[71]

When women's rights advocates weighed in on abortion and the issues of seduction, prostitution, and infanticide that were so thoroughly linked together in the popular mind, they were weighing in on an issue that unified an incredibly diverse array of American activists and pointed to particular Reconstruction and Gilded Age anxieties. There were few issues that the radical free-love advocate Tennessee Claflin and Presbyterian minister Theodore Cuyler agreed on. Disapproval for abortion was one of these. Both also saw abortion as indicative of major societal flaws. If women expressed doubt about the efficacy and justice of tightening legal restraints on abortion, they did so in the company of Protestant clergyman such as Eddy. But where many religious and secular sources saw women's moral ignorance as the largest social problem, women's rights activists saw inequality in marriage, the sexual double standard, ignorance about sexuality, maternity, and embryology, and insufficient economic opportunities for women as the root structural causes.

Chapter Two

THE REVOLUTION AND 'RESTELLISM'

"*The Revolution* has adopted a new designation for a crime which is unfortunately becoming too common. It is 'Restellism,'" several Midwestern newspapers announced in June 1868.[1] They were wrong. The newspaper had not invented the term; it had been used, albeit sparingly, nearly a quarter-century earlier. A *Louisville Journal* article in 1844 cited the prevalence of "Millerism, Mormonism, Locofocoism, and Madame Restellism" as explaining a perceived lack of progress in the United States. Four years later, a number of newspapers used it to describe a case in Boston where a girl died from infection after obtaining an abortion at five months pregnant. And in another case in 1848, "Restellism" was used to describe the allegations made by a domestic servant in Boston who accused her employer of being an abortionist.[2] But *The Revolution* appears to have been responsible for increasing use of the term, principally by its publication of a punchy letter to the editor in May 1868.

"RESTELLISM to the right of us—Restellism to the left of us—Restellism in front of us, everywhere meets us. Restellism with the poor to save expense. Restellism with the rich to prevent exposure or preserve youth! Restellism has become the great crime of our day," the letter began. It went on to laud *The Revolution* in extravagant terms for its "independent thoughts" and "bold grasp of actualities" on these topics, expressed in its articles on abortion and its anti-quack-medicine advertising policy.[3] The *Chicago Tribune* and several other newspapers applauded the publication of this letter; the *Deseret News* announced that "*The Revolution*, the New York organ of the women, is out against the fearfully increasing crime of abortion and foeticide, which it calls Restellism."[4] These took the letter to be written by, rather than to, the newspaper's editors. Nevertheless, their praise of the newspaper's editorial and business decisions related to abortion and infanticide—which the letter had highlighted—was not altogether misplaced, as *The Revolution* continued to publish on the topic.

The Revolution's interventions on the linked topics of abortion and infanticide were not merely a response to their increasing popularity. Rather, editor Parker Pillsbury intentionally made the topic a priority for *The Revolution.* As he later told a large audience, "One of the conditions under which I consented to be connected with that journal [*The Revolution*] was that it should rebuke, in the strongest language possible, every such horrible abomination as that [the "professional infanticide" advertised in many newspapers]."[5] Pillsbury had previously lost his position as editor of the *National Anti-Slavery Standard* following his refusal to "speak the average sentiment" of the American Anti-Slavery Society, preferring instead to provide his own opinions about women's rights in the newspaper's editorials.[6] In agreeing to work for *The Revolution*, he had ensured that, on this topic at least, the newspaper's editorial position was in alignment with his own.[7]

In *The Revolution*'s first issue, published on January 8, 1868, its editors proclaimed, "A new paper is the promise of a new thought; of something better or different, at least, from what has gone before."[8] Because Susan B. Anthony, Elizabeth Cady Stanton, and Parker Pillsbury had in effect broken with the abolitionist movement, they found it necessary "to explore new alliances, new constituencies and new strategies."[9] Though *The Revolution* promised to "represent no party, sect or organization, but individual opinion; editors and correspondents alike, all writing, from their own stand point, and over their own names," it did develop a distinctive voice.[10] As Ellen Carol DuBois has argued, the newspaper's editors saw "suffrage in terms of its effect on the sexual distribution of power and privilege," and sought to link it with "the sexual and economic aspects of women's oppression."[11] *The Revolution*'s main focus—women's suffrage—went hand in hand with radical reform in "our political, religious and social world," and so the newspaper would cover these latter topics—as well as commercial and fiscal policy, at the behest of funder George Francis Train.[12]

The Revolution's staff—Anthony, Stanton, and Pillsbury—had been Garrisonian abolitionists and so insisted that every woman, like every enslaved person, had the same inherent dignity as every other human being.[13] *The Revolution* argued that righting the wrongs done to women meant both reforming social structures and assisting women in their own restoration. For both women and former slaves, *The Revolution* prescribed "education and enfranchisement," which no individual could achieve alone, and from which no individual could benefit without the exertion of personal effort.[14] The newspaper's wide-ranging content was in effect a multifaceted and ongoing argument for women's suffrage, and its news, biographies, philosophical extracts, book notices, financial exegeses, analysis of cultural trends, and political arguments provided an education intended to inculcate independence and spur action.

In *The Revolution*'s accounting, abortion and infanticide were the example par excellence of women's degradation and demonstrated the ill effect that women's low standing in the family, the church, politics, and law had had on their knowledge, moral development, and independence.[15] Some women knew so little of human physiology that they literally knew not what they did. Other women were driven to the act because of their lack of economic means or social support, or by sexual abuse within marriage or without, or because of their fear of the sexual double standard.[16] Others committed the act because "the strongest of all animal affections" had been perverted.[17] In this telling, women who had abortions were still victims, but were not passive; woman's free will was not overpowered, but rather bent, weighed down, and directed such that choices previously unimaginable became possible. In this telling, which betrayed a depth of vision into the human condition informed by critiques of slavery, society was to blame not only for the death of unborn children and the physical danger suffered by women who underwent abortions, but for warping women's consciences. This moral damage—this "degradation"—minimized individual women's guilt, but condemned a society where social and economic conditions and public opinion conspired to drive women to seek abortions.

"This crime of 'child murder,' 'abortion,' 'infanticide'"[18]

The Revolution's descriptions of the prevalence of abortion and infanticide were fairly standard. Citing numbers drawn from *The Medical and Surgical Reporter*, the *Boston Banner of Light*, the

New York Express, the *Toronto Globe*, and authorities including Horatio Storer, *The Revolution*'s editors concluded with them that these crimes were "on the increase to an extent inconceivable."[19] Abortion and infanticide were, in their language, "a crying evil," "revolting outrages against the laws of nature and our common humanity," "an evil most frightful," and "slaughter."[20]

By covering these topics, *The Revolution* contributed to conversations already taking place across mainstream publications. The first explicit reference to "child murder"—which, in the mid-nineteenth century, was used variously to mean deaths from neglect (including the intentional neglect of infants by "baby farming" institutions), infanticide, and abortion—came in *The Revolution*'s fourth issue, published in late January 1868.[21] "Infanticide" began with a quote from *The New York Times* on the attention lately given by the press to "the remarkable mortality among natural or illegitimate children" and closed by asking, "Where lies the remedy?" *The Revolution* gave a simple response: "In the independence of woman."[22]

That same week, the *New-York Tribune* published an editorial lamenting that "the murder of children, either before or after birth, has become so frightfully prevalent that physicians...have declared that were it not for immigration the white population of the United States would actually fall off!" As a remedy, the editorial called for "*well-conducted* foundling hospitals"—the common term for homes for abandoned infants. It excoriated a certain "notorious 'boarding-house,'" "where mothers, married or unmarried, can be delivered of their offspring in the strictest confidence, and relieved of all the bothers of maternity"—and where it was understood that children placed in its care would most likely die.[23] Yet the editorial called for reforming, rather than abolishing, such institutions because, while all care should be taken to reduce infant mortality in them, to prohibit them altogether would be to encourage another form of "child murder." The *Tribune* was straightforward: "If you place difficulties in the way of disposing of illegitimate children, you do not prevent illegitimacy; you only foster murder." The experience of well-run foundling hospitals, it argued, showed that they could "greatly diminish child-murder and abortion." While acknowledging that foundling hospitals might not decrease prostitution, the article added that "at any rate, murder is worse than prostitution, and we see no way of preventing the wholesale slaughter of infants which goes on every day around us, except by the establishment of asylums where the children which would otherwise be sacrificed may be received in secrecy, and conscientiously cared for."[24]

Less than two weeks later, *Harper's Weekly* picked up the topic, publishing its own editorial titled "Child Murder." Citing the increase in "mysterious advertisements in otherwise respectable newspapers," the decrease in the size of the average American family, the high infant mortality in Massachusetts's almshouses, and a recent discovery of an infant who had died of malnutrition, *Harper's* argued for "the establishment of foundling hospitals as the surest method of diminishing child murder." More than "vehement denunciation and exclamations of horror" was needed to address the issue, the article insisted, because "we have no right to make the sacrifice of those who are wholly innocent a means of restraining the guilty."[25]

Jumping back into this fray, *The Revolution* published not just one article titled "Child Murder" but four spread out over the next four months. The first of these addressed the *Tribune* article directly. Its author, a Mrs. J. Sumner, agreed with the necessity of foundling hospitals but suggested that they should also provide refuge for the mothers of the babies sheltered there, in "an additional wing at each end of those hospitals for the benefit of the mothers of those poor victims." There, she proposed, these women could be surrounded by "such reclaiming influences as will lift them out of the horrible pit, on to an impregnable rock of safety, where they may look down upon their degradation with disgust and up to the god-like destiny they might achieve for themselves—warding off a necessity which God never created, of making a compromise with evil, disaster and death." Sumner decried the popular press's unwillingness to "aim a distinctive blow at the root" of the "moral evil," evidenced by their willingness to sustain the sexual double standard. She wrote that New York ought not to "wait for the terrible effects of moral evil to remove the cause that produced it, thereby inviting the fate of Sodom to overtake the city," and she lauded *The Revolution*'s management for having "volunteered to place our half of the race above the reach of those gilded snakes that hail from the rank and file of our 'protectors.'"[26] Sumner's letter began a conversation in the pages of *The Revolution*, and the responses to it received and printed by the newspaper's editors reiterated how intertwined most saw abortion, abandonment, and infanticide to be.

The second "Child Murder" article, which appeared in March 1868, reported that officials in Androscoggin County, Maine, had discovered "*four hundred murders annually produced by abortion*" there. Identifying the same problem pointed out by the *Harper's Weekly* and *Tribune* articles, it suggested different causes and, therefore, different solutions. A large percentage of these shocking numbers, the unsigned editorial suggested, were due to "forced maternity, not out of legal marriage but within it, the complete power of the stronger over the weaker sex." In suggesting that more abortions were obtained by married than unmarried women, *The Revolution* reflected the growing consensus. Yet its editors did not avoid the potentially uncomfortable questions thus suggested, but rather met them head-on: "There must be a remedy even for such a crying evil as this," *The Revolution* insisted. "Where shall it be found, at least where begin, if not in the complete enfranchisement and elevation of woman?"[27]

One reply, which came in early April—and was yet again titled "Child Murder"—arrived from a woman living in Androscoggin County who claimed to know "several of the women who got to make up the four hundred" who had had abortions. She objected to the idea that education would be enough to reduce the incidence of abortion, writing, "I must confess that I do not think this knowledge would deter one out of ten, if it did one out of a hundred, with us, from the commission of this deed." Education was not an apt remedy for "forced maternity," and while she implied that ignorance might mitigate an individual woman's culpability, no woman was motivated to seek an abortion by her own lack of knowledge. Instead, women sought abortions *despite* the knowledge that doing so might be tantamount to suicide, and so would not be immediately dissuaded by a deepened understanding of the reasons for the act's immorality. Attempts to decrease abortion ought instead to respond to the reasons *why* women sought them. And to understand those reasons, the author wrote, one ought to look at "the wretched homes where heart-broken women work day and night, for the most shameful pittance, to provide food for the little ones whom the brutal lusts of a drunken husband have forced upon them." Marital rape and women's lack of economic independence were at the root of the problem. The author signed herself "Conspirator," explaining at the end of her letter that "it is time to conspire against an institution which makes one human being the slave of another."[28]

The Revolution's fourth "Child Murder" article, published in May 1868, was a very short editorial that cited regulations in Liverpool, England, intended to fight the increase in abortion and infanticide. *The Revolution* ironically noted that, despite the obvious need for measures to mitigate the problem, the "virtuous British public continue to oppose foundling hospitals lest they should encourage vice!"[29]

Though these articles made up a small percentage of those published in *The Revolution* on the topics of abortion and infanticide, they demonstrate where the newspaper's coverage of those issues aligned with—and ran against—mainstream coverage. *The Revolution* did not dispute the incidence of abortion in the United States, whether married or unmarried women were more likely to seek abortions, or whether abortion was morally wrong and deleterious to the country. Rather, the newspaper's editors focused on understanding the reasons that women sought abortions and on measures that could decrease that demand. As with the other topics it covered, *The Revolution* provided deepened analysis of this subject.

"Enforced motherhood is a crime"

In her contribution to *The Revolution*'s "Child Murder" discourse, Matilda Joslyn Gage wrote that the discussion of abortion by married women in Androscoggin County had "touched a subject which lies deeper down into woman's wrongs than any other. This is the denial of the right to herself."[30] Gage conceded that much progress had been made on many topics within the field of "woman's rights," citing the relatively new abilities of some women to hold property jointly with their husbands, to control their own separate property, and to possess their own earnings. Yet the idea that a married woman had given her once-and-for-all consent to sex at her husband's will at her wedding had not faded; "in no historic age of the world has woman yet" had "the right to herself." Consequently, she wrote, "I hesitate not to assert that most of this crime of 'child murder,' 'abortion,' 'infanticide,' lies at the door of the male sex." Gage explained that "tens of thousands of husbands and fathers throughout this land are opposed to large families," because of the cost of providing for children. Yet "so deeply implanted is the sin of self-gratification, that consequences are not considered while selfish desire controls the heart." It was not surprising that women sought abortions when their husbands pursued contradictory ends—the at-will satisfaction of sexual desire and the curtailing of family size—with similar insistence, and without discussing "this subject of deepest and most vital interest" with their wives. Both women and children were the losers in this scenario: "Enforced motherhood is a crime against the body of the mother and the soul of the child."[31]

The Revolution's second "Child Murder" article had similarly argued that "forced maternity" lay at the root of the apparently increasing rates of abortion.[32] As Linda Gordon has written, "Few in the nineteenth century advocated or even accepted the separation of sexuality from reproduction."[33] Taking the close connection between sexuality and reproduction for granted, when *The Revolution*'s authors argued against "forced maternity," they implied forced sex. Thus, they argued that women rather than men should decide when to have sex—and, therefore, children. This insistence that marriage did not mean broad consent to sex in any circumstance was aimed against an existing understanding of marriage, but it was also a hearkening back to an older—and perhaps distinctly American—understanding of marriage as companionate, in which husband and wife were understood as equal partners within their family.[34]

Both Gage and "Conspirator" also pointed toward economic issues as drivers of abortion, including a woman's ability to earn a living wage for herself and her dependents, and a married woman's ability to control jointly held property. Some of these issues could be addressed by legal means, and so suffrage could give women a concrete means of improving their own lives and reducing stressors that drove women to commit "revolting outrages against the laws of nature and our common humanity."[35] While "the strongest feeling of a true woman's nature is her love for her child," that instinct could be distorted: When "woman is dependent on man... she will despise herself and hate him whose desire she gratifies for the necessaries of life; the children of such unions must needs be unloved and deserted." *The Revolution* decried this state of affairs: this was proof that "all things are inverted."[36]

"What has become of the babies?"

Anti-suffragists used the slogan "What will become of the babies?" to imply that when women became interested in politics and civic affairs, they would lose interest in or neglect their children. Eleanor Kirk, writing in *The Revolution*, responded to these critics bluntly: "Why don't [sic] somebody ask—what *has become* of the babies? Ask Restelle [sic] and thousands of physicians, male and female, who have been engaged in their work of destruction for years... who pocket a big fee and a little bundle of flesh at the same time, and nobody's the wiser!" Children were already suffering because of women's degradation.[37] This state of affairs was, Elizabeth Cady Stanton wrote, due to "the ignorance, folly, and selfishness of women," and would only be resolved by their "the education and enfranchisement."[38]

Suffrage would work against infanticide and abortion by allowing women to remove some of its causes. To the extent that the sexual double standard was enshrined in law, law encouraged abortion. When women had the power to change the laws—including raising the age of consent and improving the legal definition of statutory rape—women's motives for seeking abortions would be decreased.[39] Additionally, the changes that would have to take place in society for women to receive the vote would be good for both mothers and their children. As Julia Crouch succinctly put it, "Babies are not at all in the way of Woman Suffrage, but rather their existence is a great reason why their mothers should have a right to assist in making the laws that these little ones must grow up under and obey."[40] Giving women equal citizenship could foster companionate marriage, by making women more obviously equal to their husbands, and might, by motivating and allowing them to fulfill their civic duties, spur them on to additional responsibility for their children, too. Women's oftentimes primary responsibility for raising and educating their children gave additional weight to the argument that they should be granted a voice in the laws.

The usual abortion-and-suffrage argument said that granting women suffrage would reduce the incidence of abortion. Parker Pillsbury offered a slightly different version—comparing anti-suffrage women with women who sought abortions. Because women who were aware of their political duties would likely also view the pursuit of such legal changes as part of their parental duties to protect their daughters, "women who do not desire the ballot, who are willing to trust their daughters to such protection as the laws and courts now give them, would add little to their present fearful culpability, by openly proclaiming and defending, as well as perpetrating the crimes of foeticide and infanticide." Open violence toward one's own children was not so different from allowing one's children to be abused by others, Pillsbury argued. Women needed the vote, and were *morally obligated* to fight for it, to protect their young daughters from the deleterious effect of the legally enshrined sexual double standard.[41]

The Revolution's editors and contributors seemed to understand the power of "education" to minimize the incidence of abortion in two ways. One method was simple enough: while medical practitioners were aware that a fetus has life prior to quickening, this knowledge was not universal. Consequently, Dr. Anna Densmore could argue, "It is only through ignorance that it ['the crime of abortion'] has become such a wide-spread evil. But few women, even among the educated and intelligent, realize that the embryo child is imbued with the life element prior to the moment when its physical movements become conscious to her."[42] Education was understood to function in another way, too, beyond simply providing context. Many in the nineteenth century were "genuinely convinced that the ability to read and write well would result in improved morals and a more perfect society," and this principle extended beyond literacy and numeracy to other areas of education as well.[43] Consequently, Bostonian women's rights advocate Elizabeth L.

Daniels could say that children's rights included the "right to the best maternal conditions prior to birth, the right to be born (which is now denied to thousands), and the right to *that kind of education which will develop them to perfect manhood and womanhood.*"[44] And Eleanor Kirk could insist that when "education, moral, physical, and intellectually practical" became widespread, then "men and women will come together, attracted by mutual respect."[45] When women were better educated in all aspects of their life, their demoralization would decrease, and they would gain the freedom necessary to behave more morally.

Martha "Mattie" Brinkerhoff

Some of *The Revolution*'s most trenchant writing on the topic of abortion came from Martha Brinkerhoff. Little is known about Brinkerhoff's early life, but like Stanton and Anthony, she was a veteran of the 1867 Kansas campaign for the vote.[46] She began writing to *The Revolution* in the newspaper's second month, and at first primarily reported on the lectures she was giving in Missouri and Iowa and on her successes in raising subscriptions for the newspaper. One early exception came in September 1868, when she reacted against a letter to the editors that had argued, citing Sanger's *History of Prostitution*, that vice could not be abolished.[47] On the contrary, she rather witheringly insisted, "That man who honestly believes that prostitution can never be abolished is to be pitied; for his faith in the progress of the world is evidently very weak." While offering significant concessions to her interlocutor—"We cannot abolish horse-stealing by hanging men or confining them in State Prison. . . . we do not expect to legislate an evil like this out of existence"—she argued that means of abolishing evils did exist.

"The very fact that we have men and women who would rather die than debase themselves under any circumstances is conclusive evidence that all may attain to that standard, for we are all children of the self-same God," she insisted. This standard could be attained by individuals' learning "a higher consideration of life and of themselves." By this "true education," which would help them to "truly 'love themselves,'" they would be enabled to "abide by the decisions of the moral judge that sits enthroned in the council chamber of their own beings."[48]

After her letter about prostitution, it was fifteen months before Brinkerhoff again wrote to *The Revolution* about a controversial social issue other than women's suffrage. She spent much of that time continuing to report on her pursuits on behalf of women's rights in Missouri, Illinois, and Iowa. When she pivoted from this coverage, it was to take exception to an article in the *New Yorker Staats Zeitung*, the leading German-language newspaper, a translation of which had been provided to *The Revolution* by another reader. As it did with some frequency, the newspaper had printed the *Staats Zeitung* article with the purpose of refuting it. The article pilloried women's rights advocates by claiming that they wanted all men and women "to be regarded as hermaphrodites, who have like functions and equal rights."[49] It cited abortion as one example of the effort radical women evidently undertook toward this end: "American women have long been ardently engaged in the endeavor to free themselves in a mechanical way from the discharge of those functions which are essential to the continuance of society and which cannot be shared with them or performed for them by men."[50] This effort would ultimately end in failure, the author argued, with "the female portion [of mankind occupied] with the home circle."[51] *The Revolution*'s brief commentary accompanying the piece had dismissed it as evidence of "what foreign legislation will be on the woman question."[52]

Brinkerhoff's suffrage reporting had been effective and to the point, if lengthy. But when she began to address the topic of abortion and infanticide, she became eloquent. In a letter to *The Revolution* printed in early September 1869, Brinkerhoff indignantly zeroed in on the evidence offered by the *Staats Zeitung* article: "The boldness with which many men blame women for the crime of infanticide without assuming themselves, in the case, a shadow of responsibility, I should think would rouse every *mother*, at least, to utter words in self-defence [sic]."[53] Like *The Revolution*'s editors, she did not argue with the author's implication that "American women are more guilty of this practice than the women of any other nation," but rather asked why that was the case, and how this situation could be reversed.

"When a man steals to satisfy hunger, we may safely conclude that there is something wrong in society," Brinkerhoff insisted. "So when a woman destroys the life of her unborn child, it is an evidence that either by education or circumstances she has been greatly wronged." While she cited Stanton's argument that "education and enfranchisement" would decrease the incidence of abortion, she argued contra Stanton that women's education was not lacking. Rather, "the masses of American women, not only know how to read and write, but so much of the 'tree of knowledge' have many of them eaten, that they have learned it should be for them to decide when and how often they shall take upon themselves the sacred duties of motherhood." Similar to the *Circular*, she argued that the resulting disjunct between knowledge and circumstances proved untenable for many women: "Knowledge and slavery are incompatible. Teach a slave to read, and he wants to be his own master." Yet "as law and custom give to the husband the absolute control of the wife's person," women were sometimes "forced to not only violate physical law, but to outrage the holiest instincts of her being to maintain even a semblance of that freedom which by nature belongs to every human soul."[54] Brinkerhoff was not defending the practice of abortion, but was broadening the blame assigned for it, to marriage and rape law, custom, and individual husbands. Like the Androscoggin County "Conspirator" and Matilda Joslyn Gage, Brinkerhoff identified men's abuse of women—and the public opinion that sheltered such men—as the fundamental cause of abortion and infanticide.

In her next letter to *The Revolution*, published later that month, Brinkerhoff chose the topic of unwed motherhood. She again responded to Stanton, who in an earlier article had advised a girl who found herself pregnant to "keep these matters out of our courts and journals," rather than suing her seducer, and "in self-dependence and self-support [to] learn the virtue and dignity of a true womanhood."[55] While Brinkerhoff agreed that this was good advice in the case of a woman whose family was supportive of her and was able to provide for her, she pled the case of the unwed mother who needed to support herself by her own work. She reminded the audience of *The Revolution* that "more than ninety per cent of our own sex will shut their doors against [an unwed mother who needed to support herself] and refuse her even the privilege of doing their most menial work." This fact, she argued, indicated the need for a specific charitable work. Brinkerhoff acknowledged that foundling hospitals were "better than no protection for such little ones," but asked her readers to consider "what mother would yield her innocent babe to the care of strangers... if there were any chance for her to care for it herself." What was needed was an initiative to assist unmarried mothers in gaining the ability to support both themselves and their children. She was not overly saccharine: "Unwelcome children, in and out of marriage, are the fruit of the dependence, ignorance, and consequent degradation of woman," and the former, in particular, "show the degradation and demoralization of our sex." But she insisted that society should recognize that an unmarried mother was "only an erring one," not an evil or thoroughly debauched woman. The public opinion that guided unwed mothers toward prostitution by disallowing any honorable means of support—that, therefore, "forced her to do it, and now refuses her an opportunity to reform"—meant that, in Brinkerhoff's telling, "it is the duty of the true and noble among our sex to inaugurate some plan by which means can be had to support such mothers, or to see that they are provided homes with noble, cultivated women, where they can, when able, support themselves."[56]

In her Midwestern lecturing, Brinkerhoff had established a reputation as an impressive speaker on behalf of women's rights. In late 1868, *The Revolution* reprinted an article from an unnamed "Western paper," lauding her as "a popular lecturer, [with] a brilliant future." She was described as "modest and lady-like in her deportment, earnest and candid in her reasoning, interesting and entertaining as a speaker," and as the equal of famed lecturer Anna E. Dickinson. Her frequent letters to *The Revolution* on the state of the lecture field were long and interesting. And in early 1869, she was listed as a speaker at the Equal Rights Association's Anniversary, along with Elizabeth Cady Stanton, Lucy Stone, Amelia Bloomer, and other prominent women's rights advocates. Yet her September 1869 letters to *The Revolution* are some of the last remaining evidences of her public activities until she suddenly resurfaced in the national news in 1873.[57]

In May 1873, newspapers from Sacramento to New York City reported on "the new departure of Mrs. H. M. [sic]

Brinkerhoff," which resulted in "a very unhappy question [being] thrust upon the public—as to whether she is a victim of emotional insanity or of hereditary idiocy."[58] Brinkerhoff, who was married, had fallen in love with a married Battle Creek, Michigan, shoemaker, appeared to travel with him on a lecturing tour, moved into his house as a housekeeper while his wife and children traveled east, and finally held a public lecture to defend her behavior before her scandalized neighbors.[59] This event was given widespread coverage, which led many women's rights advocates to leave her out of their histories entirely, not wanting her scandal to be lastingly associated with their cause. One woman explained her omission of Brinkerhoff from her account of the history of suffrage work in the Midwest, saying, "She so hurt our cause here.... I thought I would not serve the matter by her name." Even though Brinkerhoff "spoke well," the woman stated, "It is better to tell too little than too much."[60] Nevertheless, Stanton, Anthony, and Gage did not entirely dissociate themselves from her, showing that they did not think that her missteps had entirely negated the contributions she had made to the women's rights movement. Their *History of Woman Suffrage* would report that "in 1868 Mrs. Martha H. Brinkerhoff made a very successful lecture-tour through the northern counties of Iowa. She roused great interest and organized many societies, canvassing meanwhile for subscribers to *The Revolution*."[61]

More Than Just Words

Beyond merely providing commentary on the linked issues of abortion, infanticide, and prostitution, *The Revolution* also concretely worked to repair their root causes. Like other commentators on those topics, its editors understood that changing public opinion—about the morality of abortion, about the dignity of motherhood, and about women's right to determine when to become pregnant—was one key practical remedy. Newspapers shaped public opinion, and so, to name a problem, to probe its sources, and to suggest solutions in the pages of one's newspaper was to move toward resolving it.[62]

The Revolution also took a more deliberate step toward addressing the increase in these crimes—or at least, made a decided effort to ensure that it did not contribute to it—by refusing "quack medicine" advertisements. In its opening issue, Susan B. Anthony, Elizabeth Cady Stanton, and Parker Pillsbury signed the newspaper's editorial policy, which proclaimed, "It will indulge in no Gross Personalities and insert no Quack or Immoral Advertisements, so common even in Religious Newspapers."[63] In the second issue, this assertion, published under the heading "The Revolution Will Advocate," changed slightly to "Dedicated to Morality and Reform, THE REVOLUTION will not insert Gross Personalities and Quack Advertisements, which even Religious Newspapers introduce into every family."[64] In phrasing its advertising policy this way, the newspaper was making a very pointed, though not entirely explicit, statement.

The connection between the press and the apparently increasing incidence of abortion was widely noted, whether the only somewhat veiled advertisements were understood as evidence of encouragement or of existing demand.[65] Horatio Storer had noted in 1859 that there was "hardly a newspaper through the land that does not contain their open and pointed advertisements, or a drug-store whose shelves are not crowded with their nostrums."[66] An article titled "Foeticide" published in the *Northwestern Christian Advocate* in March 1867 and republished in the secular press unequivocally stated that "a newspaper whose satanic advertisements of quack nostrums and quack doctors further this fearful evil should be treated as a social enemy and its unscrupulous publishers should be socially outlawed."[67] And a few months later, the Oneida Community's *Circular* questioned the reasoning behind the observed frequency of such advertisements in an article titled "Murder of the Unborn":

> How an editor can hereafter give place to one of those carefully-worded, villainous advertisements of nostrums which have been so common in our advertising sheets, is more than we can tell. He must know that his readers will ask him questions like these: "Are you so stupid as to think you are doing good?" "Are you so ignorant as not to know what you are doing?" "Are you so poor that you can't possibly do right? Or are you too wicked to care what you do?"[68]

In *The Revolution*'s third month, editor Parker Pillsbury made the connection between the newspaper's advertising policy and the broader discourse on abortion unavoidably explicit. While "quack medicine" might generally refer to medical services offered by untrained or unlicensed persons or to patent medicines, Pillsbury was more specific: "Quack Medicine venders, however rich, proud and pretentious, Foeticides and Infanticides should be classed together and regarded with shuddering horror by the whole human race." This was because, "by arts the most wily and diabolical," abortionists were able "through the newspaper press to beguile the wise and prudent, the high as well as the low, the rich, the poor, the religious, [and] the reprobate," so that "these frightful evils become almost incorporated into the very bone and marrow of our moral and material existence."

Quack medicine venders, he said, were easy to condemn. But, he asked, "what shall be said of those editors and proprietors of public journals who give them and their murderous work currency, respectability; nay, baptize them into the sacred name of religion by their co-operation!"[69] Later in the year, *The Revolution* would critique a new Ohio anti-abortion law for failing to make the publishing of such advertising illegal.[70] Pillsbury went on to explain the jibe against the religious press in *The Revolution*'s advertising policy. In an address given before the Lakeshore Medical Association at Painesville the previous summer that had been widely reprinted, Dr. E. L. Plympton had decried the influence of these advertisements by recalling that "our daughters have been trained under the influence of such reading, with a knowledge that it was welcomed in the best family circles."[71] Pillsbury expanded on this claim and vivified it in his article, saying that

> It is not in the *Herald* and *Sunday Mercury* alone that such advertisements are found. They are in the most orthodox and widely read of the religious newspapers. And in these papers they are borne into the most godly households; laid on the same center table with the Bible, the prayer book, and Sunday school catechisms. They are in papers that lie on family altars, that are mentioned gratefully in the morning family prayer as blessings enjoyed under the smile of Providence;

> papers that are taken by good men and godly women to the conference meetings, that the revival and missionary intelligence may be read for the encouraging and quickening of the church.[72]

He explained the pragmatic reason this might occur, saying that "it is well known to newspaper publishers" that "advertising patronage [by the business of 'child murder'] pays far more than any other." Yet citing principles given by Thoreau and Goethe, Pillsbury recommended that *The Revolution*'s readers "judge of newspapers largely by their advertisements." Since Pillsbury, Elizabeth Cady Stanton, and Susan B. Anthony—*The Revolution*'s editors and proprietor—refused this cooperation with evil, even with the great financial losses this would entail, the imputation was clear: *The Revolution*'s refusal of "quack advertisements" gave indisputable evidence of its "true quality and character."[73]

Change in Ownership

In 1870, no doubt in part due the rising debt accumulating in *The Revolution*'s name, Susan B. Anthony concluded that "so far as my own personal efforts are concerned, I can be more useful on the platform than in a newspaper."[74] In May of that year, Anthony sold *The Revolution* to Laura Curtis Bullard for a dollar, and personally assumed the newspaper's debt to that point. Bullard had previously been a contributor to the paper, as well as a member of the women's club Sorosis, a cofounder of the Brooklyn Women's Club, and a founding member of the National Women Suffrage Association. In Susan B. Anthony's description, her "refinement of manners, knowledge of literature, acquaintance with leading minds and enthusiasm for the cause" made her a fit candidate for the job.[75] Former abolitionist and women's rights advocate Edwin A. Studwell was elected to serve as the newspaper's business manager, or publisher.

When Bullard and Studwell assumed control of *The Revolution*, some things changed, but many did not. The newspaper lost its occasional apocalypticism and began including fashion tips, gossip, and jokes.[76] It published fewer letters and more articles without bylines. But it covered similar events, organizations, and topics, including the progress of women's rights in England, proposals for licensing prostitution, workingwomen's concerns—and the paired topics of abortion and infanticide.[77]

What *The Revolution* under Stanton, Anthony, and Pillsbury had termed "quack," it now termed "thug." A March 1871 *Revolution* editorial titled "Thug Doctors" discussed a proposed New York State bill "for the purpose of punishing abortionists." Abortionists were, in *The Revolution*'s language, "the vampires of both sexes," "the wealthy madams who, we fear have pledged their souls to the devil more effectually than Dr. Festus ever did in the old legands [sic]" and "the Thugs of the other sex [who] will brew their hell-broth, and bottle it, and write some innocent inoxious [sic] moral looking name upon the label which shall spread the work of death and still give license to the safe exercise of unbridled passions."[78]

The Revolution expressed skepticism about the proposed law's potential efficacy, because "the ruling power of this city have too vital an interest in helping the class of practitioners it is ostensibly designed to crush, continue their business, to allow us to entertain a contrary hope." Where the newspaper had earlier found corruption in society at large, it now found corruption also in the highest levels of government: "How many underground passages are there running from these palaces of sin to the public offices of this city?"[79] *The Revolution* described the New York police force as "whitening sepulchers, full of all uncleanness," because its members "shut their eyes and play there are no Keno or Faro banks, panel houses, abortionist establishments, or lottery swindles, until informed of their existence by a daily paper."[80] Consequently, *The Revolution* stated, "Governed as we now are, there is every reason to suppose it [the proposed law] will, if passed, remain a dead letter upon the statute book."[81]

While Bullard permitted patent medicine advertisements in *The Revolution*, she held with Stanton, Anthony, and Pillsbury's opposition to advertisements of potentially abortifacient drugs. A September 1871 editorial applauded a recent uproar over abortion in New York City newspapers—and then went on to point out the hypocrisy inherent in the newspapers' behavior: "The solemn and undeniable fact remains that some of these very papers which have exhausted the language of vituperation and condemnation in scathing abortionists, advertise their business in displayed type for exorbitant prices, and thus invite and incite weak-minded women to become parties to a crime against nature, society, and God." Again expressing a lack of faith in the capacity of law enforcement effectively to put an end to this activity, *The Revolution* argued that "these culprits"—the major New York City newspapers—"should be arraigned and condemned by public opinion, and made to feel the keen edge of public censure in loss of patronage and circulation."[82]

Bullard transferred ownership of *The Revolution* to J. N.

Hallock and Rev. W. T. Clarke in October 1871, and the newspaper survived only months before being subsumed into Hallock's *Liberal Christian*.

Chapter Three

WOMEN'S ELEVATION AND THE MEDICAL PROFESSION

By the end of the 1860s, Caroline Dall found herself a persona non grata in the Boston women's rights community, despite her vocal calls for improving women's educational and economic opportunities. Thomas Wentworth Higginson attributed this to Dall's being "such an *intensely* unpopular person!" While she was indeed known for her strong personality—her biographer has written that "she was outspoken, frequently dogmatic, more than occasionally abrasive"—in February 1869, Dall realized that there was more to the animosity she had been receiving from women associated with the New England Hospital for Women and Children (NEHWC) and the New England Women's Club.[1] She wrote in her diary that "all of a sudden, without reason, it flashed across me that my letter to Dr. Storer on abortion, printed by him, was the cause of the animosity. . . . The women there are evidently too small to understand that I may sympathize with Dr. Storer in one point, yet not be 'guilty of all.' "[2] Dall's June 1866 letter praising Horatio Storer's anti-abortion *Why Not? A Book for Every Woman* and asking for a companion volume directed at men had been printed in his 1867 *Is it I? A Book for Every Man.* In August 1866, Storer had angrily resigned from the NEHWC, publicly denigrating it and doubling down on the "physiological incapacities of women," in particular their supposed incapacity to be physicians, which became known as Storer's "favorite subject."[3] Storer's opposition to women's medical education was what Dall referred to as the "all" of which she was not guilty.

Horatio Storer and Caroline Dall were in some respects cut from the same cloth. They were well-educated Bostonians who moved in similar social circles and were both genuinely concerned for women's well-being. But Storer's version of caring for women's needs tended to be patriarchal and patronizing, and Dall was a champion for women's empowerment in every respect she could imagine. Because she understood that a decrease in abortions would be good for women, she was willing to publicly support someone who could be an ally in this, if not in all. But between Storer's obstinacy and Dall's desire to prove herself, he lost any real chance of gaining the women's rights movement as a key ally in his campaign against abortion, and she succeeded in further excluding herself from the Boston societies of which she wanted to be a part.

Historians commonly point to Horatio Storer's misogyny as proof of an inherent and unavoidable opposition between women's rights and the anti-abortion movement. Storer's reputation is not entirely undeserved: he did not believe that women were in all ways equal to men, and he fought against most women's participation in the medical profession, leading to a rift between him and those in the women's rights movement. Nonetheless, such a narrative ignores women's voices, including those of the women doctors who worked with Storer.

Two and a half years before Dall came to her realization, Horatio Storer had been employed at the NEHWC, opened by Dr. Marie Zakrzewska in July 1862. He was one of the few male physicians to be on its staff during the first ninety-some years of its existence. In joining the hospital, he had intended to do "what little I personally could do towards the real enfranchisement of women." Sounding a rather different tone than he would only a few years later, he embarked on this work in the hopes that "by elevating the few women who might be better educated than the mass of those of their sex assuming medical honors and responsibilities," the medical profession "might be purged, to a certain extent at least, of many claimants utterly unfitted for its membership."[4] In this view, providing medical education to women who had the interest and talent to pursue such a career would be good for both women and the medical profession. In this, his motivation was similar to Zakrzewska's.

Pioneering women doctors like Zakrzewska and Anita Tyng agreed with Storer's condemnation of abortion. They also considered the increasing prevalence of abortion as an important reason why there should be more women in medicine. Storer's opposition to abortion was, like that of women's rights activists, folded into an argument for women's bodily autonomy within marriage. He explicitly condemned marital rape and eventually listed it as one of the primary reasons women sought abortions. Yet despite Storer's close association with women's rights advocates during the years he worked at the NEHWC, he never made direct overtures to the women's rights movement.

Founding the New England Hospital for Women and Children

In 1855, Marie Zakrzewska was attending the Cleveland Medical College. Three years earlier, the Berlin-born daughter of Polish parents had, at only twenty-two, briefly served as the chief of the midwifery program at Berlin's Royal Charité Hospital. Seeking greater opportunities to practice medicine, she had left Germany in 1853.[5] Her first year in New York City did not proffer such hoped-for opportunities. Then she met Dr. Elizabeth Blackwell. The first woman in America to earn a medical degree, Blackwell taught Zakrzewska English and became her preceptor. More than a mentor, a preceptor was responsible for a medical student's clinical education; as Zakrzewska explained, a student "studied the preliminaries necessary for entering a medical college or school" and "visited patients with this preceptor and assisted the latter in every way possible."[6] Experience gained under a preceptor's tutelage counted for much: "Any student who could bring certificates from an acceptable preceptor could easily procure a diploma by attending the medical school of any college for two short successive winter sessions."[7] Blackwell gained admission to the Cleveland Medical College for Zakrzewska and supplied her with books.

During the same year, Horatio Storer began working as an attending physician at the Boston Lying-In Hospital (BLIH), which had just reopened in newly built quarters.[8] That fall, Storer's father, David Humphreys Storer, gave an introductory lecture at the Massachusetts Medical College of Harvard University, entitled "Duties, Trials and Rewards of the Student of Midwifery." In it, he denounced the "existing, and universally acknowledged evil" of criminal abortion, which he characterized as an "unholy transaction."[9] The lecture was later published—without the section on abortion. The *Boston Medical and Surgical Journal* noted the omission in an editorial and questioned the rationale behind this decision. "It would appear that sheer ignorance, in many honest people, is the spring of much of the horrible intra-uterine murder which exists among us; why not, then, enlighten this ignorance?"[10] In early 1856, the BLIH began admitting unmarried pregnant women—many of whom, it was argued, "are the victims of seduction, rarely of deliberate vice; they are deluded and unfortunate, and by a charitable reception and kind care may be saved from utter ruin." This change in admission policy was understood by the medical community to tend to "counteract the evils of procuring abortion and of later infanticide so frequent in our midst."[11]

When Zakrzewska returned to New York in 1856, she found it difficult to find lodgings and a place to set up a practice. Elizabeth Blackwell, several years earlier, had had the same experience.[12] It was nearly impossible to put a sign for a woman physician on a building, as "ladies would not reside in a house so marked, and expressed the utmost astonishment that it should be allowed in a respectable establishment."[13] As Zakrzewska later explained, "The name of 'Madame Restelle' [sic] was on every one's tongue as typifying the 'female physician.' She was then the leading abortionist."[14] Zakrzewska wrote to a friend that, due to Restell's notoriety, "to be addressed in public as doctor was painful, for heads would turn to look at the woman thus stigmatized."[15] She and Blackwell decided to try to "stop her [Restell] in her vile career," and so consulted with a lawyer, who told them, "'She is a social necessity, and she will be protected by rich and influential personages.'"[16]

It was in large part because "so wide a stain"—and Restell's stain in particular—"could be diffused over innocent persons by a single evil reputation," that Blackwell had been motivated to pursue the study of medicine in the first place. She later wrote, "The gross perversion and destruction of motherhood by the abortionist filled me with indignation, and awakened active antagonism. That the honourable term 'female physician' should be exclusively applied to those women who carried on this shocking trade seemed to me a horror." By becoming a "female physician," with "a great reverence for maternity—the mighty creative power which more than any other human faculty seemed to bring womanhood nearer the Divine"—Blackwell aimed to bring some light and truth into what was then "an utter degradation of what might and should become a noble position for women."[17]

Blackwell and Zakrzewska went into private practice, working separately but in the same building. They also began making plans to open an infirmary where women physicians could practice and women interested in medicine could gain clinical experience. During this time, Emily Blackwell, who was studying in Europe, wrote to convince her sister and Zakrzewska to cross the Atlantic. According to Zakrzewska, in London "we could not there have to live down or fight the nefarious and criminal practice which was being carried on chiefly in New York City, but also more or less in smaller places, and by which its advertising in the newspapers had created such a strong prejudice against 'Doctresses,' as its practitioners were styled."[18] But they were not persuaded, and decided to continue on with their work in New York City to provide high-quality medical education for women who wanted to practice professionally and honorably.

In 1856, two years after Blackwell had established a small dispensary for poor women and children, she and Zakrzewska decided to considerably enlarge it. *An Appeal in Behalf of the Medical Education of Women* described the institution they intended to create. It would provide women medical students with both didactic instruction and practical experience, thus producing women doctors who would be "thoroughly qualified to meet the responsibilities of their positions worthily," through the possession of "good acquirements, good character, [and] good sense."[19] In 1857, after doing considerable fundraising in both New York and Boston—and gaining the support of Anna Cabot Lowell, Ednah Dow Cheney, Anna Huidekoper Clarke, Samuel Sewall, and others—Zakrzewska and Blackwell founded the New York Infirmary for Women and Children. Zakrzewska served as the hospital's "resident physician, superintendant [sic], housekeeper, and instructor to the students."[20]

After the Boston Lying-In Hospital closed its doors in November 1856, citing financial difficulties, Storer immersed himself in anti-abortion work. His first efforts were local, working with the Suffolk County Medical Society and the State Medical Society of Massachusetts to lobby the Massachusetts legislature to revise its criminal statutes on abortion. He then set to work on a series of articles for the *North-American Medico-Chirurgical Review* on the intersection of medicine and law on the topic of criminal abortion, under the heading "Contributions to Obstetric Jurisprudence," and reviewed W. F. Montgomery's *Signs and Symptoms of Pregnancy* in the *North-American Medico-Chirurgical Review*, arguing that the only entirely reliable evidence of pregnancy was the identification of a fetal heartbeat.[21] He chaired the American Medical Association's Special Committee on Criminal Abortion, and presented a paper, "On the Decrease of the Rate of Increase of Population Now Obtaining in Europe and America," to the American Academy of Arts and Sciences. He quickly made a name for himself as the foremost anti-abortion campaigner in the country.

When Zakrzewska returned to Boston in 1859 for a vacation, she was invited to join the New England Female Medical College (NEFMC) and create a "clinical department," which would provide "for the accommodation and medical treatment of lying-in and other women and children" and would contain "facilities for instruction and practice...[with] advantages as ample, it is believed, as can be had at any medical institution to which females are admitted."[22] The Bostonians who had helped her raise funds for the New York Infirmary encouraged her to make the move. Because the Infirmary was by then on a stable financial footing and its operations more established, she took the opportunity. The NEFMC was, in her estimation, "by no means yet what we wish it to be," yet it was "deserving of every effort to raise it to the position that it ought to take among the medical institutions of America."[23] Zakrzewska joined the NEFMC's faculty as its professor of obstetrics and diseases of women and children and became the chief resident of its new clinical department. Lucy Sewall, whose father, Samuel Sewall, was one of the NEFMC's trustees, was among the twenty-two students enrolled during Zakrzewska's first year.[24] Anita Tyng, a student from Newburyport, Massachusetts, who was a cousin of abolitionist and women's rights advocate Thomas Wentworth Higginson, enrolled the following year, along with nineteen other students.[25]

Despite her high hopes at the outset, after two years at the NEFMC, Zakrzewska realized that her aspirations for the institution could not come to fruition. "Not one of my expectations for a thorough medical education for women has been realized," she wrote to the NEFMC's board of trustees in June 1861, explaining that she would leave the school at the end of the following spring semester. By February 1862, Zakrzewska was looking for other ways to advance the women's movement, and she visited Caroline Dall to ask her to serve as an editor for a proposed *American Women's Journal*, which Zakrzewska planned to publish with the motto "Equal Rights for All Mankind."[26] She left her teaching position at the NEFMC in March and her position in its clinical department in June.[27] Tyng left the NEFMC with Zakrzewska, as did many members of its board of lady managers and board of trustees, including Samuel Sewall.[28]

Almost immediately after her departure from the NEFMC, in June 1862, Zakrzewska founded the New England Hospital for Women and Children (NEHWC). As with the other institutions she had led, the new hospital was intended to provide clinical experience for women studying medicine.[29] In November 1862, the abolitionist *Liberator* reported on its first annual meeting, explaining that it had begun as Zakrzewska's clinical department at the NEFMC, and had become an independent institution in July. In her address at the meeting, Zakrzewska "urged the continued reception of unmarried women needing humane and friendly care in confinement," and insisted that "it seemed one of the parts most urgently demanded by duty, conscience and humanity."[30] She reiterated this point at a public lecture she gave in January 1863 to raise funds for the NEHWC. "Help and sympathy extended to such persons, so far from being an encouragement to vice, as some suppose, is indispensable as a safeguard from vice. It is one of the clearest of the duties, both of justice and humanity."[31] The following month, Horatio Storer visited Zakrzewska and, as she told Lucy Sewall, "invited me to call upon him, as he is anxious to extend colleague-ship to me."[32]

In November 1863, the NEHWC issued a fundraising appeal for a new building with a larger capacity.[33] Sewall, who had graduated at the end of Zakrzewska's final term at the NEFMC and traveled to Europe to further her education in London, Paris, and Zurich, was listed as resident physician.[34] By this time, Anita Tyng, who had had joined Zakrzewska at the NEHWC for its first year to gain clinical experience as an *interne*, or student assistant, had left to conclude her medical education at the Women's Medical College of Pennsylvania.[35] Drs. John Ware and John Cabot were listed as the NEHWC's consulting physician and consulting surgeon. And under Zakrzewska's listing as attending physician, Storer was identified as the NEHWC's attending surgeon. Storer's and Zakrzewska's names were now publicly allied.

Horatio Storer at the New England Hospital

Storer's time at the NEHWC showcased his own odd mix of both sexism and a strong desire to aid women. Storer later claimed that he had put his own professional reputation on the line by working at the NEHWC, because many people disapproved of training women to be doctors—one of its key functions. Storer himself didn't believe that most women were suited to the profession, but he was nevertheless impressed with both Zakrzewska and Tyng. He later described Tyng, who worked under him both at the NEHWC as an Assistant Surgeon and as an assistant in his private practice, as possessing "such natural tastes and inclinations as fit her, more than I should have supposed any woman could have become fitted, for the anxieties, the nervous strain and shocks of the practice of surgery."[36] Storer thought the NEHWC's mission was a good one, and he approved of its small size and the privacy it provided for its patients. He lauded its employment of specialists, himself included, "who have made the female organization a special study."[37] He would later say that he admired the charitable function of the NEHWC, and expected that it would become "a public hospital for invalid women."[38] It also seems clear that he valued the opportunity for research that being a surgeon attached to a women's hospital would afford him.

Storer's work while at the NEHWC reflected his continued worries about induced abortion. During his first winter there, he published a paper on "The Surgical Treatment of Amenorrhea."[39] In it, he warned of the inherent danger of mistaking the real character of amenorrhea by failing to consider whether a woman might be pregnant. He insisted that this possibility must be "borne in mind, even though the patient be unmarried, no matter how respectable her position, correct her general history, extensive her hymen, or of what standing the absence of her menses."[40] Because the detection of early pregnancy was difficult, with fetal pulse at the time the only reliable indicator, "the necessity of extreme caution in deciding upon the existence or not of pregnancy" could not "be overestimated," due to the risk of "unintentionally inducing abortion." This was not a theoretical warning, he made clear: "I have known, from the use of these instruments, more than one direct occurrence of the accident against which I would now guard the profession."[41] In addition to ending the pregnancy, such mistakes also did damage by suggesting that the medical profession "directly, or by implication, sanction[ed] the induction of criminal abortion."[42]

But Storer's anti-abortion advocacy was not limited to cautioning the medical profession. When the June 1864 American Medical Association meeting issued a call for "the best short and comprehensive tract calculated for circulation among females, and designed to enlighten them upon the criminality and physical evils of forced abortion," Storer penned the winning entry.[43] Its title was taken from the call—"The Criminality and Physical Evils of Forced Abortions." Though first printed and published by the AMA, Storer republished the essay, with minor additions related to a controversy over anesthesiology, as *Why Not? A Book for Every Woman* in spring 1866.

Storer's book attempted to appeal to women, though it also revealed his strict attachment to traditional gender roles. One the one hand, he highlighted the danger abortions posed to women's health. Given the danger of any surgery at a time before antiseptic practices, and given the number of abortionists without medical training, the warnings were hardly unusual or surprising. Storer was convinced that abortions were almost always detrimental to women's health. And he argued for oversight in the few instances where an abortion was necessary to save the life of the mother. In general, he insisted that "there is hardly a conceivable case where the invalidism could not be relieved in some other mode, or where by an abortion it would not be made worse." The risks of giving birth, also still quite substantial, he argued, were "in reality less than those of an abortion."[44]

On the other hand, Storer insisted that married women who were "prone to conception" would bear children and that this was "the end for which they are physiologically constituted and for which they are destined by nature."[45] Financial difficulties, he argued, could be met with sufficient thrift. Because Storer, like most of his contemporaries, believed that most women did not particularly enjoy sex, he believed that sex for pleasure was essentially degrading to women. Accordingly, to honor the procreative aspect of sex was to honor women. Thus, toward the end of *Why Not?* Storer summed up his position by arguing that if woman were "intended as a mere plaything, or for the gratification of her own or her husband's desires, there would have been need for her of neither uterus nor ovaries, nor would the prevention of their being used for their clearly legitimate purpose have been attended by such tremendous penalties as in reality is the case."[46]

Yet Storer also expressed sympathy for unmarried women tempted to abortion, and argued that America ought to have more foundling hospitals. "A certain amount of illicit intercourse between the sexes will always take place, no matter how condemned by the law," he insisted, and the fact could not be "frowned out of existence." He, therefore, urged society "to provide for its innocent victims, its irresponsible offspring, [rather] than, as now, to permit the so frequent destruction of both." He declared it "foolish to assert that by such provision we but pander to sin.... Should [a woman] be driven by what is comparatively a venial, and not so unnatural an offence, to one of the deadliest crimes?"[47]

The NEHWC's admission of unmarried pregnant women was one concrete way of providing for "both," as the BLIH had earlier. As Zakrzewska wrote in its 1865 annual report, at the NEHWC, "Unmarried women are saved from moral and physical ruin by finding here a hand extended which is willing to lift them up and hold them to usefulness and self-respect."[48] She continued: "We hear the remark made, that *almshouse care is all that such women ought to expect*." But to do so would only exacerbate the difficulty of such women's situations, because "being sent to the common almshouse demoralizes them still more, by destroying the little self-respect yet left them."[49] By treating unwed mothers with dignity, the NEHWC's doctors and staff could instill self-confidence and self-respect in these women, which might give them the strength to pursue moral and productive lives.

There is no evidence of any trepidation felt by Marie Zakrzewska or others on the staff or board of the NEHWC about Storer's anti-abortion work. Rather, there is every indication that consensus on this topic was one of the things that enabled Storer to work well with its women physicians. However, tension between Storer and the women of the NEWHC did arise over his adventurous surgical operations. Storer's desire to advance women's reproductive medicine led him to risk the death of his patients through experimental surgeries, troubling the directors of the NEHWC. These tensions eventually led to Storer's angry resignation from the institution.

Storer explained his approach in a paper published in the *American Journal of the Medical Sciences* in January 1866. He detailed an ovariohysterectomy that he, Tyng, and two other doctors had performed on a woman with a thirty-seven-pound uterine tumor. His operation was the sixth of the twenty-three known cases of the surgery being performed in which the patient did not die.[50] He acknowledged the risks and his hypothetical responsibility if his patient had died, but noted that "in no department of surgery is the common proverb more constantly true, and I apply it to the life of an otherwise condemned patient, and not to the operator's reputation alone, 'Nothing risked, nothing obtained.'"[51]

In the months that followed, Storer seems to have taken that maxim to heart, taking risks and making gains in three operations that were, unfortunately, less successful. At the May 1866 meeting of the AMA, he described a surgical instrument he had invented and its mechanical success in a case in which "my patient rallied completely from the shock of the operation, and succumbed only to an increase of the previously existing peritonitis, on the third day."[52] While it is not clear where this operation was done, his affiliation with the NEHWC was clear in the published proceedings; he was identified as its surgeon, in addition to being listed as an assistant instructor at Harvard and a professor at Berkshire Medical College.[53]

Far more controversial, however, was a case involving abdominal surgery to correct an umbilical hernia. Despite the fact that this patient, too, died, Storer posited that the method he had used "will be found worthy of being followed as a precedent in a large and varied class of diseases." The novel operation Storer undertook was uneventful, and his patient "rallied perfectly" afterward, but Storer reported that the following day, "she received a sudden fright, whose effects were immediately perceptible upon her." Mary Lynch's death on February 5, 1866, less than forty-eight hours after the operation, was ascribed to "secondary shock." However, in the article he published about the operation, Storer pointedly stated that the autopsy found that the wound had healed exactly as he had hoped, and that "the operation therefore, as an operation, was a success."[54]

This operation generated considerable controversy in the medical community, and when Storer wrote about it in *The Medical Record*, he prefaced his narrative with a notice that he would acknowledge the "several criticisms that have already been vouchsafed me." He had presented the case to the Suffolk District Medical Society and, having recorded his colleagues' criticisms, presented them in his article. Taken together, they amounted to the claim that almost any other course of action, or inaction, would have been preferable. In his response to Dr. Calvin Ellis—who had co-signed the Suffolk District Medical Society's report on criminal abortion with him in 1857—Storer implied that any criticism from him was utter hypocrisy. He referenced Ellis's eight-years-earlier autopsy of an executed convict, during which Ellis had discovered that the man's "right auricle was in full and regular motion, contracting and dilating with beautiful distinctness and energy."[55] Needless to say, Ellis was not pleased, and a very public fight, conducted in meetings, in letters, and in print, ensued. The conflict ended with Storer losing his position as assistant instructor at the Harvard Medical School.[56]

Mary Lynch's death was one of three that occurred at the NEHWC during the hospital's 1866 fiscal year. Like Lynch's, the other deaths had taken place "in the Surgical wards after hazardous operations."[57] Storer, as attending surgeon, would have conducted or overseen them all. In late summer, the NEHWC's board of directors passed a resolution that had the result of significantly limiting the scope of Storer's decision-making capabilities:

> Resolved, that in all unusual or difficult cases in medicine, or where a capital operation in surgery is proposed, the Attending and Resident Physicians and Surgeons shall hold mutual consultation, and if any one of them shall doubt as to the propriety of the proposed treatment or operation, one or more of the Consulting Physicians or Surgeons shall be invited to examine and decide upon the case.[58]

Ednah Dow Cheney, the secretary of the NEHWC, wrote to Storer on August 13 to inform him of the resolution. Seventeen days later, Storer responded with a long letter in which he not only responded to the change in policy by offering his resignation, but gratuitously offered his opinion on the value of the hospital, on how he felt he had been treated by it, and on the broader question of the capacity of women to become "fitted to practice as general physicians."[59]

Despite the fact that Storer had advocated two physicians' agreement on the medical necessity of an abortion, he wrote that the NEHWC mandate for consultation on surgeries would "relieve me of all responsibility in reference to the treatment of my patients, a responsibility which I could not in justice to them relinquish." He offered his resignation with the explanation that conforming himself to the mandate would be "alike incompatible with my own self respect, my duty to my patients, and the best interests of the hospital."[60]

Storer's rage spilled over into a denunciation of women's involvement in medicine. The hospital, he claimed, "has been degraded below the level of an ordinary boarding house," and functioned as "a mere aid to establish any individual reputations" and "a means of compelling the success of a measure that was obnoxious to physicians generally." That measure—the establishment of medicine as an appropriate field of work for women—was not only obnoxious, but impossible: while excepting Marie Zakrzewska and Anita Tyng, he stated that "women can never, as a class, become so competent, safe and reliable medical practitioners as men, no matter what their zeal or opportunities for pupilage. . . . in claiming this especial work of medicine, women have mistaken their calling."[61]

At the NEHWC's September 10 board meeting, its directors unanimously voted to accept Storer's resignation.[62] Tyng remained at her post, working with her colleagues to fill Storer's place.[63] Perhaps to the surprise of everyone at the NEHWC, the September 27 issue of the *Boston Medical and Surgical Journal* contained a copy of Storer's letter to Cheney—making what must have been a frustrating situation an embarrassing one for all involved.[64] Tyng resigned from the NEHWC two months later, at the close of its fiscal year.[65] The hospital's annual report for 1866, published in November, noted the board's receipt of Storer's letter of resignation, and their acceptance of it. Formally, they wished him well: "The Directors would however take this first public opportunity to express their sense of the value of Dr. Storer's professional services, and of the aid which he has rendered to the Treasury of the Hospital. Cheerfully bearing witness to his talent and active zeal for his profession, they offer him their best wishes for his future success."[66] The annual report noted obliquely the role that Tyng had played since his departure, but gave no notice of her own resignation.

From Why Not? *to* Is It I?

While Storer's relationship to the NEHWC had ended, his anti-abortion activism continued. And here, despite his denunciations of women in the medical profession, his arguments came to be more closely aligned with those made by women's rights advocates: the crime of abortion ought to be laid at the feet of men.

In June 1866, Caroline Dall wrote to Storer to thank him for *Why Not?* She had sought out the book after reading his essay on criminal abortion, which he had mailed to her for inclusion in the American Social Science Association's library.[67] Her long letter began by thanking Storer with "all my heart for having written it." Saying that she had been "very slow to be convinced that any woman of decent character would herself consent to abortion," she had since discovered, in talking with the "large class of women who privately appealed to me," that it "is easier to induce the victim of seduction to take the consequences of her weakness, than to persuade the fashionable woman to refrain from crime." Her letter, however, ended by commanding Storer to acknowledge that there was more to the problem than the question of female vice or virtue: "Your book needs a counterpart addressed to men.... No woman dreads her travail as she dreads the loss of what she calls, in her unhappy blindness, her husband's love."[68]

Caroline Dall was not the only woman who found Storer's diagnosis of the causes of abortion within marriage incomplete. A November 1866 *Boston Medical and Surgical Journal* article titled "A Woman's View" criticized Storer's *Why Not?* for failing to acknowledge that women's sufferings led to abortions. The author, who merely identified herself as the wife of a "Christian physician," chided Storer for his lack of sympathy for women afraid of the pains of childbirth. She argued that, even as a doctor, he simply did not understand how painful it was, and pointed out that most doctors did not, as he suggested, use chloroform (or anything else) as an anesthetic during labor. She decried the common statement, the "thousand time reiterated fact" that "'it is a woman's *duty* to suffer this,' and that it is 'the end to which she was created.'" This lack of sympathy, or any attempt to alleviate women's pain in labor, she argued, promoted abortions, and moral injunctions about duty would never "of themselves... work reformation."[69]

But the author's central critique was far more serious. Like *The Revolution*'s correspondents, she argued that the largest cause of abortion among married women was marital rape.[70] Husbands had corrupted marriage to "a convenience for revelling [sic] and grossness." They claimed that they were exercising "marital rights... ordained of society and Heaven" and that by marriage, a woman had consented to this arrangement. The author did not challenge the principle of marital rights, but she insisted that "power does not necessarily imply right of abuse." The "intellectual, spiritual woman" might not wish to publicize the state of her marriage, "for pride's sake, or honor's sake." But she might still "rebel."[71] The author argued that, at least among the upper class, marital rape was so traumatizing that it might drive otherwise upright women to seek abortions. While containing a deeply classist bias, this analysis is surprisingly modern in its psychologizing the nature of sexual assault and rape.[72] Storer, she wrote, "fail[ed] to see that no choice is allowed [women] in many cases." "Save themselves from the *cause* they cannot," she continued, but the "consequence is mainly within their power, and the temptation is strong to throw off the bond which confines them to the fireside."[73] The author insisted that she was not "justifying abortion." Abortion, she wrote, "is a crime, and women are guilty of it, but they sin not alone. While attention is being called to the fact, why not also to the cause?"[74] She did grant, at the end, that some women might procure abortion for lesser reasons, and concluded, "For those to whom fashion is god, I have not a word to offer. Let them plead for themselves."[75] The author ended her review by asking that Storer write a book for men.

Storer obliged both the review's author and Dall with the pamphlet *Is It I? A Book for Every Man*, published in June 1867. He praised and reprinted both "A Woman's View" and the full text of Dall's letter to him in it, but he also made sure to illustrate a demand for such a book from men, citing comments by "Drs. Abbot and White, of the Medical School of Harvard University," who were "generally considered men of a conservative cast of mind, very conservative indeed for Massachusetts, and in the least prone towards recognition of any 'woman's rights' that are at all of a doubtful character."[76] And unlike *Why Not?*, *Is it I?* began with a lengthy exposition of Storer's professional qualifications. Despite these appeals to the masculine mind, Storer went on to argue that "we must pillory *the man*, who under the guise of affection, steals from the maid her pearl of great price; who, under the plea of a husband's prerogative, enforced, perchance, by scriptural texts, makes of his wife, disappointed, suffering, perhaps despairing, but the constant object of his savage lust, and makes of himself what is worse than the savage, a brute."[77] That is, such a man was acting not as an uncivilized human, but as an animal, as though possessed of neither reason, sympathy, nor conscience.

Storer's pamphlet for men focused far less on abortion than his pamphlet for women had. Here, he covered everything from proper reading material for adolescent males (no Ovid), to why long engagements and masturbation were bad for health, to an argument that husbands should have more sympathy for their wives' illnesses, especially gynecological ones. A large portion of his work, however, consisted of an analysis of the "marital right." While he sought to challenge a popular conception of the right of a husband to his wife's body, he did not want to be mistaken for any sort of extreme advocate for women's rights. He declared that he was "neither a fanatic nor professed philanthrope." He hoped "in loosing . . . some of woman's chains" to "increase her health, prolong her life, extend the benefits she confers upon society—in a word, selfishly to enhance her value to ourselves." This care was due, also, out of "gratitude for her for the love with which she has solaced us, as mother, and sister, and wife, and daughter." His advocacy was not for "unwomanly women." He believed that women should stay in their "proper and God-given sphere," though he would "undoubtedly open to single women every legitimate avenue to an honorable self-support, and thus keep them free from many of the pitfalls which so closely environ them."[78] In short, Storer insisted that he was in no way trying to upset societal gender roles.

Nonetheless, Storer's reasoning on these issues mirrored that of the more radical women's rights advocates. He had strong words for men whom he believed abused their rights as husbands: "Many a married man has, as I have said, virtually committed a rape upon his wife: though the crime may not be recognized as such by the law, it is none the less this fact, the element of consent having been wholly wanting."[79] And he explicitly linked the importance of consent within marriage (not simply *to* marriage) to legal reforms that gave women the right to continue to control their property after marriage. As progress had been made on this front, he asked, "Will the time come, think ye, when husbands can no longer, as they now frequently do, commit the crime of rape upon their unwilling wives?" Storer did not stop there. He then explicitly tied marital rape to abortion, accusing the same husbands of persuading or compelling their wives "to allow a still more dreadful violence to be wreaked upon the children nestling within them—children fully alive from the very moment of conception."[80]

Thus, Storer, at least when speaking to men, described abortion as part and consequence of sexual and domestic violence. He argued that after a "forced union," one should not "wholly . . . blame the woman if she seek to avert her impending maternity, even though at the risk of her life; forced upon her, it is repulsive, and her whole nature rebels, even her most natural of instincts. It is rather the husband who is to be condemned; his selfish hardness of heart, his brutality, are the cause of her crime."[81] Because of the assumed danger of an abortion to a woman's life, putting a woman in a position where she might seek an abortion was a continued act of violence against her as well as against her child.

Anita Tyng Advances Women's Work

During the year that led up to Storer's resignation from the NEHWC, Lucy Sewall and Anita Tyng applied for admission to Harvard's Medical School, believing that "they should have further medical education."[82] But as they likely anticipated, they were "politely informed by Dean Shattuck that no provision has been made or exists for the education of women in any department of the University."[83] After her departure from the NEHWC, Anita Tyng moved from Boston to Rhode Island, where she was the only regularly educated female doctor. She re-immersed herself in medical studies, this time independently; Caroline Dall sent her eleven medical textbooks on a variety of specialties, and she began to "study chemistry practically" in her kitchen.[84] She established a successful practice and a dispensary in Providence, and initially also maintained an office in Boston, where she saw patients twice a week.[85]

After two years, Caroline Dall came to believe that there was a conspiracy of sorts against Tyng because of her close association with Storer. In September 1868, Dall wrote to him to say that "Dr. Tyng has been very shabbily treated here by those who ought to have shown themselves her friends, chiefly on account of her being a favorite of your own," and that she wanted Tyng "to succeed in spite of the efforts to prevent it." She urged him to encourage Tyng to retain her Boston office, which she was thinking of giving up, saying that she wanted "a woman here of first-rate ability, who is a lady in her nature, and whose principles moral and religious can be wholly trusted."[86] Storer responded to say that he had written to Tyng to tell her that, despite his position against women's capacity to "practice medicine with safety to themselves or their patients," he was nevertheless "willing to do all that I can consistently for her interests—believing that in many respects she is more competent than those of her sex who have here essayed the experiment."[87]

Despite Storer's now faint praise, Tyng's medical career progressed. In 1870, Tyng applied for membership in the Rhode Island Medical Society, but her application was denied, in part because there was "doubt whether a woman could legally be elected a Fellow."[88] Tyng re-applied for Rhode Island Medical Society membership in 1872, and in early 1873, she discovered that her application had been accepted. She became the Medical Society's first woman member, and the fifth woman admitted to a medical society in the United States.

After Tyng first applied for membership in the Rhode Island Medical Society, she discovered that she could insist that she was a member based on the number of votes her application had received, since her denial had been due to a conflict between the society's charter and its bylaws. But determined to prove her worth, she said, "I declined doing so on the ground that I would not force myself upon them, but would be admitted by their own uninfluenced voting and pushing it would make an unfavorable impression of me. I think my silence has been respected, and I think that women who make least talk gain most, generally."[89] This comment, written in a letter to Caroline Dall after Tyng's 1873 election, succinctly expressed how she understood her own contributions to the women's rights movement.

Two years earlier, Tyng had attended the annual convention of the Rhode Island Woman Suffrage Association, which had featured an impromptu speech by Sojourner Truth, as well as presentations by Paulina Wright Davis, Olympia Brown, Mary Livermore, and her cousin Thomas Wentworth Higginson.[90] This meeting had been of particular national interest because of the ongoing split in the women's rights movement, and the expectation that "there might be a sharp contest over the little State of Rhode Island as to which of the two associations this State should be made auxiliary to, the American or the Union Woman Suffrage Society."[91] Tyng had found it to be "plenty of fun," even though "there was very little that I had not heard before."[92] She had been invited to tea with Higginson and Livermore, and had a long talk with the latter, who promised to send the *Woman's Journal* to her. But the following year, Tyng decided to take a step back from an active public role in the movement.

Tyng decided not to attend the 1872 meeting, telling Dall that she did not "see the use of conventions, speeches, petitions—all the same thing over and over every year." Higginson had told her that she had "failed in duty" by her absence, arguing that "women who have achieved special licenses should stand by the movement which has, in a general way, helped them so much." She defended herself, arguing that missing the conference did not in any way mean that she was abandoning the movement. Rather, she believed, it was precisely by pressing ahead in the career she had chosen that she could do most for the women's rights movement. "I have written him [Higginson] that I am doing as much in my way as any other woman," she told Dall. "I have more respect for myself and such other women who by their example and practical work advance women's work, education, etc."[93]

Marie Zakrzewska did not appear to disagree. In her 1875

NEHWC annual report—nine years after Tyng's departure from the hospital in the wake of Storer's storm—Zakrzewska claimed Tyng's success as proof that "seed sown here, has fallen on fertile ground." She listed Tyng among the second group of women founders of institutions for women's medical education because of her Providence dispensary. Supporting the New England Hospital meant "helping women to their share of the privileges of all the schools and all the work our common humanity provides," and Zakrzewska credited Tyng with both fully participating in and leading that effort.[94] Similarly, Mary Putnam Jacobi, in her chapter on "Women in Medicine" in the 1891 *Women's Work in America*, acknowledged Tyng's role in the NEHWC's early years and therefore in the broader "history of woman's slow, but sure, training to stand balanced upon her own feet."[95]

Following her admission to the Rhode Island Medical Society, Tyng began to take on a more public role. She presented papers to the Alumnae Association of the Women's Medical College of Philadelphia, published her research in the *American Journal of Medical Sciences*, and contributed two reports to the Rhode Island State Board of Health's annual reports: "On Causes of Ill Health Among Women" was published in 1878, and "Heredity" was published in 1880.[96]

In "On Causes of Ill Health Among Women," Tyng renewed her public association with Horatio Storer. She listed nine predisposing causes for the "diseases peculiar to women," among which was "induction of abortion."[97] She credited Horatio Storer and his father for drawing public attention to "the increase of this evil," and listed their public interventions, particularly lauding *Why Not?*, which she said "should be read by every man and woman."[98] "The ignorance as regards the guilt and the low morale of the community on this subject, are so perfectly appalling that the boasting of repeated and successful accomplishment passes unreproved," Tyng said.[99] Her insights into women's motivation for seeking abortions were probably the result of her professional experience, as she earlier "had to stave off applications for abortions, many in Boston from the middle class."[100] Abortion was "confined to no class of persons; it prevails among the married and educated, even more than among the ignorant, the poor, the unmarried." Expressing pity for the latter—they "might be supposed to have an excuse, if an excuse for a crime could ever be offered"—she nevertheless argued that few women truly freely chose abortion.[101] She identified three main causes of "this crying sin of the age": women's abuse by men, widespread ignorance, and the commercialization of abortion. The "mental suffering" that some women were subject to because of their pregnancies was "far more acute than that from the fear of, or care for personal pain and discomfort, often amounting to the temporary insanity of despair." These women were "driven as it were, to abortion as the only relief, and often encouraged thereto."[102] Primarily, though, Tyng believed that "ignorance is the first chief cause, at the foundation of all causes."[103] Many women labored under the "erroneous idea" that "in the early months of pregnancy, there is no sin, and little danger to the woman's life."[104] Though "this is the very reverse of the truth," Tyng argued, both "legislators and the public fail to recognize the true character of the crime." Even where laws against abortion were on the book, there was "no cognizance of the murder of the child" or of "the ill health of the woman for the remainder of her life." This ignorance was encouraged, Tyng, believed, through newspapers' "advertisement of quack doctors, of medicines, and even of so-called private hospitals, where the secrets of the victims may be buried with their mortal remains."[105]

Physiological education, Tyng believed, was key to reducing the incidence of abortion. Therefore, "the responsibility should be taken up earnestly by those who have charge of public education and public health."[106] She acknowledged arguments that such topics should be left "to the private judgment or tact of individual parents," but firmly stated that "it cannot be so left, for the parents themselves are too ignorant, as I have seen in several instances, and also the terrible results of such ignorance."[107] However, Tyng believed that parents still played an important role in their children's education in this area. Admitting there was also a moral aspect to the rise in abortions—"Ignorance and selfishness rule both men and women"—Tyng argued that parents should "teach their children early in life, the wisdom of subjugating appetites to morality and to cultivate a regard for the rights of others." Not choosing abortion—or avoiding situations in which abortion could be thinkable—might require moral courage, and that had to be built over the course of a life. Parents played an irreplaceable role in inculcating these habits in their children, and this moral education would complement the physiological education they received outside the home.[108]

Like many women's rights advocates, Tyng was somewhat skeptical about the capacity of the law by itself to effectively decrease the incidence of abortion. Regardless of laws, "however wise or however strictly enforced," there were many abortions "which occur in private, cases known only to the woman herself, through ignorance of the laws of life and health, ignorance of her own anatomy, of her duties to herself, her child, the community and to her Maker."[109] While she called for legislators to "look more deeply into the preventable causes," Tyng noted that "the press [is] such a power in the land, that if it chose, it alone could almost annihilate the crime." Public sentiment was a more powerful tool than law, because it could reach farther.[110]

"A change of tone in public opinion is needed," Tyng argued. "Delicacy must not be confounded with refinement, or thinness and paleness admired for beauty, rather than a comely shape well rounded by the full development of muscle and a due proportion of fat. Sickness should be considered as allied to sin,—the sin of breaking the divine laws of nature; a person should be as much ashamed of avoidable sickness as of falsehood and stealing."[111] Women had been "taught that they must do nothing to help themselves," but they needed to "cease to be invalids and sufferers" and to act upon the realization that "the regeneration of the world must come through them."[112] While she was encouraged by the proliferation of "clubs and associations for study and for practical efforts in all questions affecting the moral and physical condition of women," she believed there was much work to be done.[113] Consequently, she said in closing, "my work will not have been ill done if any word herein shall elicit food for thought and action by and for women."[114]

In September 1882, Tyng became the chief resident physician of the Philadelphia Women's Hospital, where she remained for four years.[115] She was elected a member of the Providence Medical Association and the American Medical Association and became a corresponding member of the Boston Gynecological Society.[116] In Providence, she was involved in the creation of the State Board of Health and led the creation of the Rhode Island Medical Society's library.[117] She later moved to Jacksonville, Florida, and subsequently to Los Angeles—where there is a record of her giving a lecture on physiology to a group of women.[118] When she died, the Rhode Island Medical Society wrote that "our first woman fellow raised herself to eminence in her profession, won the universal esteem of her confreres and left us an example of fidelity to duty and high ideals 'even to the end.'"[119] It seems that she would have been satisfied to know that she had thus successfully, by her "example and practical work, advance[d] women's work [and] education."[120]

Chapter Four

RESHAPING PUBLIC OPINION IN NEW YORK

Dr. Charlotte Lozier's sudden death at the age of twenty-five in New York City prompted a flood of obituaries, appreciations, and reflections. Lozier was the mother of three children, a practicing doctor, and a member of many women's social and reform organizations, including Susan B. Anthony's Workingwomen's Association and Woman Suffrage Association. But when *The Revolution* eulogized her, they didn't focus on these activities. Rather, Paulina Wright Davis wrote, "Her real strength did not reveal itself in the brief interview we had with her; it was not till she came out firmly to stay the prevalent sin of infanticide that we knew the woman in all her greatness." Lozier, when asked by a man to perform an abortion on an unmarried girl he had impregnated, had counseled the girl against that course of action and then reported the man to the police. While this action had been criticized by some as a breach of professional confidentiality, she had argued that any expectation of privacy ceased when she was asked to commit murder for hire. Davis applauded her actions, writing, "The murder of the innocents goes on. Shame and crime after crime darken the history of our whole land. Hence it was fitting that a true woman should protest with all the energy of her soul against this woeful crime."[1]

Lozier wasn't the only woman doctor in New York praised by *The Revolution* for speaking against abortion and infanticide. Dr. Anna Densmore French, some fifteen years older than Lozier, also gained the newspaper's attention, and its pages covered both her lectures and her leadership of the early women's club Sorosis. While in many ways their lives were very different, both doctors saw women who chose abortion or infanticide (the terms were sometimes, as above, used interchangeably) as victims of women's unequal place in society, and particularly of the ill-formed public opinion. Women who chose abortion or infanticide suffered from the sexual double standard and often had been left ignorant of physiology, making them more vulnerable to sexual predators and unaware of the process of fetal development. Densmore's and Lozier's proposed solutions, embraced by women's rights activists in their city, included offering women better education about their own health and fetal development and working to erode the sexual double standard. They strove to ensure that women carrying the "burden of unlegalized maternity" could survive the crisis of having a child outside of wedlock and go on to have economic and social opportunities to support themselves and their children and to live dignified lives.[2] This approach, however, did not preclude support for legal remedies.

Doctors and Mothers

Anna Densmore began her medical career after eleven years of marriage and the birth of two children, and developed it as a widow with a young daughter to support. Born in 1828 in England as Mary Ann Walmsley, Anna and her parents immigrated to the United States and settled in Boston when she was young.[3]

She married Albert Mansfield Densmore, a clerk, in an 1851 ceremony conducted by noted Unitarian divine and abolitionist Theodore Parker.[4] The couple had two children—a son born in 1853, who died at the age of seven months, and a daughter born in 1859.[5] By 1860, they were living in Worcester with Albert's parents, and Albert had become a merchant.[6] Two years later, following the outbreak of the Civil War, Anna began studying medicine at the New England Female Medical College, where Anita Tyng, Lucy Sewall, and Helen Morton were among her fellow students.[7] The next year, she continued her studies at the Women's Medical College of Pennsylvania (WMCP), where Tyng would join her after spending a year working at the New England Hospital for Women and Children.[8]

Densmore's entrée into the world of New York women's rights began when she decided to conclude her medical education in pioneering woman doctor and suffrage advocate Clemence Lozier's New York Women's Medical College and Hospital (NYWMC).[9] She graduated in its first class in 1865, when it was neither homeopathic nor regular.[10] One of the first women's medical colleges, it had been chartered by New York State in response to lobbying by Lozier and Elizabeth Cady Stanton, who would remain its staunch supporter.[11] Less than two months after her graduation, Albert died, leaving Densmore a widow with a six-year-old daughter to support.[12] She chose to remain in New York City, and maintained a private practice while also teaching and working with women's organizations.[13] It is hard to imagine that her personal tragedies did not shape her concerns as a doctor.

The brief medical career of Charlotte Denman Lozier, who was approximately fifteen years Densmore's junior, was a whirlwind of activity, including a successful practice, public speaking, and domestic life. Born in 1844 in New Jersey, Charlotte Denman grew up in Winona, Minnesota.[14] After her mother's early death, Charlotte joined the Minnesota State Normal School's first class, and she began teaching at age sixteen.[15] In 1864, at the age of twenty, she moved to New York City to study at the NYWMC.

After a year in New York City, Charlotte returned to Minnesota, where she gave lectures on physiology in the schools where she had previously taught.[16] In January 1866, she married Clemence Lozier's only son, Abraham Witton Lozier, Jr.[17] Six years her senior, Abraham had graduated from the College of Physicians and Surgeons and had been stationed with the Army of the Potomac as Surgeon to the Sanitary Corps during the Civil War.[18] He had then become a professor of chemistry and toxicology at his mother's medical school.[19]

Marriage and motherhood did little to slow down Charlotte Lozier. After their marriage, she and Abraham returned to the East Coast, and she resumed her medical studies.[20] Because the NYWMC was tending toward homeopathy by the end of its second year, its regular physicians—including Abraham and his mother—left to found a new institution, the Women's College of Physicians and Surgeons.[21] Abraham taught surgery, pathology, and microscopic anatomy at the new institution, and Clemence became its dean of faculty, the chair of both theory and practice, and the chair of diseases of women and children.[22] That summer, Charlotte, now pregnant, returned to Winona with her husband. She practiced medicine there before giving birth to her first child in November.[23] Less than a year later, she resumed her medical studies in Pennsylvania, at the WMCP, with her husband as her preceptor.[24] The Lozier family returned to New York City sometime in 1867, moving in with Clemence, who had returned to the NYWMC.[25] Charlotte gave birth to her second child in May 1868, and ten months later she graduated from the NYWMC with distinction.[26] She then lectured for the Medical College and developed a private practice specializing in treating cancer and other tumors.[27]

Doctors and Activists

The Revolution's second issue, published in January 1868, announced a lecture series on "Physiology" given by Anna Densmore.[28] *The New York Times* reported that during her first lecture, open to the press and public, she argued "that the duties of women physicians were not limited to the practice of medicine," but rather they should be both healers and educators.[29] Moreover, the duty of physiological education did not belong solely to women physicians. Densmore argued that women teachers, as well as the wives and daughters of clergy, had a duty to provide physiological education due to their influential roles, positions of authority, and "unusual opportunities for direct personal communication with young women and girls."[30] In short, all women who could contribute to this essential piece of women's uplift ought to do so.

Densmore's lectures focused on pregnancy, explaining fetal development in detail and pointing out that physicians could hear a fetus's heartbeat before "quickening," when a mother first felt her child's movement. She believed this topic to be "the one least understood, and the one of all others necessary to be well comprehended in order that the duties and responsibilities of maternity and child culture should be realized."[31] Densmore's audience was shocked to learn that a fetus's life began before quickening; one attendee reported that several women had fainted at the realization that they had been "participators in the crime of premeditated child destruction before birth."[32] *The Revolution* printed a letter from a reader who heard the lecture series, saying that it had been better attended than any medical lecture previously given in the city.[33] Shaken by Densmore's description of fetal development, she wrote: "We have not such an amount of inherent depravity, nor such a degree of reckless daring in our composition, nor such a deficiency in the motherly instinct...as to lead us into the commission of this most *deadly* crime *realizing it to be so*."[34] She pled: "Give us *knowledge* before accusing us of crime, and do not forget to gauge the caliber of our sins by the light furnished to guide us."[35] Improving women's understanding of their own physiology and the mechanisms of reproduction would reduce the incidence of abortion.[36]

Lozier also publicly lectured on physiology. She gave a talk titled "The Social Evil" at the NYWMC in May 1869.[37] Ostensibly about prostitution, it dealt broadly with duties correspondent with a woman's physiology and sexuality, and dangers posed to their fulfillment, including infanticide—which, like other women's rights advocates at the time, she conflated with abortion, arguing that infanticide could not be justified except to "save the life of the mother."[38] She was alarmed by the apparent increase in both practices, noting that "one child in eight during 1868, was known to have been born dead, while the births of a vast number were known to have been criminally concealed."[39] Like Densmore, Lozier argued that ignorance was "directly the cause" of the "social abuses" of prostitution and abortion. That is, women had "ever been denied an equal education with man," and men, through "neglect or refusal," failed "to allow her personal and spiritual being a full expansion."[40] Young women learned "everything in physics and ethics, except a knowledge of themselves," and "ate, slept and dressed in a manner that was simply suicidal."[41] She therefore encouraged physiological and moral education, less restrictive clothing, healthier diet and exercise, and increased opportunities for women to earn their own livings. But she did not think these common prescriptions were sufficient. She also called for the medical education of women—and, notably, the more stringent enforcement of the laws against abortion.[42] Only with all of these reforms would women be healthy, understand their bodies and reproduction, and have the chance to develop their full human personalities and potentials.

The intensity of Lozier's focus on legal remedies for social ills distinguished her from many women's rights activists. In arguing for the regulation of prostitution, especially, she better reflected mainstream medical opinion. Where the radical women's rights advocates argued that to regulate prostitution would be to endorse it, Lozier insisted, with William W. Sanger, that "a medical supervision of those connected with it should exist."[43] And like Horatio Storer, she expressed greater confidence than most women rights advocates in the possibility that legal intervention could prevent fillicide, arguing that the legislature "should impose the same penalties for infanticide as for the murder of an adult."[44] Yet her advocacy of stronger legal penalties for abortion and infanticide reflected her belief that both practices represented the murder of children *and* were an outrage against women.[45]

The New York press responded to Lozier's lectures with a mixture of praise and skepticism. *The Brooklyn Daily Eagle* reported that the "most startling fact" that Lozier had presented was the incidence of infant mortality, and her suggestion of the probable incidence of abortion and infanticide.[46] The

New York World reported that Lozier's speech was representative of "what the woman reformers have to say concerning the cause of the prevalence of the crime" of "ante-natal infanticide," and described her as one of the "strong-minded women" who joined the "Roman Catholic archbishops, Episcopalian bishops, [and] Presbyterian ministers" in "lifting up testimonies against the same sin and warning the people to avoid it." The paper described Lozier as "like the Catholic bishops" for ascribing infanticide and abortion to ignorance—"but, unlike them, she means intellectual and not spiritual ignorance—ignorance of the body rather than of the obligations of the soul." While skeptical of this diagnosis, the paper fully joined in her hope that the "abolishment" of infanticide and abortion was near.[47]

Neither Densmore nor Lozier was content to limit herself to medical practice and public lecturing. Both were also active in women's organizations. Their work in these organizations reflected their convictions about women's suffering from abortion and the sexual double standard, and their insistence that both could be addressed.

Sorosis takes on the "burden of unlegalized maternity"

Densmore was a founding member of Sorosis, the first woman's club in the United States, which first met in March 1868.[48] While its membership included many women who were involved in the women's rights movement, it was envisioned as an instrument of self-elevation.[49] The club declared its purpose to be establishing "'relations between women of thought, taste, culture, and philanthropy,' which should be equally beneficial to each."[50] While the club began more like a salon than a charitable organization, it took some time for the new association to fully differentiate itself and its activities from the myriad beneficent and activist organizations in New York.[51] During this period especially, Sorosis discussed important social issues, including the plight of unmarried mothers.

In June 1868, Sorosis members decided that their meetings should include time for "written Themes and conversational Disquisitions"—that is, members should present reports for discussion.[52] A few months later, Mary Fenn Davis, a noted spiritualist and women's rights advocate, put forward resolutions on "the homeless and unprotected condition of those upon whom, by misfortune or crime, is laid the burden of unlegalized maternity."[53] Davis's resolutions decried the sexual double standard that left such women "bereft of social position and debarred from all opportunity to retrieve their error and to rise to honor and preferment in respectable communities."[54] These unfortunates were "driven to despondency, loss of self respect, and that deep despair which ultimates in recklessness and ruin."[55] Their "innocent offspring" were "left to perish or live to swell the downward drifting tide of vice."[56] Banned from respectable society and her possibilities for employment further restricted, such a woman might well turn to prostitution in desperation.

Davis believed this punishment for "unlegalized maternity" grossly unjust. Those who shamed unwed mothers almost inevitably ignored the male transgressor and failed to honor the reality of motherhood. Motherhood, Davis argued, was sacred in itself, even outside of wedlock. Casting out the unmarried mother "dishonored the holy office of maternity by degrading its entire significance, and neglecting its most imperative and sacred claims."[57] By wasting both the woman's future and that of her child, casting her out also did far greater damage to society than the original sexual transgression.

Densmore was elected chairman of a Sorosis standing committee established "to investigate the causes of descent into this great evil of our civilization, and, if possible, to discover the means of protection and redemption from this bottomless pit of agony and shame."[58] The committee—alternately referred to as the "Committee on Homes for Unfortunate Women" or the "Committee on Hospitals and Asylums"—set out to determine "what public provision has been made by way of hospitals and asylums, in this city and elsewhere" and, "if such wise and human guardianship shall not be found, to consider the question of the erection of such asylums and hospitals."[59] The women of Sorosis hoped that "the desolate and despairing" might be "rescued from misery and vice, and her offspring saved to fill an honorable place in our great, intelligent, and virtuous commonwealth."[60]

Sorosis's interest in "unlegalized maternity" was not unique, but its analysis of the problem was more complex than most. The move to create foundling hospitals was encouraged by physicians and public-health reformers such as Reese and Storer, who believed that they would reduce abortion rates by giving women somewhere to leave their unwanted children. Before the Civil War, no private charity, including orphanages, accepted foundlings (abandoned children who were assumed to be illegitimate).[61] This quickly shifted in the postwar era. In New York City, the Infant's Home opened in December 1865; the (Protestant) New York Infant Asylum opened first in 1865, failed, and would reopen in 1871; and the (Catholic) New York Foundling Asylum would open in 1869.[62] These institutions also hoped to reform the mothers of the infants, when they could be discovered. However, while most abandoned infants were illegitimate, poverty, not the mere fact of illegitimacy, lay behind the decision to abandon in the vast majority of cases.[63] Most abandoned babies were not newborns but rather old enough to show that their mothers had attempted to keep them, but had been overwhelmed by poverty resulting from "marital breakdown through death or abandonment; homelessness; illness; the unwillingness of the employers of female domestic servants to house their children; and women's lack of employment options."[64]

Densmore reported the results of her committee's research at a Sorosis meeting held at her home in early December 1868. Resources for unmarried mothers were quite sparse. In New York City, Densmore reported, "Expectant mothers out of wedlock are admitted gratuitously into but few institutions." Bellevue Hospital, the public hospital that originated in the city's eighteenth-century almshouse, had an obstetrical ward that freely admitted all pregnant women; Elizabeth and Emily Blackwell's Hospital and Infirmary for Women and Children freely admitted unmarried women if they were "known to have been heretofore respectable"; and the Child's Nursery and Hospital admitted unmarried women at their ordinary fees ($20 in advance and $5 per week).[65] Densmore noted that the Lying In Hospital only admitted women who could provide their marriage certificate and references, and that the Woman's Hospital had no obstetrical division. The committee's survey of other cities indicated that these sparse accommodations for unmarried pregnant women were more than other large cities provided. In Philadelphia, Pittsburg, Providence, and Chicago, almshouses were the primary or only "refuge for unmarried mothers not able to pay for private accommodation."[66]

Densmore's report also laid out the provisions then available within the city for the care or adoption of illegitimate children. The Children's Nursery and Hospital would provide care for infants for a fee of $10 per month. At Bellevue Hospital, women who "do not desire to take their babes" could leave them there. They would be taken to the city's orphanage at Ward's Island to be raised, taught trades, and "as soon as capable be sent out to earn their livelihood." Despite this lofty goal, the orphanage had a track record of appallingly high infant mortality rates: "Two or three years ago 90 to 95 per cent of the entire number of infants died in their first year." The introduction of wet nurses had helped, but 1867 still saw an infant mortality rate of 70 percent.

The report also described the nascent Massachusetts Infant Asylum as "one little step in the right direction," explaining that "the enterprise is still young and of limited capacity, but the results thus far have been even more satisfactory than the incorporators had dared to hope." Nevertheless, Densmore said, "We can but realize the while, and *keenly*, its inadequacy" to slow "the growing crime of infanticide." This inadequacy—whether due to its small size, or to its newness, or to other factors—should not discourage such work but rather "awaken earnest convictions in the heart of every true woman that there is a field of labor opening up to her from which she *cannot* recede without outraging both conscience and womanhood."[67]

Densmore argued that both infanticide and abortion would be decreased by the institution of infant asylums "for the promiscuous admittance of all infants presented." These institutions, while far from eliminating the sexual double standard, could help to temper some of its worst consequences for the most desperate of women. Infant asylums, therefore, might indeed mean that "more [illegitimate] children might for a time be born" because they would offer desperate women the opportunity to "resume their place in society, and to command reputable employment."[68]

While condemning abortion and infanticide in no uncertain terms, Densmore urged compassion for unwed mothers as the best preventative. Like many women's rights advocates, she found society at least as much at fault as the women who actually committed these crimes. She was convinced that abortion, "now become one of the most prominent demoralizing features in American life," was only sought by women under extreme duress. She pointed to "the despair that must sink deep into the soul of an erring woman in her dark hour of trial" at the thought that "the babe she has passed through such overwhelming agony to evolve will be to her but the passport of exclusion from every hearth and home, from every friend." Under the threat of such cruel ostracism, Densmore argued, it was no wonder "that the promptings of maternity are sometimes driven back to their source—that the brain reels—that the mother ceases for a time to be human." Therefore, it was "because of our inhumanity . . . that a little life is so often immolated on its shrine."[69]

To slow the incidence of abortion, Densmore argued (as she had in her public lectures) that women needed to understand human physiology better. Specifically, they needed to know that "the living principle is there from the first moment of fecundation, and should be fostered and nourished and brought into the world in every instance that conception takes place—at *no* period can it be interfered with, from the first to the last moment of *utra* [sic] *uterine* life, without tampering with a life that God alone can give." Densmore appealed to her audience to join in this work of education, urging "you each and severally, to stretch out a helping saving hand in this direction, that its suppression may to some extent at least be accomplished."[70]

Two months later, in early February 1869, Sorosis held a special closed meeting "to consider and dispose of" the topics of "Household Laborers"—which had risen in tandem with the discussion of "unlegalized maternity" and foundling hospitals—and "Homes for Unfortunate Women."[71] The meeting had evidently been meant to lead to concrete action on these topics, but it ended in chaos after a few of its members reminded those present that "Sorosis could not, according to the circular, engage in any business or charity."[72] When this discovery was made, Densmore declined to discuss her committee's work, evidently seeing the meeting's futility.[73]

She did not, however, drop the issue, but continued to write reports and thereby kept Sorosis engaged with it for a little longer. At the end of her "Hospitals and Asylums" report, Densmore had promised to provide an overview of Europe's foundling hospitals and the different principles guiding each, "together with such plan or plans as the committee as a whole may desire to bring forward with the view of rendering our work thoroughly practical."[74] She made good on this promise, presenting a "long and elaborate report" on European institutions and one in San Francisco that had been recently established.[75]

Densmore's presentation of this report began something of a symposium at the May 17 Sorosis meeting.[76] Ernestine Rose, the outspoken abolitionist and suffragist who would be formally elected to Sorosis later in the meeting, questioned the prudence of focusing on foundling hospitals, prompting vigorous responses from other Sorosis members. Rose stated that she "would advocate the foundling hospital with all heart and soul, but she thought prevention was better than cure."[77] By "prevention," she meant "stringent legal measures for the suppression of the crime of seduction," which would make men as "deprived of every hope for the future" as women facing out-of-wedlock pregnancies.[78] Mrs. Oliver Johnson, wife of a radical abolitionist and New York journalist, critiqued Rose's call for new laws against seduction, because "these could be of little use, unless sustained by public opinion." Instead, she said, "Women ought to try and create such a public opinion, and mete out to men the same measure of justice and retribution as fell upon women."[79] If the suffering felt by unwed mothers was due to social pressure, to punish men similarly ought to mean exerting similar social pressure, rather than resorting to legal means.[80] Paulina Wright Davis, an abolitionist, suffragist, and early lecturer on women's physiology, countered Rose's suggestion that, despite their necessity and beneficial effects, foundling hospitals might "increase the number of unhappy births."[81] Instead, Davis argued, foundling hospitals respected the "existence [of] a fact that we were bound to accept"—that infants would continue to be born in precarious situations—and suggested that they should remind the public that "life [is] a gift, of which, if necessary, we should be taught the value."[82]

At the May meeting, Sorosis celebrated news announced two months earlier, when the *Galveston News*, the Memphis *Public Ledger*, and other papers reported that a New York woman had set aside $10,000 "as a nucleus of a fund for the endowment of a new charity, comprising a city bureau at which new-born infants will be received without any questions, and a farm upon which they will be carefully cared for, until they are adopted, or some other provision made for their future."[83] By October, Sorosis's Committee on Foundling Hospitals stated that there were "gratifying indications of progress" and "promise of substantial aid."[84] While it is unclear what became of this specific effort, Sorosis had at least contributed to rising public awareness of the need for such institutions through the coverage of its meetings by the *New York World* and *The Revolution*.

Jane Cunningham Croly would later insist that the Committee's work had been a success, claiming that as a consequence "the press took up the subject," and that the founding of the New York Foundling Asylum in 1869 and the 1871 reopening of the New York Infant Asylum had been direct results.[85]

The Life and Myth of Charlotte Lozier

Charlotte Lozier was also very active in women's organizations and women's rights work. She served as one of the incorporators of the Working Women's National Association (WWNA), collaborating with Susan B. Anthony, Celia Burleigh, Sarah Francis Norton, Augusta Lewis, and others.[86] The WWNA's first vice president, she occasionally led its meetings, was listed as its financier, and played a key role in its defense of Hester Vaughan (see Chapter 5).[87] She also proposed that the WWNA lobby for women's admittance to New York College and chaired the committee for that project.[88] She was praised for her "ability to sift the good from a mass of Utopian schemes which would sometimes be projected by members with more enthusiasm than judgment."[89] Lozier did not limit her activism to the WWNA. She was engaged in the suffrage movement.[90] She also attended a meeting to form the "Social Science Club of the City of Brooklyn"—which would later become known as the Brooklyn Women's Club—during which she agreed to be the chair of its board of directors.[91] Despite all this work in women's organizations, Lozier's untimely death at the age of twenty-five meant that perhaps her greatest impact on public opinion was through her posthumous characterization as a sort of martyr for maternity.

Six months after her "Social Evil" lecture, Lozier made the national news again for the saga that led women's rights advocates to praise her following her death. In November 1869, eighteen-year-old Caroline Fuller came to Lozier's office and announced her pregnancy, implying that she wished to terminate it.[92] Lozier tried to dissuade her, writing later that "I did 'advise,' and 'caution,' and 'remonstrate;' more than this, I plead [sic], with her hand in mine, that she would relinquish her terrible purpose, and not add to the misfortune she already suffered, but bear her child honorably, and enjoy an approving conscience at least." Lozier "offered to aid or befriend her to any extent in my power" and "begged that she would at least take time to consult" her child's father. She "assured her he would agree with me, if he was the true friend she had declared him to be." Lozier further volunteered to "consult with him" about finding Fuller "some good place in this city till the child was born, and then consigning it [the baby] to safe hands for care."[93] Fuller, however, was unmoved, and after threatening that she would kill herself if she could not find someone else who would provide her with what she wanted, she left. She returned with a man who introduced himself as Andrew Moran, a married plantation owner from South Carolina. He had traveled to New York City with both Fuller and his wife. Explaining that he was the father of Fuller's unborn child, he "with great effrontery and every-day, off-hand business air," proposed that Lozier "bring about premature delivery" and offered to pay her well and protect her "from any possible legal consequences, should there be a fatal termination."[94] This last statement likely meant that he would shield Lozier from prosecution if Fuller died, as the "fatal termination" of the fetus was the evident intent. Lozier responded that "he had come to the wrong place for any such shameful, revolting, unnatural and unlawful purpose." She then reported the incident to the police.[95]

The *New York Herald* described the legal case as "certainly, in this city at least, a novel one."[96] The paper reported that "she was prompted to this course solely by a desire to check the present systematized and 'professional' crimes of infanticide and foeticide, and it is well known that she has frequently made it the subject of severe denunciation in public meetings."[97] Lozier's own explanation for why she chose to go to the police, instead of simply refusing to perform the abortion, shows that she both thought abortion constituted the murder of an infant and that it was profoundly damaging to women, especially in its new commercial and professional iteration. Like Blackwell and Zakrzewska, she probably also resented the assumption that as a female doctor she must be an abortion provider. She later wrote that she "felt myself and all womankind so outraged that I am willing to leave it to any public, to any press, or to any court of law or of justice, if I was not justified in arresting him."[98] Perhaps the fact that she was herself pregnant at the time amplified her outrage.[99]

Lozier's approach reflected not only her stated belief in the efficacy of using the law to restrain abortions, but also her understanding of who was at fault when a woman sought an abortion. Moran and Fuller were both arrested under the 1864 law that the *Herald* described as having been "practically a dead letter," which had made the attempted procurement of abortion a crime.[100] Lozier had not wanted Fuller to be arrested, but she "reluctantly acceded" when she was told that one party would not be arrested without the other.[101] However, at the hearing held the following Tuesday, Lozier made sure that Fuller was not punished further by, with some equivocation, testifying that the young woman "had not solicited the operation in any manner, therefore not being amenable to the law, though she had in her great mental distress, consequent upon her disgraced and painful position, tacitly consented to submit to anything to hide her shame."[102] Fuller was then freed, whereas Moran had his bail set at one thousand dollars. He reportedly unsuccessfully offered to bribe Lozier with the same amount of money if she would withdraw her complaint.[103] Moran's purported wealth and power, his apparent belief that these entitled him to manipulate the women he encountered, his willingness to risk Fuller's life, and his decision to end the life of their child probably all contributed to Lozier's desire to see him prosecuted. Given the amount of time she spent with women who had been active in the abolitionist cause before the Civil War, his introduction as a plantation owner from South Carolina likely made Lozier even less inclined to sympathy. It would have been difficult to conjure up a better villain.

Nonetheless, Lozier's defense of her course of action focused on her role as a physician rather than on Moran as a living example of the need for women's rights. She responded to claims that by going to the police she had somehow violated "professional privacy" in a letter to the *New York World*, which also appeared in the *New York Star* and was substantially reprinted in the *New-York Daily Tribune* under the headline "Infanticide and Bribery."[104] There she gave the basic outline of her interactions with Fuller and Moran and her reasoning for having them arrested. She argued that "as the commission of crime is not one of the functions of the medical profession, a person who asks a physician to commit the crime of ante-natal infanticide can be no more considered his patient than one who asks him to poison his wife."[105] *The Revolution* applauded her reasoning, saying that her letter "most triumphantly vindicates her course in the very disagreeable position in which she was placed."[106] The *World* wrote that Lozier "seems to prove conclusively that neither law nor professional honor forbids physicians handing over to the police persons who apply to them to commit murder; but that law, professional honor, moral obligation, and social duty all unite in compelling them to thus aid in the punishment of these attempts to procure the slaughter of innocents."[107]

The press immediately used Lozier to make broader arguments about public policy. On November 23—a day after reporting Moran and Fuller's arrest—the *Herald* cited the case in an editorial arguing for state support of the New York Foundling Asylum, opened by the Catholic Sisters of Charity the previous month. The editorial claimed that police reports had shown a decrease in infanticide since its opening, and that "the infamous trade of that most abhorred of all, our mock medical professionals, has considerably diminished."[108] This was progress in the right direction, according to the *Herald*, which regularly covered developments related to the asylum.[109] "This kind of business," it said, was exemplified by "the case of the man Moran and the strong-minded female doctor, Mrs. Lozier," whose "conscience and a decent respect for morality consigned the tempter and would-be criminal to the station house." Institutions like the Foundling Asylum were similar to Mrs. Lozier, the paper argued, because they were both "instruments of good and sources of prevention against crime." While Lozier had gained public esteem for her actions, the paper argued, these institutions should gain public support of a more tangible nature.[110]

Lozier's sudden death, which occurred less than two months later, following the birth of her third child, produced a steady stream of eulogies, commemorations, and resolutions in her honor, which described her as a model doctor, a model woman, and a model of altruism and sanctity.[111] The Brooklyn

Women's Club, which she had helped to found months earlier, honored her life for being "filled and permeated with Christian philanthropy, and consecrated to the Divine work of doing good."[112] One of the ministers who spoke at her funeral said that the lesson of her life was "'Have a purpose," and in her memory urged his listeners to "Be not content with a mere butterfly existence.... Devote those years of early womanhood, which so many leave vacant or full up with chaff, to intellectual and moral development by solid reading and study, to useful work and to benevolent activities.'"[113] Another minister described her personality as "tenderness blended with force," saying that "so thrilling and tender were her feelings of pity for the evil that their unfortunate distresses were unbosomed to her, and their place filled with peaceful resignation for the past and hopeful determinations of good for the future."[114] Sorosis passed a resolution expressing "grateful remembrance and profound esteem... for what she has done for the women of the nineteenth century."[115] *The Revolution*, in its first note of several about her death, stated that Lozier's "family and friends, the cause of woman, society generally, and especially the Medical Profession, into which she seems to have come commissioned as a leader and bright particular star, have all sustained an almost irreparable loss."[116] Eulogy rapidly turned to hagiography as her life became a means to instruct the public in different virtues.

Lozier's complaint against Moran had been national news, and her death was as well. The *Chicago Tribune*'s notice described Lozier as "the well-known female physician, who, a week or two since, caused the arrest of a Southern gentleman on the charge of requesting her to commit an abortion on the young lady accompanying him."[117] The South Carolinian *Daily Phoenix* printed nearly the same thing.[118] Many took Lozier's action in the case to be direct evidence of her sanctity. The *Home Journal* found in her actions a testimony to personal integrity and courage, explaining that Lozier's "brave stand in invoking the law against infanticide, which, through the criminal neglect of practitioners and the public, had long remained a dead letter, were not exceptional acts in her career, but the consistent expression and outgrowth of her daily life."[119] Some went as far as to imply that Lozier was, in a certain sense, a martyr. One of Lozier's friends recalled, in a letter to the Buffalo *Evening Courier and Republic*, that when Lozier decided to have Moran arrested, she had appeared "weary-eyed and sorrowful, but with a look in her face as if she had lifted her soul up to the heights of self-immolation, and could calmly meet whatever a misjudging world might say of her." Lozier had received a death threat by mail afterward, and told this friend, "If God wills that my work is done, I might as well go this way and now." The friend saw this as prophetic, as "she has done what her keen sense of a Christian's duty bade her, and no more, and now she is dead."[120]

Commentators used her life not only to teach virtue, but also to register their approbation of her public opposition to abortion. In one of the eulogies given at her funeral, a minister lauded the "conscientious convictions" that "led her to earnestly remonstrate against a fearfully prevalent evil. She boldly asserted and ably argued the right of the human immortal to life even from the earliest stage of its existence, and merited the gratitude of all right-minded people by her earnest efforts to counter what she believed to be 'the social evil.'"[121] The *Evening Journal* lauded her for Moran's arrest and her subsequent defense of her actions, saying that that "by her example in practice, by her voice and pen, she protested against a crime that degraded the womanhood of America."[122] *The Revolution* reiterated this message; Paulina Wright Davis wrote that Lozier's "recent action, prompt and decisive, against a high-handed crime cannot be too much commended.... It was not till she came out firmly to stay the prevalent sin of infanticide that we knew the woman in all her greatness."[123]

Lozier's acclaim in the press is somewhat remarkable and illustrates the quiet success that the women's rights movement had had in redefining women's place in society. Lozier was a working mother, a woman with significant professional success in a profession in which men were seeking to secure their dominance. She frequently spoke publicly on topics relating to sexuality including initiating the controversial prosecution of an attempt to procure an abortion in which she took down a wealthy man who clearly saw himself as immune from any possible social or legal censure for his actions. For Lozier, campaigning against abortion was simply part of a life that declared broad human equality.

Lozier and Densmore's activity within women's associations, their public lecturing, and Sorosis's advocacy all illustrate that these women discouraged abortion and infanticide using the institutions of civil society, whether the lecture hall, the press, associational life, or charity. They focused on offering support to other women. Sorosis's focus on encouraging the creation of more lying-in hospitals open to all women and foundling hospitals implicitly asserted that society needed to honor both the maternity of any pregnant woman, regardless of the origins of that pregnancy, and the life of any child, regardless of her origins. The social cost of higher tolerance for illicit sex, they quietly implied, was more than justified by the moral imperative of assisting vulnerable women and children, both of whom could and ought to be encouraged to contribute to society, not condemned. Nonetheless—as Lozier's willingness to have Fuller and Moran arrested, and the positive response to that action in *The Revolution* show—that preference for civil society, celebrating maternity, and women helping women was not construed to mean that there should be no legal aspect to restraining abortion and infanticide.

Chapter Five

DEATH OR DISHONOR: WOMEN'S RIGHTS, ECONOMIC EQUALITY, AND THE SEXUAL DOUBLE STANDARD

"The New York Workingwomen's Association seems to have undertaken too large a job, or rather several jobs that are too large," opined the editors of *The Brooklyn Daily Eagle* in late 1868.[1] Susan B. Anthony, who was not known for the timidity of her ideas, had founded the association several months earlier. While "its legitimate purpose . . . is the helping of women to get more work and better pay," the *Daily Eagle*'s editors stated, the association "addresses itself to the problem of suffrage, to the question [of] whether infanticide ought to be regarded as a crime or as an ameable [sic] weakness chargeable to the treachery and tyranny of man, to the propriety of putting insane women in lunatic asylums, and to the expediency of establishing foundling hospitals."[2]

The *Daily Eagle* was responding to the recent sponsorship by the Workingwomen's Association (WWA) of a large public meeting on behalf of Hester Vaughn, who had been convicted of infanticide and sentenced to death. The WWA sought public support for a stay of her execution and a possible retrial, as well as funds to care for the woman upon her hoped-for release. Contrary to the *Daily Eagle*'s assertion, WWA members argued sufficient reasonable doubt existed that, in the eyes of the law, Vaughn should have been considered innocent of infanticide—not that infanticide ought not to be considered a crime. But the meeting—like the WWA itself—was the culmination of efforts begun by Anthony's newspaper, *The Revolution*, and the argument presented in its pages had not always been so straightforward.

The WWA hosted the meeting in defense of Vaughn, Anthony explained, because "the workingwomen were going to defend the defenceless [sic] of their own sex."[3] This intention motivated *The Revolution*'s coverage of workingwomen's issues, as well as the WWA's foray into areas the *Daily Eagle* considered illegitimate. Like others concerned with social issues, many in the women's rights movement saw workingwomen as particularly vulnerable to seduction, abandonment, and prostitution—conditions closely tied to abortion and infanticide in the popular imagination. Women's second-class social and economic citizenship led them to resort to infanticide and abortion.

Death or Dishonor

In a lecture given in Boston almost a decade before the WWA's public meeting, Caroline Dall had argued that "the question which is at this moment before the great body of working women is 'death or dishonor': for lust is a better paymaster than the mill-owner or the tailor."[4] Dall drew heavily from William Sanger's *History of Prostitution*. While she spoke disapprovingly of his work ("his historical retrospective furnishes every possible excuse to the vices of youth, and is open to question on every page"), she cited his figures and agreed with his conclusion that the main drivers of prostitution were the paucity of professional vocations open to women and low wages.[5]

She also quoted French hygienist Dr. Alexandre Jean Baptiste Parent-Duchâtelet's 1836 *De la Prostitution dans la ville de Paris*: "Compare the price of labor with the price of dishonor, and you will cease to be surprised that women fall."[6]

When Dall drew her listeners' attention to prostitution, she wanted them to "realize that what a noble friend of ours has called the 'perishing classes' are made of men and women like yourselves."[7] In her lectures on women's work and wages, she aimed both to cultivate moral horror at the state of affairs in the United States that had resulted in "five hundred ordinary omnibus loads" of prostitutes in New York City, and to motivate sympathy toward those individual women.[8]

Dall pointed to two primary causes for women becoming prostitutes, each of which mitigated their individual culpability: "ill-paid labor" and misplaced love that led to illicit sex. "Among those whom ill-paid labor forces into sin, there are women nobler and more disinterested than many who remain pure," Dall told her audience, and advised its members to "always remember, that, in nine cases out of twelve, she [a 'fallen woman'] sold herself, not to vice, but to what seemed at least, to her longing heart, like love."[9] She meant that when a woman had been found to have had illicit sex, she was seen as ruined, and prostitution became one of the only means of self-support open to her. The sexual double standard meant that for women the consequences of such seeming love could be permanent loss of status and respectable employability.

Caroline Dall is hardly representative of women's rights advocates in any general sense. She did not, for instance, get along well with many of the women in the Boston women's rights circles. Nonetheless, her approach to the struggles of workingwomen was shared by *The Revolution*'s editors and contributors, who would argue that women in economically precarious positions faced the choice of "death or dishonor" that Caroline Dall had defined so aptly in these lectures.[10] They insisted that behind the sensational scandal of increasing prostitution lay a moral crisis with its roots in women's struggle to access justly-remunerated work and in the deleterious effects of the sexual double standard.

The Revolution *Pleads for Workingwomen*

The Revolution had been publishing for only two months when it began issuing a steady stream of articles on the struggles faced by workingwomen.[11] These pieces tended to reflect antebellum tropes about the working class. They drew heavily on the figure of the "sentimental seamstress."[12] The pathetic image was a favorite mode of stirring sympathy for the "worthy" poor that arose in antebellum evangelical reform literature. It created a feminized image of poverty defined by economic dependence and continuous decline. The virtuous seamstress might die alone in her garret; the vicious one might succumb to prostitution.[13] This feminization of poverty mirrored the increasing association of masculinity with participation in the market and economic success.[14] Unsurprisingly, not everyone responded to this gendering of poverty in the same way.

While these narratives often presented female poverty and dependence as "natural," female reformers used the linked images of the seamstress and the prostitute to argue that women were systematically, and unnaturally, victimized by male power. As Ellen Carol DuBois has written, "The degraded working woman can be said to have replaced the degraded slave woman in the post–Civil War period as a staple of popular imagery and superficial social criticism."[15] Workingwomen's victimization was twofold: economic and sexual. And low wages made women even more susceptible to the injustices of the sexual double standard. The female victim called for a female rescuer: in evangelical literature, the figure of the virtuous and genteel middle-class woman as rescuer and provider of moral-uplift dominated.[16] *The Revolution* embraced these conventions wholeheartedly: most articles on these issues made the case that economic inequality caused prostitution. Many sought to encourage middle-class women to assist their less fortunate "sisters."

There were, however, some distinctive features of *The Revolution*'s coverage. The Civil War had drawn more women into work outside the home, but they hardly enjoyed equality in the workplace. Workingwomen's struggles were, therefore, cast as a part of the project of Reconstruction; creating a more moral republic in the aftermath of so much bloodshed needed to include justice not only for former slaves, but for women as well. *The Revolution*'s articles also included a wider array of workingwomen. While they continued to worry about low wages leading women to choose prostitution, they extended that worry beyond the solitary seamstress to the shop girl and the typographer.[17] For instance, the author of "Female Compositors," a correspondent identified as "M.C.B.," described how the Civil War had allowed women to pursue new avenues of work, but the resulting glut of female labor contributed to their low wages. In the field of typography, female compositors made too little to save, and like seamtresses, when they lost work, "They must starve, or do worse!"[18]

Some articles went further, arguing for solutions such as wage equality and the empowerment of workingwomen themselves. In mid-February 1868, *The Revolution* published a three-article series on "The Working Women of New York." In these pieces, "Tupto" extended the traditional linking of the seamstress and the prostitute to the department store. She described it as if it were a brothel—"a marble palace, where polite dolls . . . show off goods and themselves at the same time."[19] There the male capitalist not only ground "poor sewing girls to the dust," but also took advantage of the "nearly empty purse of a genteel person . . .who would rather die than have anybody know she would descend to sewing even as a means of eking out a scanty income."[20] Women in all areas of life were imposed upon and defrauded by employers and business owners "simply and solely because we are women."[21] Consequently, Tupto wrote, it was strange that more fortunate women "should not make an effort to grab one or two of their sex from the brink of destruction to which high board bills, low prices for work and high prices for clothing are leading unfortunate women every day."[22] She especially faulted Christian women of means for not intervening on these women's behalf.

Tupto was not merely playing with tropes. Rather, she matched her detailed exposé of workingwomen's daily sufferings with calls for practical solutions. She described the poor ventilation of the department stores' work rooms and the long hours their inhabitants were forced to work, and reported that the "great majority seemed to be suffering with lung and throat diseases." Where cheerfulness could be found, she wrote, it was "because they fancy they are making an honest living," though they "allow themselves to die by inches."[23] For these women, the choice to pursue this line of work was the choice of a slow death. Therefore, instead of arguing for benevolence, Tupto demanded economic and wage equality. While the Civil War had opened a wide variety of professions to women, they were "not admitted in equal numbers with men, and when admitted are paid inferior salaries."[24] Both of these injustices needed to be remedied.

In particular, Tupto argued that the concept of the family wage needed to be extended to acknowledge that "if the father is the head of the family, so in many cases is the mother."[25] Indeed, in two of New York's census districts in 1855, some 355 of 599 wage-earning women were the breadwinners for their households.[26] The widows who featured in the more sentimental narratives that *The Revolution* published that spring dramatized their struggles. While marked by class bias and sentimentality, these narratives nonetheless assailed the economic injustices that left such women so vulnerable. Implicit in these critiques was the claim that the social and economic system needed to acknowledge the rights and duties of motherhood as at least equal to those of fatherhood. Without challenging the ideal of a male-supported household, these narratives insisted on the reality that many women lost that support without losing the necessity of feeding themselves and their children. Any system that made it impossible for women to meet those necessities was fundamentally unjust. While these pieces did not usually offer solutions, they did insist that women move beyond complacency.

"A Plea," written by "H.M.S.," who claimed to have been a seamstress, reiterated the argument that low wages for seamstresses led women into prostitution. She not only demanded empathy for such women, but also argued that society, especially other women, bore responsibility for their plight. Therefore, she instructed her readers "not [to] draw your skirts closer to you and shrink away in disgust from the approach of the haggard, hollow-eyed women of shame who pass you in the street." They "were once as pure as you are" and had merely not been "brave enough to choose death rather than dishonor." Women who had done nothing toward "rendering the possibility of such a choice impossible" ought, she argued, to "perceive on our skirts the blood of these poor women, our souls stained with their dishonor."[27]

Later that spring, H. M. Shepard—possibly the "H.M.S" who wrote "A Plea"—presented a nearly archetypical sentimental seamstress narrative.[28] Shepard introduced herself to *The Revolution*'s readers as "a director and worker in various benevolent societies." She told the story of "Madam Fossette," a refined widow and the most deserving of the poor, and used that story to argue against unjust wages and for the power of feminine benevolence. Witnessing many skilled seamstresses come to her charities for assistance, Shepard had set out undercover to investigate their plight. She went to "one of the largest dry goods houses in the city" and, while waiting to be given work, saw a young and attractive French woman arrive and present lacework and embroidery to the superintendent, who received them enthusiastically. The woman then inquired quietly about payment, and was told loudly that nobody was ever paid before payday. She "turned away without remonstrance, but with a look of hopeless sadness in her face that told a bitter story." After receiving her own assignment, Shepard followed the woman to the lobby and talked to her.[29]

In Shepard's telling, Fosette served to illustrate the blamelessness of the tempted seamstress. "Her husband, a wood carver, had died a few months before. His illness had taken the last cent, and she had parted, too, with most of her furniture before he died. Since then things had gone from bad to worse, and now she lived in a little room in the attic of a tenement house and supported herself and four little children by her needle." She knit lace caps for babies, making one a day, receiving thirty-seven cents for each. Shepard accompanied Fossette to her home—a "wretched, utterly comfortless place, with its broken windows, stuffed with rags; its one chair and leafless table, its cracked and fireless stove, its cot-bed, with scanty covering." There were four small children huddled on the bed, awaiting their mother's return; the oldest was eight, and the youngest only a few months old. As soon as they saw her, they began asking for food, but their mother had to respond that she had no bread and no money with which to buy any. Shepard, the figure of benevolence, ran out, purchased food and utensils and fuel for them, and returned to talk more with Fossette. Less working-class than an impoverished member of a higher class, Fossette was thus an easy figure with whom to sympathize for many readers. She was skilled—she could make lace and embroider. Moreover, she had been educated in one of the best schools in Paris and was confident that she could teach the French language. She did not pursue the more lucrative line of work that her education could have afforded her because she did not have the resources to invest in finding pupils, and she felt that her children were "very young to leave alone for so much time." Rather than neglect her children, she had gone out to beg for food for them when her income from needlework fell short.[30]

Fossette, despite her gentle breeding and her innocence in her own predicament, reported that she had "been sorely tempted, for their sake to choose dishonor rather than see them starve," since, while on the streets, she had "over and over again [been] offered that 'wages of infamy, which pays better wages than slop work.'" Despairing, she admitted that earlier she had purchased charcoal with the intent of burning it in her apartment, asphyxiating her children and herself. "I would end it all, but my courage failed," she told Shepard. "Had not the good

God sent you to me this day I fear I must have given way," she admitted, though it was unclear whether she would have chosen death for herself and her children, or prostitution. Fossette embodied Dall's insistence that virtuous women faced the choice of "death or dishonor." Economic injustice caused prostitution and bred moral corruption. And yet Shepard's account suggested that virtue could find a reward. Madame Fossette, an attentive mother, was "lifted out of the depths into which she had been cast," to her own benefit and that of her children, by the aid of one woman's material generosity and her well-timed kind words.[31]

While some articles in *The Revolution* were calculated primarily to stir sympathy, others argued that the burden of securing a better future lay on workingwomen themselves. Rather than waiting for rescue, vulnerable women needed to enliven their own imaginations and participate in their own elevation. The best benevolence would encourage and support this self-improvement. One contributor to *The Revolution* wrote: "If they raised their eyes a little higher they would have seen a road broad and smooth into which they could have entered and walked erect!"[32]

A melodramatic morality tale under the heading "Life and Death by the Needle" criticized women's economic dependence but blamed the individual woman for participating in the unjust system. "L" described a widow with three small children. Not possessing any particular skills, she sought sewing work at an establishment with bad circulation and cramped conditions, where she eventually contracted consumption. Meanwhile, her children suffered from her absence and developed "habits of idleness and aimlessness." The woman died, leaving her children orphans. "L" lamented that the woman and her husband had not purchased land on which to support themselves by farming; if they had, "she might have secured life, comfort, happiness for herself and her children, instead of premature death and early orphanage for those she died to save." That life on a farm would almost certainly have required the woman to promptly remarry does not seem to have occurred to "L." In her view, the seamstress's story was triply tragic: not only had she lost her own life, but she had neglected her parental duties of moral formation, and in her death had further failed those who depended entirely upon her. However much sympathy readers might have for those children, "L," wrote, "tears will not feed them, will not clothe them, will not prevent others from being added to their number. What shall be done about it? How shall we prevent these woes of womanhood and orphanage from multiplying?"[33]

"What shall be done?" tended to be followed by suggestions that vulnerable workingwomen, especially seamstresses, find other lines of work, as in "L's" wish that her widow had taken up farming. Most commonly, middle-class women argued that workingwomen's problems would be solved if they would only take up work as domestics. *The Revolution*, like women's rights activists in general, was not immune from this argument.

The Revolution's commentary on the plight of the workingwoman was part of a broader conversation. In "A Word to Our Sewing Girls," Eleanor Kirk made a contribution to a discussion that had begun with the publication of William Wirt Sikes's "Among the Poor Girls" in the April issue of *Putnam's Magazine*.[34] Like *The Revolution*'s contributors, Sikes had described workingwomen as "at the entrance of the ghastly avenue of sin," goaded toward "its tawdry attractions" by "Starvation, Cold, and Cruelty."[35] He estimated that there were thirty thousand sewing girls, or perhaps poor girls total, in New York City. The number of prostitutes in the city, he claimed, was probably half that.[36] Few women could be converted from that life of sin, he held, so concern first ought to be given to those in danger of entering it. A good starting place, he argued, would be to ensure that women were paid enough to provide for themselves.[37]

One reader of Sikes's article had reacted by trying to offer a young woman employment as a domestic and, when that experiment failed, wrote to *Putnam's Magazine* to announce that the problem was workingwomen's pride.[38] Eleanor Kirk concurred with this disappointed do-gooder and wrote in *The Revolution* that "Until young women do look at this matter sensibly and practically, the ranks of those who are rushing to social destruction and death will continue to fill."[39] Addressing herself to an imagined category of workingwomen without dependents, with freedom in their choice of employment, who were opposed to taking domestic positions, she bluntly stated, "The prejudice you have to places of this description is foolish and unwarrantable." All honest work is respectable, she wrote, and "If you desire to be respected, if you love truth and value culture, it will not make the slightest difference what position you occupy." She urged workingwomen to seek positions as cooks or maids or anything else that would guarantee them a home, and "keep your feet from straying among the hedges."[40] However, women such as Kirk and the *Putnam's* letter writer seem to have been unaware that work as domestics placed young women in a more sexually vulnerable position than did industrial work; the Working Women's Protective Association, which Sikes lauded, often assisted domestics in legal disputes demanding payment.[41] Fortunately, women's rights advocates never relied exclusively on such prescriptions. Eleanor Kirk, who had become a consistent contributor to *The Revolution*, would go on to play an important role in the practical efforts on behalf of workingwomen led by its staff.

The Workingwomen's Association

In the fall of 1868, Anthony and Stanton called a meeting at *The Revolution*'s office to organize an association of workingwomen.[42] Unlike previous organizations for workingwomen, this one was structured for and by women. Its mission was "the amelioration and elevation of all women in New York who labor for a living," through assisting its members in their own "self-extrication and elevation."[43] Formally naming the new association, however, required some negotiation. The methods by which women should best self-extricate and elevate themselves were not universally agreed upon.

The women of *The Revolution* placed their hope in suffrage. A few weeks earlier, a short editorial had claimed that the newspaper existed "for the one specific purpose, more than any other, of ameliorating the condition of working women." The Woman's Suffrage Association, it continued, "was constituted with the same end in view," and "possession of the ballot equally with man [was] believed to be a powerful if not all sufficient means to secure that end." As Aileen Kraditor has argued, the vote held more promise of effecting real change in the lives of workingwomen than in upper-class ones—so the witness of working-class women might carry especial weight in the battle for suffrage.[44] Not surprisingly, then, Stanton proposed that the *new* association be called the "Working Woman's Suffrage Association."[45]

Many of the members, if not all, were involved in the printing business, as typesetters and compositors—they were "the elite of the female wage-earning force."[46] While they were strongly in favor of improving conditions for women, not everyone saw suffrage as the most promising means of improving women's station. Perhaps, in private, Anthony was more willing to grant the possible insufficiency of the ballot to fully remedy these women's wrongs; in a letter to unnamed friends in Kansas nearly a year later, she would write, "If the ballot in the hands of women shall fail to do the desired work of elevating women—then I shall not despair—but look in some other direction for help."[47] But during the meeting, Anthony responded to the workingwomen patronizingly, saying, "If those present did not feel that the ballot was the fulcrum by which they could gain their ends, she was sorry; but [she] did not desire them to pass resolutions beyond what their present mental status sanctioned."[48] Answering Anthony's sneer, Emily Peers, the forewoman in the *Anti-Slavery Standard*'s printing office, argued that suffrage shouldn't be the sole goal of the association, because suffrage would not by itself accomplish the goal of amelioration and elevation, and "however we altered or amended the law, custom, more tyrannical than law, would remain."[49] While debate over the role that suffrage could play in addressing workingwomen's concerns would continue, the organization would be known simply as the Workingwomen's Association (WWA). Suffrage would not become its primary purpose. Instead, it set about expanding—"No. 1" was soon appended to the flagship's name—and pursuing concrete ways to assist workingwomen in their day-to-day lives.[50]

The first meeting of the "Workingwomen's Association No. 2" (WWA2) took place at the Working Woman's Home, a location that reflected the concrete direction the Workingwomen's Association was taking.[51] Established the year before by the trustees of the Five Points House of Industry, the home sat at 45 Elizabeth Street, just north of the upper border of the ill-famed Five Points neighborhood.[52] The institution housed "tailoresses, dress and cloak-makers, milliners, hoop-skirt and artificial flower makers, book-folders, workers in confectionery, tobacco, cigars, etc., with a great number of shop or store clerks."[53] It provided room and board for single women as well as "facilities for education and self improvement," where women would be "withdrawn from temptations, and brought under moral and Christian influences."[54] Here, Anthony tried to rouse working-women to fight for better wages through press agitation and unionization of particular industries.

Anthony clearly doubted whether the workingwomen she was attempting to organize were sufficiently invested in their "self-elevation." She exhorted the crowd to "have a spirit of independence among you, a wholesome discontent, as Ralph Waldo Emerson has said."[55] While the women's rights movement has been characterized as the crystallization of mounting discontent among American women, its success at the popular level depended on the fostering of such discontent among women whose thoughts might not have tended in that direction naturally.[56] This purposeful dissatisfaction would provide the motivation to change public opinion: "Talk to one another, and I will come and talk to you, and the press will support you, for the reporters put everything down . . . and by and by we will have an immense mass meeting of women, where all can talk if they choose, and all the good men and women of America, listening to your appeal will come forward and stand by you."[57] Agitated minds would shape organized agitation, which would reform public opinion. In the next meeting, citing the adages "Where there is a will, there is a way" and "God helps those who help themselves," Anthony told the women that she was sure that when they got to work, they would find the resources they needed to succeed in their aims—"hence her persistency in trying to make them do something."[58]

Anthony's admonitions simultaneously implied that workingwomen were victims and that their sufferings were their own fault. This paradox lay at the heart of her program of self-extrication and elevation. Women suffered because of injustices imposed upon them, but they were also supposed to be powerful enough to cease being victims. The key to this conundrum, in Anthony's eyes and others', seems to have lain in associational life. Despite the classist tone that some suffrage leaders had in speaking about the plight of workingwomen, the model of the new association was less in the tradition of the genteel reaching down to the helpless poor than it was a model of universal cooperation. Bourgeois women associated among themselves, and they could assist working-class women to do likewise. This system did not eliminate a top-down approach, but it did emphasize horizontal relationships.

The "self" in self-elevation and self-extrication was not a lone individual, but rather a woman within a network of other women, even when it came to economic progress. Anthony, for instance, appealed to the members of the WWA2, who lived so close to the center of prostitution in New York City, not only to work for their own benefit but also to protect those whom temptation threatened. "The streets would not be crowded every night by what are called fallen women if it were possible by honest industry to get bread," Anthony said. "There is no solution thereof but to open the avenues of trade so that each woman when she finds herself thrown upon her own resources may support herself in honor, honesty, and integrity."[59] Anthony was trying to move beyond a model of the genteel helping the poor to one of more general cooperation, in which the workingwomen also helped each other, though not to the exclusion of top-down help from wealthier women.

Indeed, the first meeting at the home focused on wage equality. The approximately one hundred women who gathered, most between the ages of fifteen and thirty-five, reported an average daily wage of one dollar. Although these were relatively high wages for workingwomen, Anthony noted that they were less than those paid to men for similar work, because they were based "on the supposition that every woman had a man to support her, and, therefore, that every man ought to be paid wages to enable him to support a wife and family."[60] That supposition was false, however, and therefore the practice was unjust. Like Tupto in *The Revolution* months earlier, Anthony insisted that "a vast majority [of workingwomen] in this city not only support themselves with the scanty price they receive, but also support and maintain a brother, father or children."[61] Neither the women nor their employers should be ashamed, she continued, "but public sentiment should be."[62] Public opinion, however, was not the only means at women's disposal. At the next meeting, Anthony encouraged the formation of profession-specific unions. Mrs. Lozier—either Charlotte or her mother-in-law, Clemence—was chosen to organize the embroiderers present into a union, and a number of other attendees would later go to *The Revolution* offices to discuss the creation of a Sewing Machine Operators' Association.[63]

Again emphasizing the importance of cooperation, Anthony convened a meeting in early November to discuss whether it would be "expedient" to form a single Workingwomen's Union, or Association, open "to all who claim to be workingwomen."[64] A platform for the new association—evidently written in advance of the meeting—was introduced for discussion. The document contained four headings: "The Dignity of Labor," "Excellence of Performance," "Social Interchange," and "Immediate Aims." It lauded the importance of workingwomen having the opportunity to meet "in friendly conference," which "gives hope to the worn spirit, opens anew the avenues of friendship, and reinspires the flagging energies to action."[65] These acts of associating underlay the possibility for practical assistance, but also were intended to enrich the everyday lives—practically, socially, even spiritually—of the women involved.

One of the first actions of the newly united WWA was the organization of a lecture by abolitionist and women's rights orator Anna Dickinson at the Cooper Institute on November 5.[66] Titled "A Struggle for Life," it was partially autobiographical; the *Burlington Free Press* reported that she "detailed many of her own experiences when battling for bread with the rough world" and "entreated those who exalt purity to make its paths less rugged, and closed with a touching picture of the many instances of poverty and temptation which had come under her own observation."[67] Dickinson also relayed the story of Hester Vaughn (or "Vaughan"), a young English immigrant under sentence of death for infanticide in Philadelphia, and in so doing, "touched many a heart."[68] The WWA would go on to fight for Vaughn, playing an important role in her eventual release.

Hester Vaughn's Trial

Hester Vaughn's trial had begun on June 30. That day, the Philadelphia County Court of Oyer and Terminer heard the cases of two women in their late teens—Vaughn and Rose Solomon—

who had both been employed as domestic servants and who had both been accused of infanticide.[69] Rose Solomon's dead daughter had been discovered in a backyard sewer by her employer, who brought it to the Philadelphia Coroner. Solomon had admitted that she had given birth to the child and shortly thereafter had thrown her where she was found, but refused to say anything else that would suggest a cause of death. The coroner, Dr. Shapleigh, testified that there was physical evidence that the Solomon child had breathed independently; her stated cause of death was asphyxiation, though no signs of trauma were present.[70] Solomon was discharged from the custody of the court after the district attorney claimed that there was no proof "that the child met its death by violence, or whether the voluntary act of the mother caused it." Vaughn, however, was not so fortunate.[71]

Vaughn's case had come to the attention of the criminal court due to the report of a neighbor in her building. The woman claimed to have visited Vaughn in her room, and that—as Vaughn admitted—she had shown the body of her dead child to her, and asked her for a box in which to bury the infant and to "keep the matter secret." The neighbor, rather than complying with Vaughn's request, went to the police. The coroner retrieved the infant's body. Vaughn's lawyer, John Goforth, testified that she had been startled by a woman coming into her room with a cup of coffee, and had fallen on her child, killing it. The woman who had brought the coffee to Vaughn testified that she had heard the infant cry. According to the coroner, the infant's cause of death was blunt force trauma to the skull. The trial of Vaughn for murder in the first degree continued, adjourning until the morning of July 1, so that the defense could gather witnesses.[72]

When Vaughn's trial resumed, her lawyer gave evidence of

her good character and made three arguments in her defense. He argued that the infant's death was probably accidental, that Vaughn might have been "bereft of reason" because of the agony she suffered in giving birth, and finally that—as in Solomon's case—there could be little evidence as to what had actually happened beyond the testimony he had given. Vaughn was the only witness to her child's death, and she was prohibited from testifying in the trial, as defendants in criminal cases were not allowed to testify, per then-unchallenged common law.[73] The district attorney countered that there was no evidence that Vaughn had lacked reason, and that her unwillingness to announce the child's birth to her neighbors or supposedly to show its dead body to them and the wound to its skull "proved it to have been a deliberate, premeditated murder, by a mother to her first born."[74] He told the jury that they "should not be moral cowards, but should support the law intended for the preservation of human life, and stamp the foul deed of this false woman with the name the law had made for it—murder of the first degree." After deliberating for several hours, the jury found her guilty.[75] Judge Ludlow instructed Vaughn to "Hope not against hope; the only pardon which can in any event cleanse your soul from the stain of this guilt must be granted by that Divine Being who was the author of your child's life, and who made it in his own image." He then sentenced her to death by hanging.[76] Observers noted that she did not appear to comprehend her fate.[77]

The Revolution *Responds*

The Revolution's initial coverage of Vaughn case accepted the judge and jury's assessment of the facts but challenged the justice of the death penalty. The typical press account of abortion was "seduction, abortion, death," and *The Revolution* cast Vaughn's story in that mode. In an article titled "Infanticide," *The Revolution* provided the text of Judge Ludlow's sentencing, and then pronounced Vaughn's death "a far more horrible infanticide than was the killing of her child." At that time, an individual below the age of majority (then twenty-one) was referred to in the law as an infant; Vaughn was reportedly eighteen or nineteen. In *The Revolution*'s telling, she was a "poor, ignorant, friendless and forlorn girl who had killed her newborn child because she knew not what else to do with it."[78] She had been seduced by society, "by the judge who pronounced her sentence, by the bar and jury, by the legislature that enacted the law (in which, because a woman, she had no vote or voice), by the church and the pulpit that sanctify the law and the deeds." Having been her "joint seducer," these would also "become her murderer." She was "the child of our society and civilization, begotten and born of it."[79] And she, as much as her child, was the infant victim, and her death, like her child's, would be the culmination of a multitude of wrongs.

Perhaps improbably, Vaughn was on her way to symbolizing the structural wrongs done to American women through the sexual double standard and their lack of political and legal rights. A month later, a submission titled "Hester Vaughn" appeared in *The Revolution.* The article was not in response to "Infanticide," but rather rebutted an article on "The Working-Women" published in the Philadelphia newspaper *The Press*. The *Press* article had expressed sympathy for the "wrongs" experienced by workingwomen, but stated that their remedy should be found in benevolent activities rather than in the extension of political and civil rights to women.[80] In *The Revolution*, "M" protested this claim, saying of the author of the *Press* article, "She would have the *women* of a *republican* government 'protected' by 'charity.'" She mocked the idea, saying that it was the same protection "that slavery gave to the Africans... that the English government gives to her subjects... that Mahometanism gives to woman; protects her as a slave to man's basest passions, while she has not the right to say how her own body shall be used."[81] For "M," the link between workingwomen's unjust wages and sexual vulnerability was self-evident, and the tragedy of Vaughn's life was its proof case. "Hester was taught to confide in man," wrote "M." "She did so, and he robbed her of her character before the world. In hopes to save herself—and no doubt she reasoned that her babe would rest more sweetly in the grave than in this unkind world—she committed murder; and again she is in the hands of her 'protectors.'"[82] Infanticide was proof of women's dependence on men and utter lack of autonomy. And it proved that a woman's dependence rendered her far less virtuous. Women, like the men of a republic, needed independence to be fully virtuous.

These defenses of Vaughn no doubt resonated with those who could recall abolitionist and women's rights advocate Lucy Stone's passionate defense of Margaret Garner.[83] Garner, a slave captured in Ohio, slit her toddler daughter's throat rather than see her returned to slavery. Garner was tried for the destruction of property rather than for murder, and at her trial Stone had explained Garner's act as at least rational if not heroic: "The faded faces of the negro children tell too plainly to what degradation female slaves must submit. Rather than give her little daughter to that life, she killed it."[84] The analogy between women's condition in society, in which infanticide could become a thinkable act, and the "seething hell of American slavery" was clear. Readers of the early narrative of Vaughn's case presented in *The Revolution* would understand the similarities between the two cases. In this telling, both Vaughn and Garner had been taken advantage of by men with power over them, and in the throes of despair, had decided to choose death for their children rather than allowing them to be subjected to the dishonor they themselves had experienced.

While these earlier pieces sought to reinterpret the significance of Vaughn's impending execution, Anna Dickinson's November appeal marked the beginning of the actual campaign to save Vaughn's life. At this point, *The Revolution*'s narrative began to shift. Rather than arguing for mercy toward a guilty woman who had committed a crime under extreme duress, the newspaper's editors began to insist that Vaughn was actually innocent. Two weeks after Dickinson's lecture at the Cooper Institute, Stanton wrote a new article that gave a description of the infant's death that was closer to the defense testimony than to her own earlier assertions that Vaughn had murdered her child. She described Vaughn's utter solitude while giving birth, writing that she had cried for help fruitlessly. When someone finally came to bring her water, "she was found in a fainting condition, and the child dead by her side."[85]

Despite the shifting description of the facts of the case, the lesson Stanton took from it remained nearly the same—that women needed rights. She made the same argument, broadly, without applying it to Vaughn. She reiterated that a woman who killed her own child was one who had been victimized by the father and by a society in which some held her death preferable to her "dishonor." Men could not understand the devastating effects of the sexual double standard, "the terrible mortification and sorrow of a girl's life when betrayed into a false step" and her deep fear of her "future exposure, disgrace and degradation." They, therefore, could not understand her desperation "when in the crisis of her danger, she denies herself, through fear, all human sympathy," because she had "no hope of future love and happiness...every natural pulsation of the human heart, the deepest and holiest affections of a mother's nature...[were] crushed in concealment and violence."[86] Consequently, "men have made the laws cunningly, for their own protection," Stanton wrote. Returning to Vaughn, Stanton now argued that regardless of what might actually have happened, Vaughn had been "tried and condemned with most inadequate proof" by the male-dominated legal system.[87] Because Vaughn's guilt had not been *proven*, her conviction was mistaken, regardless of her moral guilt.

The Revolution, presuming innocence unless the reverse was proven, found that it was an easy step from finding Vaughn "not guilty" to declaring her free of fault, morally and legally. Two weeks later, at a WWA meeting, Eleanor Kirk described Vaughn as "falsely accused of killing her newborn child, and under sentence of death."[88] The narrative turn complete, the group took action.

The Hester Vaughn Meeting at Cooper Institute

On December 1, 1868, the WWA sponsored a large meeting at the Cooper Institute to protest Vaughn's conviction and "to take such steps as may be deemed necessary to obtain the liberation of the unhappy young woman."[89] Among the nine officers for the meeting were Horace Greeley, editor of the *New-York Tribune*, as president; Jane Cunningham Croly, founder of the woman's club Sorosis, as a vice-president; and Charlotte Lozier as a secretary. While it appeared to be largely a top-down endeavor, *The Revolution*'s editors later claimed that Anna Dickinson's speech had inspired "several members of the 'Working Women's Association,' as well as many outside of this organization, [who] called at the office of 'The Revolution,'. . . to see what steps could be taken in the wretched woman's behalf."[90] Eleanor Kirk led initial efforts for Vaughn. She suggested petitioning the governor of Pennsylvania, John W. Geary, on Vaughn's behalf and served as head of a committee to coordinate the petition. She also went to Philadelphia with Mrs. Dr. Lozier (probably Clemence Lozier) to interview Vaughn in person.[91] Upon her return, Kirk instigated, and spoke at, the meeting for Vaughn's benefit.[92]

To replace the narrative of Vaughn as exemplar of the evil of infanticide, the WWA argued that Vaughn represented systematic social and legal injustice. Greeley opened the meeting by opining that no other argument for Vaughn's release should be made than that "a friendless, feeble person is under sentence of death of a murderer, under circumstances which at the very worst afford strong grounds for doubt whether any crime at all was committed or meditated by her."[93] The WWA's petition to Governor Geary asserted that, as Vaughn "was condemned on insufficient evidence and with inadequate defense, justice demands a stay of proceedings and a new trial." If that were impractical, the petition added, the governor could instead "grant her an unconditional pardon."[94] Stanton argued, "Hester Vaughan is a workingwoman, unjustly accused, tried and condemned, and as the poorer classes cannot avail themselves of the fraud, concealment, bribery, or bail, that the rich can, they are pre-eminently interested in seeing that justice is done to the poorer classes of women in our courts." Most of the speakers at the meeting, however, insisted that saving Hester Vaughn mattered for women, and workingwomen in particular.[95]

Suffrage advocates saw Vaughn as a dramatic example of the urgent need for legal and political rights for women.

Anthony argued that "the workingwomen were going to defend the defenceless [sic] of their own sex, and act on the doctrine that the crime of women shall be condemned no worse than the same crime by men." Anthony, therefore, presented the WWA's petition with a series of resolutions that called for legal equality for women: "that in all civil and criminal cases woman shall be tried by a jury of her peers; shall have a voice in making the law, in electing the judge who pronounces her sentence, and the sheriff who, in case of execution, performs for her that last dread act"; that the existence of the death penalty ought to "startle every mother into a sense of her responsibility in making the laws under which her daughters are to live or perish"; and finally that "the gallows—that horrible relic of barbarism—be banished from this land; for human life should be held alike sacred by the individual and the state."[96] The meeting at the Cooper Institute, Stanton argued, should "rouse thought and attention to the unjust laws and public sentiment that make crimes for women that are not crimes for men, and visit on the victims of society all those penalties that in justice should be shared by the makers and administrators of law."[97]

In her speech, Kirk recounted her meeting with Vaughn, and how it left her and Lozier convinced of the young woman's innocence. Vaughn was attractive with "a girlish figure; a sweet, intelligent face; soft brown eyes; broad forehead; [and a] warm, earnest mouth." She carried herself with a "quiet, womanly dignity." According to Kirk, Vaughn had been raped rather than seduced and betrayed: "Overcome, not in a moment of weakness and passion, but by superior strength—*brute force*—Hester Vaughn fell a victim to lust and the gallows."[98] As she and Lozier were leaving, Kirk reported, Vaughn had told them, "Ladies, I know you will do all for me that lies in your power, but my trust must be in God." Based on "all that I saw and heard at Philadelphia," Kirk declared that "Hester Vaughn is no more guilty of infanticide than I am, and I am right sure that I never killed a baby in my life."[99]

Lozier provided more concrete arguments for Vaughn's innocence. In addition to meeting with Vaughn, she had consulted with a Dr. Susan Smith, "who has been a practicing physician for fifteen years, a woman of large influence and a neighbor of the judge who condemned Hester Vaughan." Smith had met with Vaughn at least once a week for five months and, after interviewing her extensively, had come to the conclusion that the girl was not guilty. Both Smith and Lozier came to the conclusion that Vaughn had probably suffered from puerperal mania and blindness.[100] According to Lozier, Vaughn said that she had never seen her child, and that her vision was still weak. When Lozier directly asked Vaughn what had happened to her child, and to explain the indentations on the child's skull, she responded that "I must have lain on it; when I waked up, the child lay under me." Lozier granted that the "poor woman, in her agony, alone, without fire, without life, may have injured the child, but not willfully." Lozier then cited Vaughn's maternal affection as evidence of her innocence, reporting that the girl had told her, "No one ever loved children more than I do—no one. I dearly love them. I wish I had my poor little babe. It would be some comfort to me."[101]

Vaughn's sentencing had been a serious miscarriage of justice, Kirk argued, especially because Judge Ludlow's opinion of Vaughn seemed to mirror her own: "I do not think her a bad woman naturally," he had told Kirk; "She has an excellent face, but there was no other course open for me but the broad course of condemnation; she was, in the opinion of the jury, guilty of the murder of her child." But that was not all. "You have no idea how rapidly the crime of 'infanticide' is increasing," he had continued. "Some woman must be made an example of. It is for the establishment of a principle, ma'am."[102]

While Kirk and the rest of the WWA agreed that infanticide was wrong, they doubted that the public's understanding of the principle could be strengthened by condemning a woman like Vaughn, whose guilt and culpability were so much in doubt, to death. The *New York World*, reporting that Ludlow's argument "made the blood of the Ladies Committee boil in their veins," understood this. In a lengthy article published on the day of the Cooper Institute meeting, the *World* opined:

> Probably the committee thought more—thought that the crimes of foeticide and abortion were very prevalent, and that the germ of many a life was destroyed, not alone by poor girls, and not alone out of wedlock, but that better examples might be found perhaps among ladies who sit cosily [sic] wrapped up in elegant boudoirs, with abundant means and good husbands, and who destroyed life not through shame, or poverty, or despair, but because they did not like the trouble of fulfilling the office for which nature fitted them. Besides, infanticide is only discovered on the part of poor girls who have not the means of secrecy.[103]

When Parker Pillsbury spoke to the meeting at the Cooper Institute later that day, he also argued that Vaughn's execution could not serve as an effective way to rally society against infanticide or abortion. If Vaughn were innocent, her execution would be the first murder committed in her case. And if she were guilty, he said, it would be the utmost in hypocrisy for society to condemn a woman who had suffered such abuse, poverty, and illness, when "before tomorrow's sun shall rise both in New York and Philadelphia infanticide will be perpetrated in hundreds of instances, both fathers and mothers assenting to the horror, and paying largely for it." He reminded the audience of the media's encouragement of abortion and infanticide, asking "Have you not in your own city professional murderers? How many newspapers have you [that are] too pure to advertise these murders from week to week?" To applause, Elizabeth Cady Stanton responded, "*The Revolution* has none."[104]

The WWA did not just seek Vaughn's release. They also intended to offer her some practical assistance. Reiterating the familiar argument against the assumption that men were women's natural protectors, Ernestine Rose rallied the audience to not only sign the petition to Geary but also "give your means to enable that poor child after she shall have been liberated from that dungeon to re-enter the path of virtue." During the meeting's intermission, Anthony asked the audience for $500, or as much as $1000, to provide for Vaughn upon her potential release. She also proposed that Dr. Lozier, or "some other competent female physician," care for Vaughn after her hoped-for pardon, and that she be sent back to England after fully regaining her health.[105]

For these women's rights activists, Vaughn was clearly first and foremost a symbol. Anthony, in the midst of her "begging," told the audience, "As soon as we get Hester Vaughan out of prison we will get somebody else to work for. We intend to keep up the excitement."[106] Advocating for Vaughn was, as Greeley would later complain, "an occasion for a grand dress-parade of women's suffrage and women's rights."[107] Anthony readily admitted that this had been the case, and argued that her use of the occasion had been just. "Yes, we did make a 'grand dress-parade,' and so we have had grand dress-parades for the negro for the last thirty years," she was reported to have said. "We have had specimens of the great stalwart negro brought up for exhibition upon the platform, and have had his back uncovered to see the great streaks from the lash. Henry Ward Beecher brought a little girl with bright blue eyes upon the stage, and said that she was yet a slave. . . . We see the parallel."[108] In the Cooper Institute meeting, the radical women's rights advocates' argument that the position of women in American society mirrored that of the slave had been given shocking, tangible form.

Anthony repeated this sentiment to the WWA in May, after discovering that the Pennsylvania governor had pardoned Vaughn and had spirited her out of the country secretly, sending her to England on a ship that departed from New York City. "If I'd have once seen Hester Vaughan, or got hold of her in any way," Anthony said, "I would have exhibited her on the platform of the Cooper Institute, on the same principle that we used to exhibit fugitive slaves on that platform."[109] Anthony deplored the way that Vaughn, like so many women, had been violated by men, and she deplored the judicial and political system that allowed men to blame the women they seduced or raped, and abandoned or pressured to obtain abortions, for committing infanticide or obtaining abortions under the duress they themselves had caused. Yet the governor's secretive dispatching of Vaughn to England was, Anthony said, "a tremendous acknowledgement of [the governor's] fear of us women, although we do not vote.[110]

Vaughn and the Politics of Motherhood

Vaughn's story dominated the December 10 issue of *The Revolution.* The more than 6,700 words on her included an editorial, an article written by Elizabeth Cady Stanton, an article by Parker Pillsbury, and an additional unsigned piece. Stanton reiterated her critique that Vaughn's defense had been essentially nonexistent. She insisted "there was so much room for doubt in the case that if she had been properly defended, the jury would either have acquitted her, or disagreed, which latter would have ultimately resulted in her discharge."[111] Vaughn's case, she said, proved the need for "girls who have brains to understand the science of jurisprudence and hearts big enough to demand justice for the humblest of God's children" to become lawyers.

Pillsbury's article, however, dealt with criticisms of the meeting. Despite his annoyance at the direction the meeting had taken, he defended the appropriateness of the Workingwomen's Association taking up Vaughn's cause. She was "a working woman, like the members of the Association; and possess[ed] special claim to their regard on that account." If women had a particular responsibility to look out for other women on the basis of shared sex, the same principle applied to class. Responding to criticisms that the meeting had gone beyond its stated purpose, he responded, "There is a horrible harvest of Hester Vaughan victims every year," and "how to prevent the enemy from sowing the seed whence it grows, is as well the work of the Working Women's Association as the rescue of one specific victim." Like Anthony, Pillsbury tied the use of Vaughn's plight as propaganda for women's rights to the strategies of the abolitionists who were "long accustomed to that type of humanity and philanthropy." Pillsbury also countered the accusation that "not one of them [the meeting's speakers] spoke of the terrible increase of the crime of infanticide." To the contrary, he responded that "this was the burden of at least one of the Cooper Institute addresses"—his own—"and some of the others were surely not silent on the subject."[112]

The WWA's defense of Vaughn became a reference point in debates over the significance of women's rights for women's role as mothers. The first speaker at the founding convention of the Illinois Woman Suffrage Association in February 1869 asserted that women could not exercise the franchise without neglecting their families. He pointed to the "ten thousand women in this land now [who] have the guilt of murder upon them for having destroyed their unborn infants," arguing that the opportunity to vote—and to be elected to office—would further deter women from childbearing. Rev. Robert Collyer, a Unitarian minister with strong anti-slavery bonafides, responded by asking, "If woman is criminally disposed to reduce the rate of births, is it not true that man, as the accessory, is equally guilty?" He described Lucretia Mott as having told him that she "never neglected her children for public duties," and "so it would be with every true woman." Stanton spoke after Collyer and went further. She claimed that Vaughn's story stood for the whole cluster of issues being discussed, and was an exemplar of the effects of "manhood suffrage" and women's exclusion from political life. Anna Dickinson, in turn, insisted that woman suffrage was "the cause of purity" because it would "strengthen young girls" and "give them dignity, which is to give them self-respect." Suffrage would "put these girls on their feet; that is to say, 'You are human beings, you are to earn the clothes that cover you, you are to walk with steady feet through rough places.'"[113]

At the May 19 meeting of the WWA, Sarah F. Norton read an essay on the decrease in the marriage rate.[114] She denied the premise of her subject, arguing that the marriage and birth rates in New York and major European cities were very similar and therefore not disproportionately low.[115] She nonetheless acknowledged that the number of stillbirths reported in New York City was twice what ought to be expected and attributed that to infanticide and abortion. These, she argued, were increasing due to "a growing dislike among certain classes to assume the duties and responsibilities of parents," and "the unblushing effrontery with which of late the professional perpetrators of foeticide advertise their business."[116] According to the *World*, Norton's argument echoed those Charlotte Lozier had made in her "Social Evil" lecture less than two weeks earlier.[117]

Speaking next, Anthony explained that a man had asked her what the study of statistics about marriage had to do with workingwomen. "It has a great deal to do with it," Anthony told the meeting. "All the arrangements of society are made on the supposition that every woman is supported by some man, and every door of profitable occupation is closed against them." The basic economic and legal inequalities between men and women lay at the root of many social ills, within marriage and without, and those ills couldn't be resolved until men and women were acknowledged everywhere as equal. That would happen, Anthony said, "the moment woman holds the ballot in her hands—the moment she begins to help make the law of marriage—she will be the controller of her own person, and her own earnings, and no husband will have the right to make her violate her conscience."[118] The moral injury that men inflicted on their wives when they pressured them—either explicitly, or by simultaneously wanting sex and being opposed to children—into obtaining abortions was the result of the same bias against women as competent agents of their own welfare and that of their children that made it difficult for workingwomen to support themselves and their dependents.

Norton, Lozier, and Anthony all flatly denied that increasing women's legal and political rights would increase the number of abortions and infanticides. Rather, they saw these, as exemplified in the case of Hester Vaughn, as symptoms of broader social ills. Abortion indicated a lack of feminine autonomy. That lack of autonomy took various shapes, including women's ignorance of their own bodies and their lack of power, especially within marriage. Moreover, the supposed choice between "death or dishonor" that led women to choose an abortion or to commit infanticide was itself a sign of grave social, political, and economic injustice. To pursue either option, a woman had to violate her conscience, and this showed that moral, if not also physical, violence had taken place. The WWA's defense of Vaughn was premised on the belief that she had been presented with this false choice, through seduction or even rape—and could not have been presumed to have committed infanticide freely. The freedom that Anthony and others sought for workingwomen was economic, legal, and moral, and would allow women to fulfill their capacities and duties; it would allow them to choose the good.

Chapter Six

THE CREATION OF THE MASSACHUSETTS INFANT ASYLUM

"The Massachusetts Infant Asylum, incorporated by the Legislature of 1867, and generously endowed by the people of Boston, will open in a few weeks," Frank Sanborn announced in the pages of *The Revolution* in early 1868. "A modest house in Dorchester has been rented and furnished, and will soon be filled with these poor babes, under the care of skilful [sic] women."[1] This announcement came in the middle of some friendly sparring with Parker Pillsbury in the pages of the newspaper, begun when Pillsbury cited research Sanborn had undertaken as the secretary of the Massachusetts Board of State Charities (MBSC) in a front-page article discussing "the frightful increase of foeticide, infanticide and child murder in every form."[2]

On March 26, *The Revolution* ran Pillsbury's "Foundling Hospitals" article on its front page. The article began with paraphrasing, not wholly accurately, Sanborn's research on the death rate for the infants sent to Massachusetts's almshouses. Pillsbury claimed that "ninety per cent of [the] infants in those institutions die before they reach the end of their first year!"[3] Because of the high infant mortality in these institutions—in particular, the mortality of foundlings (abandoned infants) and illegitimate children sent into this system "in great numbers and [who] die almost as fast as they are sent"—Sanborn had recommended in MBSC's first annual report that "a foundling hospital should at once be established to receive children of this class."[4] Noting this suggestion, Pillsbury wondered "whether foundling hospitals could be conducted with so much humanity and success [as suggested by Sanborn] even in Massachusetts." Nevertheless, he wrote, "Under the superintendence of the excellent and indefatigable Mr. Sanborn, Secretary of the Board of State Charities, we earnestly wish to see the experiment fairly and fully made."[5]

A few weeks later, Sanborn responded to the "Editors of the *Revolution*," and more specifically "my friend, Parker Pillsbury," with a letter apologizing for "offer[ing] corrections in return for the too flattering mention which you made of your present correspondent." Like Pillsbury, Sanborn had been a devoted abolitionist—he had been the youngest member of the "Secret Six" who supported John Brown—and a supporter of women's suffrage.[6] Though Pillsbury was twenty years older than Sanborn, it seems very likely that they were personally known to each other. Perhaps because of their shared commitments, Sanborn had no qualms in, somewhat gently, accusing Pillsbury of making "statements and intimations which may mislead your readers." Sanborn went on to provide detailed statistics about infant mortality in the Tewksbury Almshouse, his opinions about the causes of infant mortality, and corrections to Pillsbury's description of his plans for providing for vulnerable infants.

In the first annual report of the Massachusetts Infant Asylum (MIA), published within weeks of this exchange in *The Revolution*, Sanborn would make it clear that the MIA was not strictly speaking a foundling hospital but had been "designed to take the place of such a hospital, and to render that unnecessary."[7] Unlike continental foundling hospitals, which admitted all infants brought to them, the MIA's staff would review the cases of infants presented for admission individually. They would accept children in three categories: foundlings, who were deserted by unknown parents; orphans or children deserted by known parents; and "the infant children of women unable to support them entirely, but who can pay a part of their cost or can take some part in the care of them."[8] Rather than housing all the infants together and providing little individualized care, the MIA planned to primarily "board out" its infants in the homes of foster parents, who would receive a stipend for their care, with its centralized institution serving primarily as a place to care for medically unstable infants, and as a hospital for those who became ill. Parents who placed their infants with the MIA nonanonymously were required to provide financial support for their infants if they were able to do so, were strongly encouraged to visit them, and were encouraged to remove their children from the MIA and resume primary care for them when they became competent to do so. The MIA also allowed some destitute and unskilled mothers to live in the "home" with their infants and work as wet nurses. In this way, while the MIA cared for abandoned infants, it also worked to prevent infants from being abandoned and to keep their mothers with them.

From the first discussions leading to its founding, the mission of the Massachusetts Infant Asylum was conceived of as doing more than caring for infants. It was also intended to support women who might be tempted by abortion or infanticide—or who might be forced to abandon their children. Dr. Lucy Sewall had noted that she knew that many of the infants who died very young were born to mothers who left the NEHWC "not knowing how to provide for them." At least one half of the unwed mothers Sewall saw would take care of their children "if they could do so," she said.[9] Matilda Goddard had agreed, saying that about twenty mothers came to her with infants each week, and that the first question they asked her was, "How can I take care of my child?"[10] While the philosophy that underlay this system did see women who bore children out of wedlock as in some sense fallen, it did not see them as irreparably damaged. In this way, the project implicitly challenged the sexual double standard and functioned to allow individual women the opportunity to strengthen their lives. In essentially providing long-term child care for the infants of vulnerable women, allowing them to find employment and work toward stable homes for their children, the MIA would help women take care of their children in the long and the short term.

In his letter to *The Revolution*'s editors, Sanborn wrote that, despite his lengthy criticism of Pillsbury's article, he was nevertheless grateful for it because "so little is known in this country of the management or mismanagement of foundling establishments, that to direct inquiry that way is a public benefit."[11] Pillsbury responded to Sanborn by writing that "we cheerfully accept and publish the corrections of our excellent friend Mr. Sanborn"—and then proceeded to continue ribbing him for being "too good a student in history and human nature" to disbelieve the possibility of some of the tales he had related about Russian Orthodox foundling hospitals.[12]

Homes for Infants Who Have to Depend Upon the Community for Care

In Boston in the 1850s and 1860s, Dr. Marie Zakrzewska and Matilda Goddard had worked independently to provide care for infants who had been orphaned or were at risk for abandonment. Matilda Goddard was a native Bostonian, in her late forties, and of relatively modest means. She lived "in very simple fashion" in Boston's South End, and was "the most practical of housekeepers and the most perfect of economists." When Goddard's older brother died, leaving her $100,000, the only change she made was to undertake "her errands of mercy with a carryall and horse and driver, enabling her with her feeble health to do an amount of work which she could not have done unaided."[13] Unmarried, she appeared to her friends to have "consecrated herself to the cause of humanity," and in particular to the care of vulnerable women and children.[14] In the years leading up to the Civil War, she had been engaged in anti-slavery work and the organization of the New England School of Design for Women, and she would go on to support suffrage efforts as well as the Indigent Females' Relief Association and the Home for Aged Women, among many other organizations.[15]

For more than two decades, the project of caring for abandoned and at-risk infants in Boston was uniquely Goddard's. When Ednah Dow Cheney met her for the first time in 1844, Goddard had already embarked on her efforts to care for every infant "deserted by its parents, or having none able to care for it."[16] While Goddard did not bring them into her own home, or institute an organization to care for them, she found a boarding place for each child, and watched over them until they reached maturity.[17] She found adoptive parents for some of the children, and followed up on their lives, too, finding that "'in far the larger number of cases, the homes had proved good ones." By 1868, Goddard estimated that she had facilitated the adoption of more than 700 children.[18]

Around the same time, Dr. Marie Zakrzewska was engaged

in a similar project, though in scale it was much smaller and its execution more institutional. While teaching at the NEFMC, which she had moved to Boston to join in 1859, Zakrzewska noticed that its clinic treated more dying infants than mildly ill—and therefore curable—ones. Consequently, she decided "to inquire how far the law protected such little beings, and how far institutions gave relief either to poor mothers by boarding their offspring, or to foundlings," i.e., infants abandoned by their parents. "No public provision existed," she found, "save a few places in connection with a Roman Catholic institution," and so she decided to establish her own.[19] In 1861, with the financial assistance of friends, she rented an apartment close to the Medical College and established a "baby-home" there, employing a matron, a nurse, and a wet nurse as staff. The home cared for up to eight infants at a time. Zakrzewska found the undertaking expensive, with an average cost of $3.50 per person, adult or child, per week. Consequently, the little institution closed after nine months.[20]

It is hardly surprising that Franklin Benjamin Sanborn sought these women's advice when he became interested in decreasing infant mortality in Massachusetts's almshouses. Within weeks of the publication of the MBSC's first annual report, Sanborn asked Zakrzewska—by then the head of the NEHWC—to tell him what she knew about provisions for a "comfortable and respectable home for infants who have to depend upon the community for care." She was happy to respond; the subject, she told him, "has been of great interest to me as long as I can remember back to my childhood," and "there is no subject on which I feel more warmly and could speak more earnestly about, than this legal murdering of the least part of our community."[21] She swiftly described provisions for foundlings in Germany, Russia, and France; mentioned an institution for that purpose in New York City; and gave a slight nod to her own little "Home."[22]

Zakrzewska suggested to Sanborn that, if an institution were founded in Boston, it could care for more than foundlings. When she was a child, she told him, "I saw the poor infant abused by its foster mother while its own had been taken to nurse the rich man's child, whose mother wished to save herself the trouble of doing so." Zakrzewska understood the pressures burdening mothers who had primary economic responsibility for their households. In Prussia, where wet nursing was more common as a matter of convenience, poor women often left their own offspring with women who maltreated the children when their mothers went to work. In the United States, Zakrzewska wrote, "work is not easily provided for a woman with a child, and she often is obliged to desert it [the child] for want of food or shelter." Consequently, in both countries, "these little ones are abused, become crippled in health and chiefly die within the first years of their lives."[23] Sanborn's not-yet-founded institution could also function to save these children's lives, too.

While Zakrzewska had sympathy for poor women whose need for remunerative work sometimes endangered the lives of their offspring, she nevertheless believed that "The necessity to provide for these little creatures [is] the greatest need of civilization." That responsibility, she believed, fell on both the members of society and its government. As she told Sanborn, "such an enterprise ought to be carried on by private charity, but it should be made the house of the State to take care of its children."[24] Julie Miller has noted that there were two European models of care for foundlings: In Catholic countries, national governments assumed responsibility for the care of foundlings in order "to preserve the honor of married men, unmarried women, and their families." But in Protestant countries, government rarely became involved in situations that were understood as fundamentally private, with the presumption that "parents, not the state, ought to be responsible for their illegitimate babies."[25] The system that Zakrzewska proposed combined both of these models; while the state would continue to fund, if not actively provide, care for foundlings, private charity would also provide support for parents in the fulfillment of their individual duties to their children.

This Lamentable Waste of Human Life

By 1867, Sanborn had made more progress toward the goal of establishing an institution that would provide better care for Massachusetts's abandoned children, which he had initially articulated in the MBSC's first annual report, published two years earlier. He had consulted with many physicians, including Zakrzewska; Henry G. Clark; Horatio Storer; his father, David H. Storer; Samuel A. Greene; and Dr. Lucy Sewall.[26] He was making his project well known; following Sanborn's retirement from the MBSC in late 1868, the board recalled his "eloquently set[ting] forth, in season and out of season, officially and unofficially, the importance of doing something to lessen the suffering and the death rate" of Massachusetts's foundlings.[27] At the same time, progress in caring for abandoned infants had also been made in other cities.

The New York Infant Asylum had opened in early 1865, within months of the publication of the MBSC's first annual report. The Infant's Home, also in New York City, opened under the direction of Mary DuBois at the year's end.[28] In Detroit, Sanborn noted, "a society of ladies have made a beginning in this work, but have not carried it far." In Chicago, Philadelphia, Pittsburgh, and Providence, he reported, "nothing is done except in the great Almshouse."[29] In Massachusetts, as a general rule, foundlings were sent to the state's almshouses. Sanborn acknowledged that, within the state, the city of Boston was something of an exception, because its foundlings were brought to the Temporary Home on Charles Street, from which many were adopted. But those not adopted—69 out of the 156 infants brought to the Temporary Home between 1862 and 1867—were sent to the almshouses.[30]

From 1863 to 1867, 451 of the 1,161 children under the age of one year admitted to Massachusetts's three almshouses—Tewksbury, Monson, and Bridgewater—died. But the numbers looked much different when foundlings alone were considered. From 1854 to 1867, the Tewksbury Almshouse admitted 297 foundlings, of which 250 died. The foundlings had, on average, spent only five weeks in the almshouse before they died. "When they do live," Sanborn reported, "it is usually because they have been taken in charge by some special attendant who takes a fancy to them."[31] The almshouse fed its infants with cow's milk, grouped them in a large room without good ventilation, and gave them little individual attention. Sanborn insisted that this system for caring for foundlings was "little better than consenting to their death."[32] Consequently, he argued, "it is the duty of the Legislature, as soon as possible, to *stop* this lamentable waste of human life."[33]

When Sanborn referred to "this lamentable waste of human life," he was not only referring to the conditions at the almshouses. His argument was also based on what was known broadly about birth and infant mortality statistics for the fifteen years between 1852 and 1866. Following the Civil War, the general birth rate declined, but the reported number of illegitimate births in Massachusetts doubled and the number of reported stillbirths increased by 50 percent.[34] Like many similar investigators, Sanborn argued that the real numbers of such births and deaths were likely much higher, because "a great number of children reported still-born, are in reality destroyed, with the consent of the mother, or at her desire, because she does not know how, or does not wish to support them."[35] In addition to hoping that a future institution would prove better at preserving infant life than the almshouses, Sanborn hoped that women in desperate situations—both pregnant women and mothers of infants—would consider it a refuge for their children, and as providing an alternative to abortion or infanticide, as well as to infant abandonment.

The Infant Asylum Takes Shape

Sanborn held his first public meeting on January 11, 1867, "to consider the subject of Deserted and Destitute Infants and what further provision should be made for them." Horatio Storer, Ednah Dow Cheney, Lucy Sewall, Matilda Goddard, and Caroline Dall—who had been recruited by Goddard—were among the attendees that evening. He presented them with a list of twenty-seven questions that he had prepared with the intention of sending "to various people acquainted with the subject"—and to which he'd already received a few responses. It began by asking, "How many infants within your knowledge are annually left unprovided for by the death of the mother? By desertion of the mother? By the mothers' inability to support them?" and ended by inquiring whether "the establishment of such a Home [for abandoned infants] in your opinion [would] encourage or increase vice? Would it tend to diminish infanticide and criminal abortion?"[36]

In these latter questions, Sanborn gave a nod to the notion—frequently present in literature on these topics, and rarely if ever sourced—"that to take good care of foundlings is to encourage vice."[37] For those involved in creating foundling asylums, abandoned infants were "not only infants whose lives were in danger, they were also visible reminders of a connected group of transgressive activities committed by women . . . [which] included infanticide, abortion, prostitution, and baby farming."[38]

Discussion at this first meeting centered on the problem of deserted and destitute infants and the means by which it could be addressed. Storer, wholeheartedly behind Sanborn, "stated his conviction of the great need existing of an asylum for infants, and that the establishment of such a home would tend to check the crime of infanticide." By contrast, another attendee implicitly questioned the need for such a project, asking whether "a law did not exist to punish desertion of children." To that, Sanborn responded that while one very likely did, "it was very difficult to bring it to bear upon the guilty parties." Sewall and Goddard added that supporting mothers who were ill-prepared and ill-equipped to provide for their children—and yet were, in their experience, willing to do so—would go farther toward reducing the number of deserted infants in the city than would punishing parents who abandoned their children.[39]

At a second meeting held in mid-March 1867, Sanborn introduced the nascent plan. A new home would care for twelve infants at a time, at an anticipated yearly cost of $500 a year, for a trial period of three years. The project Sanborn described was a public-private collaboration; he hoped that the legislature would pay half of the home's yearly costs, and suggested that the other half could be raised "by subscription." In the discussion that ensued, meeting attendants doubled down on the necessity of the small scale of their home, and also of "opening its management to all denominations"—meaning, not excluding Catholic infants. The meeting ended with plans to instantiate the institution under discussion. A committee—which included Sanborn, as well as Lucy Sewall, Ednah Dow Cheney, and Lucy Goddard (all key members of the NEHWC staff)—was established to create an operating plan, and to find individuals who would serve as incorporators.[40]

The group met again less than two weeks later, on March 27. Seven incorporators had been identified, and Sanborn's committee agreed to meet with these individuals and, with them, "to organize an association for the protection of deserted and neglected children."[41] By this March meeting, Sanborn had received far more answers to the questionnaire he had introduced in the first meeting about the home, in January. Responses had come from several Massachusetts doctors, two of the state's almshouses, and doctors and other interested parties in Detroit, New York City, and Providence. The responses were not particularly surprising. "From these letters," the meeting's secretary noted, "it appears that there is nowhere in the country such provision for the care of neglected infants as there should be, either on the part of the public or private establishments."[42]

Two responses to this questionnaire were transcribed in full in the institution's records. These came from Marie Zakrzewska and the Detroit Home for the Friendless's Isabella Graham Duffield Stewart. Descended from Isabella Graham, who launched New York's first orphan asylum in 1806, Stewart was a huge force in Detroit's charitable scene. The Detroit Home for the Friendless had been founded in 1860 at her instigation, and she would go on to play a leading role in Detroit's Women's Christian Temperance Union, as well as several other civic associations.[43] In 1867, when she responded to Sanborn's questionnaire, Stewart was serving as the home's corresponding secretary.[44]

Outside of the Eastern Seaboard, it appeared that this institution was doing the most for vulnerable infants.[45] Stewart had reported that, to the best of her knowledge, between thirty-five and fifty foundling and deserted infants were abandoned in Detroit each year—slightly less than a third due to their mothers' deaths, and more than two-thirds due to their mothers' desertion or inability to support them. The Detroit Home for the Friendless had not been created for the purpose of caring for deserted infants, but, Stewart wrote, "*de facto*, it is the only institution of the kind taking young children" in Detroit. And it fulfilled this task very well: Only 10 percent of the infants in the Home for the Friendless died before their first year, and including children from the home who had been adopted, only 20 percent died before the age of two.[46] Taking her own institution as an example, Stewart wrote that an institution caring for abandoned infants could be expected to produce a third of its operating costs; the rest of its cost should be supported by the state and local governments through a "proper poor fund" that was administered by "a board of sensible women," as well as by private charity.[47]

On the question whether an institution caring for destitute and deserted infants would encourage vice, Stewart said that it would depend on how the institution was run. "A mismanaged institution relieving too readily a parent of parental obligation would lead to continual vice—but a home to help a woman take care of her child would tend to the establishment of a higher standard of virtue and responsibility in nine instances out of ten." In an addendum to her survey responses, Stewart admitted that she struggled with the ethics of accepting illegitimate children. "How far my feelings towards aiding and receiving illegitimate children are influenced by weakness on the one side, prejudice on the other, and principle on the third, I can scarcely define. It is a triangular duel in almost every case. If I could just see the principles clearly set forth, and then the prejudices I could better tell."[48] Prior to the Civil War, few charities would care for foundlings, who were presumed illegitimate. Julie Miller has argued that "the ability of these apparently compassionate people to turn their backs on foundlings, to, in a sense, doubly abandon them, marks them as bearers of a worldview that held that the fate of sinners and the very young was in the hands not of compassionate men and women but of God."[49]

Zakrzewska's response to the question of whether the proposed institution would "encourage or increase vice" was simple: "Not at all."[50] In her own work at the NEHWC, she had publicly argued that "unmarried women are saved from moral and physical ruin by finding here a hand extended which is willing to lift them up and hold them to usefulness and self-respect."[51] She clearly understood care for mothers and their children—regardless of their marital status or legitimacy—as part of her own vocation and the profession of medicine.[52] In the 1868 NEHWC annual report, she posed a version of Sanborn's question to herself, and answered even more emphatically: "Does the hospital favor immorality, by assisting patients, who give birth to illegitimate children? To answer this in the affirmative would be absurd."[53]

In the MBSC's second annual report, Sanborn had given his own answer to the question of whether foundling hospitals increased vice. Though "many argue how worthless are such lives to society, and others declare that to take good care of foundlings is to encourage vice," Sanborn was not daunted. "I cannot believe that either of these arguments will have weight with the humane people of Massachusetts, when they once understand how great this needless mortality is, and how easily much of it can be prevented," he continued.[54] Massachusetts' Society for the Prevention of Cruelty to Animals would be established in 1868, and the Massachusetts Society for the Prevention of Cruelty to Children a decade later, in 1878.[55] Yet appeals to Massachusettans' humanity had been made and answered for decades, in the antislavery movement, and in reactions against industrialization, which had begun in New England. The resulting "much deeper and more widespread sympathy" with suffering was manifest in Massachusetts's enactment of child labor laws, prison reform, and the establishment of institutions for the poor and disabled such as the Perkins School for the Blind.[56] While, as James Turner acknowledges, motives for these movements were complex, "compassion was part and parcel of the inseparable bundle of worries, ideals, and emotions that powered all of them."[57] Sanborn appealed to Massachusettsans' sense of moral superiority, knowing that they would not be insensitive to the implication that to ignore his call for assistance would be to allow the "needless mortality" among disadvantaged infants to remain, and that this would be a mark against their humanity.

All in all, addressing the "fancied encouragement of immorality by preserving infant life," the frequently cited concern about such institutions, Sanborn concluded, "It would be the height of injustice to visit upon the helpless child the sin of the father or the mother." Saying that he believed that there was "a great fallacy in the common reasoning on this point," he declared that "the only satisfactory decision of this question" would be by experiment. "A few years' experience in our Asylum would serve to show whether vice was increasing by reason of our efforts; if we found that to be the result, we must of course abandon or modify them; but if the contrary, we should only regret that we had not begun them earlier."[58] Storer, who believed that "these fears are groundless," echoed this assessment in his 1868 *Criminal Abortion: Its Nature, Its Evidence, and Its Law*, noting that a new "asylum for infants in Massachusetts will soon practically test this question upon a sufficiently extensive scale."[59]

Sanborn conceded that the creation of a foundling hospital would likely result in an increase in the number of abandoned infants, but he argued that this would be due to a decrease in abortion and infanticide, not an increase in out-of-wedlock conceptions. At his first meeting to consider "Deserted and Destitute Infants and what further provision should be made for them," Storer had concurred, saying that "the establishment of such a home would tend to check the crime of infanticide."[60] He had also said as much in print eight years earlier, in the seventh of his "Contributions to Obstetric Jurisprudence" articles in the *North American Medico-Chirurgical Review*. In "Its Obstacles to Conviction" (where "it" meant criminal abortion), Storer argued that "the punishment of a crime cannot be just, if the laws have not endeavored to prevent that crime by the best means which times and circumstances would allow."[61] State-run foundling hospitals, he argued, were one such means of preventing criminal abortion."[62]

In their responses to Sanborn's questionnaire, Stewart and Zakrzewska expressed some doubt as to whether an institution for abandoned children could do much to reduce abortions. While a home would tend to diminish infanticide "certainly to a measure," Stewart believed that "criminal abortion [would] be practiced just as far as women have the pecuniary means and physical courage and pride to accomplish it."[63] Zakrzewska similarly believed that criminal abortion "will not be lessened by such an institution, as it is more the educated and rich, the married as well as unmarried, which seeks such relief." The home would be a support to poor women who were driven toward the crimes of prostitution and infanticide by economic motives, but upper-class women's abortions were motivated by different causes, which the Infant Asylum could do little to address. But in agreement with Stewart and Sanborn, Zakrzewska stated emphatically, "Infanticide will diminish."[64]

The People of the Massachusetts Infant Asylum

The Massachusetts legislature unanimously approved the charter of the Massachusetts Infant Asylum (MIA) on July 11, 1867. The new institution's incorporators included socialite and later social reformer Harriet Lawrence Hemenway; Anna Cabot Lowell, the youngest living daughter of the Brahmin patriarch John Lowell; abolitionist lawyer and women's rights advocate Samuel Sewall, who was the NEHWC's vice president and legal advisor; Ednah Dow Cheney, who was the NEHWC's secretary; and Charles Donnelly, a proponent of Catholic education and a director of the Massachusetts Society for the Prevention of Cruelty to Animals. Also on the list of incorporators was Horatio Storer.[65] Less than a year earlier, Storer had publicly broken with the NEHWC, and his joining with Cheney to launch the Infant Asylum was probably the closest public association with the hospital he had undertaken since that excitement.

At the first formal monthly meeting of the MIA on October 29, officers and directors were chosen, leading to a roster that included "many of noble repute in a city whose aristocracy even England must respect."[66] Some incorporators, including

Lowell, Sanborn, and Cheney, stayed on as directors. This roster, too, demonstrated the breadth of the coalition supporting the new institution. Boston's Brahmins were represented by Lowell, Thomas C. Amory, Susan Cornelia Warren, Sarah Cabot, and Arthur T. Lyman. Many had been involved in anti-slavery work, including Samuel Cabot, Hannah Stevenson, and Harriet Minot Pitman, and were active in other charitable projects and social reforms. Emily Fairbanks Talbot, Lucy Sewall, Cheney, Sanborn, and Zakrzewska were actively involved in the women's rights movement.

Lowell, who had been one of the MIA's incorporators and became one of its directors, had initially refused an active role in the Infant Asylum's work.[67] In her late fifties and unmarried, she lived with her older sister Rebecca, who was in her early seventies.[68] Lowell was heavily involved in charitable work for the Freedmen's Aid Association and taught Sunday school at the Unitarian First Church of Roxbury.[69] Despite her determination to resist taking on this additional work, Lowell agreed to meet with Ednah Cheney and Fanny Hooper—after clearly having told the former that "I could not take any office in it."[70] Unfazed, Cheney asked her to become one of its directors. Lowell declined again, but that night as she was recording the day's events in her journal, her perspective shifted. Because the asylum might be located in Roxbury, she considered whether she ought to accept the offer. "It is a sort of thing I dread," she wrote. "There will arise many nice moral and prudential questions as to the women whose babies are taken in, etc., but ought I to shirk from taking my share of the difficulties?" In the next sentence, answering her own question in the plural, it was clear that she had already decided: "We shall make blunders, assuredly, and be blamed for it, but we must buy our experiences in this way."[71] The next morning, Lowell wrote to Cheney, telling her that "after a good deal of thought and arguments with myself pro and con, I decided to become a director of the Infant Asylum," contingent on its being located near her, and for the limited term of a year.[72] In short order, she was placed on the committee in charge of finding a house for the MIA, and later was one of four directors in charge of creating and finalizing its working plan.[73]

A week and a half after her conversation with Anna Lowell, Fanny Hooper was elected secretary of the MIA.[74] At twenty-three, she was one of the youngest people involved with it.[75] She had married Captain Edward Hooper three years earlier.[76] Before and after her marriage, first in Boston and then in New York City, she worked for the United States Sanitary Commission in Boston, an institution created to provide support for wounded and sick Union soldiers during the Civil War.[77] By mid-1866, she and her husband had returned to Massachusetts.[78] Hooper would later tell her aunt that their childlessness was "the only cloud which rested over our happiness," but it gave her comparative freedom in the use of her time, and so she was able to dive into the business of the asylum, perhaps finding her work there all the more poignant for her ability to do it.[79]

Though Sanborn undoubtedly drove the creation of the MIA, women were strongly involved from the beginning—both the committee established to find incorporators and the initial list of incorporators contained a female majority. While its act of incorporation listed only six women among its seventeen members, as the MIA became established and as Sanborn's role decreased, the number and percentage of women in its leadership increased. The MIA's first annual report showed that eighteen out of twenty-eight officers and directors—64 percent—were women.[80] In early meetings, several women had spoken out on "the responsibility of women for the recovery of their fallen sisters" and the importance of encouraging mothers "to take care of their children, and by this means be induced to return to the path of morality."[81] The makeup of the MIA's leadership clearly shows that this charge was taken seriously.

The New England Hospital and the Infant Asylum

When Cheney proposed both Zakrzewska and Sewall as attending physicians, Hannah Stevenson had opposed the close association with the NEHWC that having its founder and resident physician serve as the MIA's senior physicians would have implied.[82] While "highly honoring those ladies for their courage, benevolence and independence," Stevenson—who was herself on the NEHWC's Board of Directors—thought that it was "unwise to connect this institution with the Hospital for Women and Children. The latter was unpopular with some part of the public and this new institution should not suffer from association with it."[83] Stevenson was likely pointing to the NEHWC's mission of providing clinical experience to women doctors, as there was still considerable opposition to the idea that women were as fit as men to be doctors; her comments came after Horatio Storer had asserted that his experience at the hospital had proven to him that women physicians "have mistaken their calling."[84]

However, Stevenson might also have been referring to the NEHWC's staunch position against homeopathy and other "irregular" medical practices. A meeting attendee initially described the MIA as "this simple home for infants where neither allopathy, nor homeopathy, nor any one form of medical practice was to be relied upon mainly, but fresh air, nourishment and boarding cure."[85] Dr. Samuel Cabot took exception to this, stating that one form of medicine or the other must be chosen, and implying that he would resign if a certain Dr. Talbot, a homeopathic physician, were hired.[86] Anna Lowell wrote that it would be a great pity if he were to do so, as "Dr. Cabot's name gives confidence to the public that the Institution will be properly conducted," but noted that there were rumors that Dr. Talbot had warned that if the Infant Asylum chose modern medicine, "no homeopathist would give a cent to the Asylum!"[87]

These competing systems of medicine had caused considerable controversy across the medical fields and had led to some division within the women's rights movement. Zakrzewska had begun her medical career with Elizabeth Blackwell in New York City and had founded the New York Infirmary for Women and Children with her. In the fundraising pamphlet they published, they said that women doctors needed to be "thoroughly qualified," so that "ignorant or unworthy hands" would be kept out of the field of medicine—likely a jab at both female abortionists and "eclectic" or unorthodox physicians.[88] Despite Susan B. Anthony's best efforts, Blackwell would later refuse to have any connections with Clemence Lozier, a fellow women's rights advocate and the founder of the NYWMC, which was a homeopathic institution—because it was homeopathic.[89]

That autumn, Ednah Cheney announced the establishment of the MIA in the NEHWC annual report, explaining that "this institution will have no immediate connection with this Hospital, but it will aid us in the great work of preserving human life, and we most heartily wish it God speed."[90] Nevertheless, Lucy Sewall, the NEHWC's resident physician, became the MIA's attending physician.[91] Zakrzewska, the NEHWC's founder, became a consulting physician for the MIA. Dr. Samuel Cabot, who was Zakrzewska's mentor and had worked for the NEHWC for several years, became the MIA's president and also served as a consulting physician.[92]

More Than a Foundling Hospital

On April 18, 1868, Elizabeth Clapp, the newly chosen matron, received the MIA's first infant—a foundling.[93] In the month that followed, thirteen more children were brought to the asylum. Five of these had been brought by their mothers, with the intent that the MIA would care for them until they could be adopted; seven were the children of women "who labor[ed] as common servants," outside of the MIA; and one was the child of a woman who came to work as a wet nurse at the MIA. Clapp reported that while most of the infants arrived with "marks of neglect, uncleanliness and actual want of nourishment," the babies were all doing well after receiving "regular care and suitable food" from the MIA's staff and physicians.[94]

In his questionnaire, Sanborn had asked his respondents what percentage of women they believed would assume responsibility for their illegitimate child given the chance, and whether mothers and children should be kept together. Isabella Stewart answered that two-thirds of women would support their illegitimate children.[95] Zakrzewska had said that half would, adding that in her experience "the legitimacy or illegitimacy has very little influence" on a mother's decision to give her child up, which was most often driven by her inability to support the child.[96] Similarly, Stewart had written that mothers and children should be kept together "on every occasion in the least degree practicable," and that one way of doing this was to engage these women in domestic employment in the establishment; Zakrzewska had suggested rather that "under good control, mothers may be hired as wet-nurses, if willing to nurse a second child."[97]

In her response to Sanborn's questionnaire, Stewart had argued that if a woman had a child out of wedlock and was able to give up her child without consequence, she would be unlikely to reform. But she also believed that if such a woman was given the assistance she needed to care for her child, the experience of motherhood would likely reform her.[98] The MIA adopted this belief, as well. "Our hope and belief," Eliza Dixwell wrote in its 1870 annual report, "is that in many instances the mother love [sic], feeble at first, will strengthen as days wear on, and, instead of giving up their children, they will be ready to work to support them."[99] More concretely, the MIA was aiding "several young mothers... whose husbands or fathers of their children have deserted them... as well as their children," by allowing them to stay at the MIA and paying them full wages if they had "proved themselves trustworthy" after a trial term of two months.[100]

The MIA's structure was the result of the study of and consultation with every similar institution its founders could identify. Describing the institution's creation as "a duty too long neglected, a labor of love involving many difficulties and much patience, discretion, and perseverance," Sanborn wrote that the MIA had "the opportunity, not only of benefiting our own community, but of furnishing an example for other cities and states, which they will not be slow to follow."[101]

To Save Both Lives

"The object of our Asylum should be not only to save all the infant life we can, but also to help, in our small way, in solving the great problem of how to prevent the terrible mortality that occurs everywhere among children under one year," wrote Lucy Sewall in the MIA's 1870 annual report. She attributed this mortality to abortion, noting that every baby born at the NEHWC who was known to have been subjected to an attempted abortion had died before turning one.[102] This was not a new problem. In the NEHWC's annual report for 1867, Ednah Dow Cheney had noted that "much of the mortality among newborn infants and mothers in the Hospital, this year, has been due to previous criminal interference with the sacred right to life of the unborn child."[103] The following year, Zakrzewska noted that the bodies of the twenty infants stillborn at the NEHWC bore "indications of attempted destruction of the foetus before pregnancy had ended." And of the fifty infants who died there, she reported, "many lost their lives through this criminal process."[104]

Sanborn would later write, "To us, all these little ones to whom their Heavenly Father has given a living soul are worth saving. It is for God to determine whether they shall live or die; it is for us to see that they do not die through any fault of *ours*."[105] This nuance was telling. While reducing infant mortality was one of the main purposes of the MIA, Sanborn acknowledged that in the case of abortion its means were primarily indirect. But the MIA could care for those infants who had survived attempted abortions, so that "these should be allowed to go back to the God who gives and takes away life without having death hastened by our neglect."[106]

The women doctors associated with both the new institution and the NEHWC were also full of compassion for these unfortunate infants' mothers. Zakrzewska described "those who come to Boston to hide their condition and spare their friends the mortification of seeing an illegitimate child among them"—whether country girls or immigrants—as belonging to "the class of respectable needy ones."[107] In the MIA's annual report, Sewall described with sympathy the intensity of unwed mothers' suffering, saying that "the mother has not only to endure the desertion of her lover, and often starvation, but the weight of her sin and the knowledge that her shame must soon be known." Therefore, she asked, "is it strange that these poor women, driven to despair, often try to destroy their children before they are born[?]"[108]

Though it seems clear that the staff of the NEHWC did not often, if ever, become aware of these situations in advance, they took pride in the occasions where they were able to save both mother and child, born or unborn. These cases appear again and again in NEHWC annual reports. In 1865, Zakrzewska described the case of a woman with a deformed pelvis who seemed incapable of giving birth to a live child. She induced labor when the woman reached thirty-five weeks gestation, and thereafter "a living, healthy child was laid by the side of its happy mother."[109] The following year, Lucy Sewall told the story of a rich woman "who had been delivered successively of three still-born children, and whose physician considered it hopeless that she should ever have a living child." Similar to Zakrzewska, Sewall admitted the patient to the hospital when she reached eight months gestation, and induced labor, causing the woman to give birth to a healthy baby for the first time.[110] And in 1870, Dr. Chloe Annette Buckel described "one of those exceptional cases, where the best physicians justify destruction of the child's life in order to save the mother." A pregnant patient who was "a mere skeleton, unable to retain a mouthful of food or drink," probably due to a severe case of hyperemesis gravidarum, came to the NEHWC.[111] The hospital admitted her and its staff cared for her over two months, during which they were able to relieve her symptoms and help her to gain weight. The case had a happy conclusion, when the "happy looking woman, eating heartily the ordinary house diet," could be discharged. "Both lives were safe," Buckel concluded triumphantly.[112]

Helping Mothers to Support Their Babies

In his 1866 MBSC report, Sanborn had printed a letter written by an anonymous "lady manager" at the NEHWC in support of his plans for providing for vulnerable infants. While she was generally in favor of his ideas, she offered one significant critique: "I think any establishment should be based on the idea of helping mothers to support their babies,—not of taking them out of their hands."[113] While the MIA's staff had been amenable to that advice, and had actively sought to foster the relationship that the known parents of MIA infants had with their children, it did not fully adopt it until 1891—and even then, it wasn't fully voluntary.

The MIA's genesis was in the faults Sanborn found with the care of infants, especially foundlings, in the Tewksbury Almshouse. Sanborn argued that new institution could better care for those infants than the almshouse system could, and that the MIA should receive payment from the state for taking on this public burden. These funds received from the state for the care of its foundlings amounted, on average, to half of the MIA's yearly income. Around 1891, having "profit[ed] by the methods and experience of the Asylum, and with all the resources and machinery of the state at its disposal," the MBSC decided that it could resume care of the state's foundlings under its own auspices, "more conveniently and reasonably" than by using the MIA. This was a major blow to the MIA, and its 1891 annual report issued an urgent appeal for funds, without which "we see no resource but to largely surrender our work." Yet the other practical change effected by this policy—that "by ceasing to take the State foundlings, we shall no longer have children to give away for adoption, our object being to help a mother keep, not give away, her child"—did not hurt the MIA's mission, but rather reinforced it.[114]

Sanborn's investigative committee had, in 1867, determined that "our aim [should be] to encourage mothers to spare the lives of their children and to take care of them—not to afford facilities for giving them away."[115] Thus, when the piece of the MIA's work that involved placing children for adoption was removed, the problem posed was not primarily one of mission. Rather, the MIA was unique among social institutions because "no other Home that succeeds in saving infant life combines these three things—taking such young infants as we take, keeping them for so long a time, and keeping them for such low board as very poor mothers can pay." In this way, they were able to support "very poor working-women, struggling hard to support themselves and their infants, and struggling harder to save their infants' lives against greater hindrances and discouragements than more fortunate mothers can know."[116] This primary aspect of the MIA's work attempted to render the death-or-dishonor question facing poor women—especially poor mothers, whether married or unmarried—null. In supporting women in their duties of care to their children, the MIA's staff members and supporters worked to break down social forces that would pit a mother's well-being against that of her infant, or that would pit the well-being of society against both.

"You and your predecessors have changed the old distrustful opinion adverse to the saving of infant life, if the infants were illegitimate, into its very opposite," Frank Sanborn wrote in a retrospective essay on the success of the MIA's first thirty years.[117] At the same time, the MIA functioned to allow individual women to rise above their pasts, in contravention of the sexual double standard. This work was of equal value with, and inseparable from, the MIA's goal of preserving infant life. Consequently, despite the financial struggles that the MIA knew stood in its future with the removal of state funding, its staff were heartened and motivated by the mission to which they were now able to further devote themselves. "Many a disheartened mother, almost wrecked in the hard struggle of life, implores us to help her to save some little child, 'all she has in the world,'" Mary Parkman wrote. "Such petitions cannot be shut out from even the most happy and sheltered home. Such work as ours is never ended."[118]

Chapter Seven

HELPING DESTITUTE MOTHERS AND INFANTS

In 1912, Lilian Freeman Clarke wrote to Jane Addams, the pioneering social reformer, to tell her about "the work which we have carried on for now nearly forty years and in which we have been successful beyond our fondest hopes."[1] This charity, which Clarke did not name, was known in Boston as the Society for Helping Destitute Mothers and Infants (SHDMI). Its mission was "to enable a mother to retain the personal charge of her infant, when without such help she might be obliged to give it up for adoption or to place it in an institution."[2] The SHDMI was formed about two decades after Massachusetts's passage of the first modern adoption law in the United States, during the height of the Orphan Train movement.[3] At the core of its mission was the understanding that mothers and children who faced poverty and the social stigma of illegitimacy, and lacked social resources, nevertheless benefited from remaining together and from the relationship of dependence between them. The SHDMI's insistence on this point was radical for its time.

The three ideas foundational to the SHDMI's work, Clarke told Addams, were that the SHDMI was not an institution; that its staff made no distinction between married and unmarried mothers, but rather assisted "mothers as such"; and that it worked to keep mothers and children together, rather than liberating mothers from the care of their children.[4] The women who were aided by the SHDMI were not the mere beneficiaries of institutional charity; rather, its staff wrote, the women it assisted received "real friendship and sympathy," in addition to material assistance.[5] While they argued that the experience of caring for their infant children would be morally beneficial for these women, they also acknowledged that the women they assisted were often very lonely. The archetypal unmarried mother had been, in their experience, "a young, ignorant, friendless girl trying to earn a living in a large city, without home, without parents, without any friend whose experience may be her guide."[6] Age and experience would help these girls, but the women of the SHDMI also did what they could to supplant some of the missing roots, by assisting them in making homes for themselves and their children, and providing them with friendly and wise advice.

By 1912, the SHDMI's bare-bones operations had expanded only slightly from its beginnings, to five staff members and two consulting physicians.[7] It had begun in 1874 as the work of two women, Clarke and Bessie Greene, at the immediate behest of Dr. Susan Dimock, following a recognition by several other physicians at the New England Hospital for Women and Children (NEHWC) that more should be done for the unmarried women who came to the hospital to give birth because they had no other source of aid. The SHMDI adopted Dimock's advice to NEHWC nursing students as its motto: "Think that you see your own sister before you. Treat her in all respects as you would wish your own sister to be treated."[8] This sense of kinship among all women, binding the privileged to the destitute and the wise to the inexperienced, illuminated the SHDMI's work.

Clarke and her coworkers didn't necessarily share the New York women's rights advocates' structural analyses of the challenges facing American women, and they worked to assist individual women rather than to motivate those women to advocate for themselves and their peers. Nevertheless, Clarke's enterprise and those begun by Anthony, Densmore, and Lozier had many important commonalities. In important ways, they were oriented against the sexual double standard, arguing that women and men ought to adhere to a single standard of sexual ethics, and that a woman who had transgressed those standards ought not necessarily to be seen as "fallen." They were cognizant of the real responsibilities incumbent on women, and that many women—especially in the aftermath of the Civil War—were the primary wage earners in their households. Like their more radical peers, Clarke's team understood that fulfillment of one's duties, whether of suffrage or of motherhood, was educative and key to moral formation and maturation. They valued motherhood without oversentimentalizing it. And as women who knew their own privilege, they understood that they had a duty to help other women and that this could be accomplished best by meeting these women where they were, without snobbery or an affectation of noblesse oblige.

The women that the SHDMI assisted were the same class of women described as facing the choice of death or dishonor, due to their economic vulnerability and potentially tarnished reputations. Yet Clarke and her coworkers worked to put them on firm financial footings and to rebuild their own self-confidence and sense of self-worth. These vulnerable women had every motivation to destroy their children before or after birth—and the SHDMI took care of them over that time. These mothers would be least culpable for neglect of their children; the SHDMI gave them significant support in the fulfillment of their duties to them. The work of the SHDMI was of a piece with the work against infant mortality that concerned Storer, Reese, and others. It aligned with arguments made in the pages of *The Revolution* and in women's rights advocates' lectures against abortion and against the false choices that made women believe that they had to choose between themselves and their children. The SHDMI was united, not just in its aims but in its work, with the concrete assistance and care offered to individual women at the NEHWC and with the solicitude for individual infants found at the MIA.

New England Hospital Origins

In 1865, Marie Zakrzewska wrote that at the NEHWC, "unmarried women are saved from moral and physical ruin by finding here a hand extended which is willing to lift them up and hold them to usefulness and self-respect."[9] By this, she meant that the NEHWC accepted unmarried women as maternity patients. The alternative—the almshouse—"demoralizes them still more, by destroying the little self-respect yet left them."[10] By treating unwed mothers with dignity, the NEHWC's doctors and staff could instill self-confidence and self-respect in these women, which might give them the strength to pursue moral and productive lives.

The NEHWC's doctors soon began to believe that the moral support they could provide to these women during their few days in the hospital was not enough. In 1870, Dr. Chloe Annette Buckel, who after three years as an assistant physician at the NEHWC had taken over Dr. Lucy Sewall's position as resident physician, reported that several young women who had left the hospital in good health and "willing and anxious to keep their babies" had been unable to find work because of their offspring. Thereafter, probably as a result of neglect, "the babies soon sickened and died, leaving their unfortunate, friendless mothers, as one of them so touchingly wrote, without aim or hope in life."[11] Buckel clearly feared for the future that lay ahead of her patients. In her report the following year, she elaborated the dangers she saw by giving examples. Describing one infant brought to the hospital as a "wretched little creature... in a comatose state, with the skin drawn loosely over its bones, and its half-closed glassy eyes sunk deeply in their sockets," she decried the economic situation that had led to the child's being "boarded out" by its mother, where it had been neglected.[12] Similarly, she told the story of a young unwed mother who had been prostituted by her stepmother, yet was willing to turn away from that life and "to do even the hardest for the sake of keeping her baby with her." But when the woman tried to find work, she was turned away from every possibility because of her child. Though Buckel was confident that "she had the will and the strength to earn her living honestly," nevertheless "the hard look in her eyes, and the bitter smile... made me tremble for her future."[13]

Buckel hinted at what she saw as a possible solution to this problem: "Could such women secure places where they might work for small wages, or their board even, and care for their infants[,] their best safe-guards, both they and their children might be saved for future usefulness."[14] By the following year, this thought became a general request. "Can we not find some means to secure to infants, for the first year of their lives at least, a mother's care and love, by furnishing these mothers with some honest means of support and thus save both mothers and children?" she asked. "I leave this important question for you to consider, for it is a *sequel* to one department of our Hospital, if it is not strictly a part of our work."[15]

In 1872, Buckel ceded her role as resident physician to Dr. Susan Dimock, who had just returned to the United States after the completion of her medical studies in Europe.[16] Determined from a young age to practice medicine, Dimock had studied at the New England Hospital under Dr. Lucy Sewall and at the Massachusetts General Hospital with Dr. Samuel Cabot.[17] When her application to Harvard Medical School was rejected, due to the university's policy against admitting women, she applied to the University of Zurich in Switzerland. With the financial assistance of Dr. Marie Zakrzewska, she studied there for four years and graduated with high honors, specializing in obstetrics and gynecology.[18] Her German-language dissertation, "On the Various Forms of Puerperal Fever," was published in Zurich.[19]

On her arrival at the NEHWC, Dimock took command of the institution with "an earnestness and dignity which commanded respect and even caused an involuntary sense of awe," and she demonstrated remarkable compassion for the women in her care.[20] She was given responsibility for the training of nurses, instituted a lecture series for the students, and increased the length of their studies.[21] At the same time, she continued practicing medicine and in the space of two years gained "a deserved reputation among some of the best surgeons in the city."[22]

During her first fall as resident physician at the NEHWC, Dimock became particularly interested in the fate of the unmarried pregnant women who gave birth in her hospital. In a letter to her mentor, Dr. Samuel Cabot, she lauded a fellow student at the University of Zurich who had pursued medicine in order to help what she described as "those who suffer most, viz., women, especially poor women."[23] Dimock, too, undertook her work with a particular concern for this population. At the close of her first full year at the NEHWC, she noted in its annual report that for years it had been the only obstetrics facility in Boston and the surrounding area, and that while that was no longer the case, "still the need remains great."[24]

In 1873, after she had been resident physician of the NEHWC for a year, Dimock echoed Zakrzewska's early observations about the hospital's willingness to admit unwed mothers. She described them as mostly "worthy"; they were often sixteen or younger, and though they had been "betrayed and abandoned," their "greatest desire is still to lead virtuous and respectable lives." Were it not for the hospital's willingness to admit them and treat them with dignity, Dimock argued, "we thrust them only too surely to suicide or a life of infamy."[25] But she knew that more was needed, since many of the new mothers leaving the hospital were "homeless and friendless."[26] Dimock tried to interest others in assisting these women after they left the hospital, but she had little success until her good friend Bessie Greene was hospitalized in the fall of 1873 and was able to see what Dimock had described with her own eyes.[27] Greene, determined "that something should be done," then enlisted Lillian Clarke, and they began working to provide some concrete assistance to these mothers who, "though sometimes unmarried, are often still comparatively innocent."[28]

Lilian Clarke was the daughter of Anna Huidekoper Clarke and James Freeman Clarke, the abolitionist Unitarian minister who founded Boston's Church of the Disciples.[29] A member of the Transcendentalist Club and a Harvard professor of natural religion, he was a supporter of female suffrage and the Massachusetts Society for the University Education of Women.[30] Lilian grew up a close friend of Fanny Hooper, to whom she was related by her uncle's marriage and with whom she served as an officer of the Massachusetts Infant Asylum.[31] She would later go on to speak publicly in favor of women's suffrage, join the Massachusetts Animal Rescue League, work for the Church of the Disciple's Post Office Mission, and edit the "Cheerful Letter" published by the General Alliance of Unitarian Women.[32] But her work with Dimock and Greene, begun at the age of thirty-one, was her first significant foray into public life.

Greene and Clarke informally called their project "The Invisible Institution," because "although doing in fact the work of an institution, it was found better to aid each patient as a personal friend; not founding a 'Home,' and so avoiding the heavy expenses and cumbrous methods of institutional charity."[33] Concurring with Dimock in her refusal to believe that "one fault sunk a woman below redemption, or that even sin placed a fellow-being out of the range of human charity," they raised money to provide housing for unwed mothers before they gave birth and while they were recovering, and then assisted them in finding employment. By this work, Dimock explained, Greene and Clarke were "not only relieving and preventing terrible misery, but also lending a helping hand to those who have fallen, and who without the help must inevitably sink deeper and deeper."[34] The need understood by Zakrzewska and articulated by Buckel was finally beginning to be met.

The Appeal

Soon, Greene and Dimock realized that to continue their work, they needed to establish it in a more formal manner. In early

1875, an *Appeal in Behalf of Destitute Mothers and Infants* was issued, signed by Mrs. James Freeman Clarke (Lillian Clarke's mother), Mrs. William Bradley, and Dimock.[35] The *Appeal* asked for donations to a fund to cover the boarding costs for women leaving the hospital after giving birth who had "no home or friends to go to, and no money to live upon," during their recovery, "until they are strong enough to work."[36] The fund would provide for the two groups Dimock had described in the 1874 NEHWC annual report: "widows whose husbands have recently died, wives whose husbands have abandoned them, whose husbands are drunkards, or ill, and unable to work," and "unmarried women . . . generally motherless girls, under twenty years of age, living at service, or in working people's boarding-houses, who have fallen victims to unscrupulous and unfeeling men to whom they were bound by promise of marriage."[37] That the women in the former group ought to receive a little assistance should be uncontroversial, the authors of the *Appeal* wrote, but the proffered assistance to the latter might need a little more explanation. To begin with, these unmarried mothers were not "depraved women," but were rather "generally fully awake to the horror of their fault, and their strongest desire is to retrieve the past by a life of virtue, humility, and hard work."[38]

The *Appeal* argued that this effort would benefit both women and their children. An unmarried mother bereft of her child would be "beset by all the perils and temptations which assail a young, poor, and friendless woman, especially one who has already taken the first step on the downward path."[39] The child, separated from its mother, might be "adopted, happily or unhappily, as it may happen," die "in some boarding-place for want of a mother's care," or go on "to swell the ranks of a pauper institution by one additional union . . . grow[ing] up a thief or an honest man, a good or a bad woman, as chance may decide."[40] Thus, "two lives run the risk of ruin, which, if not separated, might have blessed and protected each other."[41] One of the "best safeguards" keeping an unmarried mother from a life of vice was "the loving care she bestowed on her child, and the holy and purifying influence of its innocence and helplessness." And each mother, they argued, "however poor, however ignorant, however weak and erring in the past, is her child's best protector, provided she is willing and eager to fulfill her whole duty towards it."[42] Unmarried mothers, they argued rather radically against popular wisdom, felt as much love toward their children as married mothers did, and were similarly capable of fulfilling their duties to their children.

While the immensity of the individual and social problems facing "these poor, helpless women and infants" might have seemed insurmountable, the *Appeal* argued that "a small sum, judiciously expended, will often raise these forlorn creatures from starvation and despair to a situation of comfort and security." Between ten and fifteen dollars would "give shelter to a poor woman during convalescence, or during the last weeks previous to the birth of her child, when she can no longer work, but cannot yet be admitted to the Hospitals." One dollar more, its authors wrote, would cover advertisements for positions which would allow a woman to support herself and a child while providing food and housing for both.[43] The *Appeal* suggested that such women could find positions as wet nurses, and that if they were willing to commit to a long-term position, they could find live-in domestic positions where their children would be welcomed with them. At the same time, they also acknowledged that many of the women they served were teenagers who had been "living at service" when they were seduced. Their perhaps questionable solution to this dilemma was to assert that, with the assistance of the "Invisible Institution" and the duties newly incumbent upon them as mothers and motivated by the love of their children, these women would be less susceptible to being preyed upon.[44]

The *Appeal* included a letter from Dr. Charles Pickering Putnam. A pediatrician, Putnam lectured at Harvard Medical School and served as one of the MIA's attending physicians.[45] Putnam concurred with the *Appeal*'s description of "the class of women" served and stated that he was "very glad to bear witness to the truth of its statements in every particular." He lauded the *Appeal*'s organizers and authors, describing their "excellence and the thoroughness of the work done" in taking "a large number of these otherwise friendless mothers and children under their charge, giving money sparingly, but freely expending their time, labor and thought."[46] The *Appeal*'s "Account of Receipts and Expenditures" showed that in eight months during 1874, the women had spent $692.34 to pay the board of twenty-nine women and their infants, to provide both women and infants with clothes and some furniture, to cover related traveling expenses, to advertise for positions, and to provide for sundry expenses and small loans. In the first month of 1875, they spent $177.65 on the same expenses for eight women and their infants. Thirteen individuals had provided the institution's funds for these nine months, including Bessie Greene and her mother, Lillian Clarke and her father and sister, and one of Putnam's cousins. No calculation of the hours that its collaborators had poured into its work was given.[47]

At the close of the *Appeal*, Clarke, Bradley, and Dimock addressed "the good and virtuous," asking them to "stretch out a helping hand to these unhappy ones, and give them the opportunity to work for their own bread and that of their helpless offspring." The "good and virtuous" had a moral obligation to do this, they argued, because "the wicked and depraved stand with wide-open doors, inviting these shame-stricken, heart-broken, inexperienced women—many of whom are so young as to be scarcely more than children—to enter in, and enjoy the pleasure and immunities of what they describe as a life of comfort, ease and luxury."[48] By helping vulnerable women to give birth in a dignified fashion, and assisting them in finding honest employment that allowed them to keep their children with them, the "Invisible Institution" worked to improve both infant mortality and individual and public morality.

The Invisible Institution Becomes Independent

In May 1875, Bostonians were startled to learn that Susan Dimock, Bessie Greene, and their friend Caroline Crane had died in a shipwreck off the coast of England. The three, all in their late twenties, had been headed to Europe for the first vacation of Dimock's professional life, after which she planned to return to the United States to resume her post as resident physician at the NEHWC.[49] The women's deaths were, Zakrzewska wrote, "not a loss to friends and relatives merely, but also a loss to all women; for each of the three represented a special type of woman's capacity, woman's industry, and woman's worth on a broader scale of life than is usually allowed to them."[50]

Neither Greene nor Crane's bodies were recovered, but Dimock's was found and returned to the United States. During her funeral, James Freeman Clarke described Dimock as having "the spirit of an apostle, who counted not her life dear so that she might finish the work which she had agreed with her own soul to fulfill," as well as "the subtile [sic], spiritual grace which turned all duty into beauty, and made her life as full of charm as it was full of heroism."[51] Greene, he described as "so full of enjoyment, always happy, bright as a sunbeam, and also taking the most serious and most noble tasks of life into her young hands; becoming an arm of aid to the weak, and a hand of help to the helpless."[52] Dimock's pallbearers were eight physicians from Boston, including her mentor, Samuel Cabot. After their arrival at the graveyard, Dr. Bowditch suggested that "instead of allowing the last services to be performed by strangers, we, who knew her and loved her in life, should with our own hands lay the earth in her grave," and the eight men filled in her grave after her casket had been placed in it.[53]

To commemorate "the noble young physician whose loss our community so deeply feels," Dimock's friends began working to raise $5,000 for an endowment, the interest of which would support a "Susan Dimock Free Bed" at the NEHWC. This memorial, they believed, would "worthily express their appreciation of her loving service to the poor, suffering women under her care at the hospital" and, in a fashion, allow her work at the hospital to continue.[54] In the NEHWC's annual report, published in September, Ednah Cheney stated that the sum had nearly been raised.[55]

Despite the deaths of Dimock and Greene, the work of the "Invisible Institution" continued. Recalling "the depth of [Dimock's] tenderness for the suffering, the weak, the sinful," who "seemed to win from her only love, pity and sympathy," Clarke soldiered on.[56] By the end of its first full fiscal year, the "Invisible Institution"—which would eventually become known formally as the Society for Helping Destitute Mothers and Infants—proved itself successful and its work increased.[57] Its yearly income rose to $3,052.26, including contributions from ninety-six individuals, of which $1,807.22 was expended. Marian Hooper Adams—daughter of the transcendentalist poet Ellen Sturgis Hooper, sister-in-law of the MIA's Fanny Hooper, and wife of the American historian Henry Adams—topped the list of new contributors. Like the MIA, the SHDMI's list of supporters included representatives of Boston's Brahmin families, and of the city's transcendentalist, abolitionist, and reform movements.[58]

In its first year, the SHDMI cared for eighty-three mothers and their infants. Its first real annual report, simply titled *Report of Aid Given to Destitute Mothers and Infants*, provided some basic demographic information about the mothers and infants it assisted. Fifty-four had been unmarried women—65 percent of the cases taken on, a percentage that would remain more or less constant in the SHDMI's future. The youngest unmarried woman assisted was fifteen years old, but most were in their older teens and early twenties. Twenty-three of the unmarried mothers were American, thirteen were Irish, nine were from Canada, two were reported as "colored," and the seven others were from different European countries.[59]

At the time of the annual report, the SHDMI remained in contact with forty of the unmarried women, all of whom were "in respectable situations, earning their living, either wholly or with some assistance; or else at home with relatives." Nine women had recently lost contact with the SHDMI, but its members had "reason to believe that they are comfortably and respectably situated." Three of the unmarried women assisted by the SHDMI had "disappeared entirely from our sight," without giving any indication of their possible whereabouts.

One unmarried woman had died while in a hospital and one had been placed in the care of an unnamed charitable institution. Three infants had died, and three had been abandoned by their mothers. Of the latter, the report's authors noted, two had been married women and the third woman had "claimed to be married, but there was some reason to doubt her statement."[60]

The 1874 annual report contained the SHDMI's first case study, which illustrated the entire premise of the society. It described a nineteen-year-old Irish Catholic girl who had been urged by her mother, "her priest," and "a benevolent gentleman, who had sometimes assisted the family," to "give the child up" for adoption. The SHDMI had been skeptical whether success would be at all likely in her case; because it "appeared that there was no reasonable hope of reclaiming her to a life of virtue," its members had questioned the wisdom of assisting her. Whether she simply seemed rebellious or distrustful, or whether they judged her to be approximately "depraved" is unclear. But seeing her "intense love for her child," they decided to help her, providing her with assistance until she was able to support herself and her child.[61]

The SHDMI came into contact with the women and girls it helped through the physicians at the NEHWC, who interviewed their prospective and current patients to find out whether they had anywhere to stay before and after they gave birth. If the answer was no, the doctor would pass on her patient's information to the SHDMI, and a member would investigate the case by talking to the woman.[62] The society made a point of avoiding "needless suffering caused by a repetition of painful questions," so that "the self-respect of the woman is not wounded by the unnecessary exposure of her private feelings and personal experiences of a trying nature, to the examination of more than one person."[63]

The woman who initially interviewed the girl maintained her contact with her, remaining her connection to the SHDMI.

The report's authors had given time and thought to investigating the larger influences behind the unmarried motherhood they encountered in their work. "From all we have been able to learn of the circumstances of these poor sisters of ours," they wrote, "it seems as if the strongest predisposing cause of the error into which they fall, is the loneliness of the life which they lead." Forty-seven of the fifty-four unmarried mothers they had assisted in the previous year lived in a broken home of some sort. Most of the women had been living with a single parent, or they had no parents, or they lived apart from their families "with no companionship or guardianship but that of other young girls, exposed in ignorant helplessness to the dangers and temptations of city life." The women of the SHDMI didn't believe that these broken homes led to sexual errors because those they helped had lacked proper oversight, but because the moral formation they had received in these homes had been lacking. They believed that lonely women were more prone to seek the intimacy they lacked at home in imprudent or illicit relationships; their loneliness "makes them an easy prey to anyone who will show them kindness."[64]

Consequently, the SHDMI saw its work as the provision not just of pecuniary support and social services, but also of friendship. Lilian Clarke later wrote that "just as some invalids are cared for by sunshine, fresh air, and exercise, so our patients need work, hope, a sense of responsibility, something to love and live for."[65] The personal connections that the women of the SHDMI strove to foster would, they hoped, inspire that hope and encourage the sense of responsibility they believed to be innate in their clients. The society strove to create a close bond with each woman in question: "The lady who investigates [the case] makes it her aim to establish a personal relation between herself and the young mother, so that she may possess her confidence, and that the poor, desolate girl may feel that it is not merely charity she is receiving, but real friendship and sympathy." They tried to use the trust that developed—rather than patronizing moral authority—as a lever in encouraging her to develop the personal strengths necessary for providing for a child.[66]

Despite the women's initial skepticism, the SHDMI's willingness to invest in the young Catholic woman bore fruit. At the time of the report's publication, they stated that "it is now a year and two months since the child's birth, and the young woman is supporting it entirely by her own labor, and leading a respectable, virtuous life." As evidence of their coup, they wrote that "the gentleman who advised her to give the child up, now strongly expresses his belief that had she done so, she would soon have been led astray again, and that the course pursued was the wisest that could have been chosen."[67]

The authors of the report recorded that the depth of gratitude that the young women in their care had expressed for the help they received had exceeded any expectations. These expressions were "more, almost, than the help and attention bestowed seemed to call for," and were often accompanied by requests for advice, rather than any material assistance.[68] One letter they printed was from a woman who told them:

> I think, I can say, on this first day of the year, that, take everything together, I am happier than I ever was before. First, I have my boy, who is perfectly healthy, bright and very good, and is said to be a beautiful child by all who see him. Second, I have friends such as yourself and

> Miss —— whose influence is all that is good. . . . I think I have a great deal to be sorry for, but more to be thankful for. Sincere gratitude for your kindness.[69]

Sometimes women who had been helped years earlier contacted the SHDMI's staff, who were left with an impression of "what those lives must be, in which any experience of real friendship and sympathy appears to be such a rare and unexpected thing," and of the consequent real importance of their work.[70]

The SHDMI in the Twentieth Century

From its founding until 1904, when it sought incorporation in the state of Massachusetts, the SHDMI continued its operations with little change.[71] In 1905, the SHDMI hired two agents to assist Lilian Freeman Clarke and Mary Parkman in interviewing candidates and working with their clients, and to enable the "Invisible Institute" to expand its reach.[72] By 1908, it was clear that the SHDMI's staff were trying both to professionalize their own operations and to become a more integral part of Boston's charitable apparatus. They hired another agent who had proven experience in charitable activities, with the Children's Aid Society and "other similar work," bringing the number to three so as to better monitor the women being assisted.[73] The following year, the SHDMI moved into new centralized offices in the Boston Children's Mission on Tremont Street. While their understanding of its mission hadn't changed, the SHDMI's staff noted that, now, "a great deal of our work necessarily consists in guiding a large number of the applications that we receive into the right channels." The society referred cases that didn't fit its mission to other institutions, including the Massachusetts Infant Asylum, and conversely received cases referred from those institutions, including the Society for the Prevention of Cruelty to Children and the Associated Charities of Boston.[74]

As the SHDMI was becoming more enmeshed in the tightening network of charitable institutions in Boston, its staff found themselves more and more on the defensive about both its mission and its methods. In 1910, they found it necessary to defend the institution's general position against sending the women they assisted to custodial institutions. "While there may be some women so weak that they require institutional methods," they argued, "there are a large number for whom the kind of help that we give is more wholesome, forming habits of self-reliance. For some, the restraints of institutional life are positively injurious."[75] The following year's annual report was a defense of the society's traditional methods against the criticisms of "some persons who have not had experience in such matters." Clarke and Parkman argued against the superficial kindness of those who would suggest that unmarried mothers place their children for adoption so that they could resume their places in society undisturbed—this would "save her reputation at the expense of her character." What was necessary in such cases, they insisted, was the redemption of past faults by the leading of "an upright life for a year or two," which would allow a woman to earn new respect and love in the eyes of her family, friends, and previous associates.[76]

In the world in which Clarke and Parkman had grown up, "the individual had appeared to be a causally potent creature, normally master of his own fate and thus responsible for his own situation in life."[77] Consequently, gaining independence was an important goal of the process of maturing into a contributing member of society—and the SHDMI insisted that "the keynote of our work" was "the principle of self-reliance."[78] Moral formation was at least as important as material support. To choose adoption was damaging to a woman, they argued; it led "to the deterioration of her moral nature" and damaged her character. But "giving too much help" or "showing too much sympathy" to an unmarried mother in need of assistance was a danger, too, because she might "expect to have every difficulty removed from her path."[79] It was neither kind nor charitable to pretend that life would be easier than it was likely to be; far better, they reasoned, to inculcate independence and strength, so that a woman could face the difficulties of her life more easily, in the long run. In this view, the woman in question had a moral nature that could be developed and purified by the exercise of virtue and the fulfillment of her duties, and degraded by the practice of vice and the neglect of those duties. Thus, she had real moral agency in crafting her future, and in creating conditions for her child's life in all its dimensions.

But by the early twentieth century, this insistence on self-reliance was rapidly becoming old-fashioned in the world of "organized and incorporated charity" that the SHDMI had worked to enter over the previous years.[80] The SHDMI staff began to make some significant changes, starting with their 1911 annual report. Perhaps responding to the above-noted criticisms that they focused on mothers more than their children, the SHDMI reports began including photos of the children who had been helped by their work. These portraits never included the children's mothers or other adults. More significantly, the SHDMI began listing the number of "defective" mothers they had rejected in their statistics.[81]

The SHDMI began to understand its work as providing the environmental preconditions for the outcomes they desired, rather than spurring women to act in their own and their children's best interest. Women's individual personal agency essentially disappeared. "Whether her future years will lead her upward into respectability, usefulness, and happiness, or downward into an abyss of sin and suffering," now depended not on an individual woman's willingness to develop virtue and self-sufficiency, but "upon the ideas and influences which surround [her]...during the first few weeks of her child's life."[82] Consequently, it was no longer assumed that a mother was the best caretaker of her own child. Rather, the SHDMI found itself in the business of proving their clients' fitness for "so important a charge" as motherhood. The 1912 annual report suggested that discovering "defectives" who were "unfitted" to care for the children they bore was in the best interests of both these women and their children; and one of the report's authors regretted that there was currently "no resource" or "method of providing for those unfitted by mental deficiency to be at large in the community."[83] This new model of charity "shifted away from the effort to inculcate thrift, prudence, and the other elements of self-mastery," preferring instead "the design of institutional shelters where the poor might be shielded from life's worst hazards."[84]

As late as 1908, the SHDMI had maintained that its mission was "to assist a mother to retain her infant in her personal charge, when for want of such temporary aid she might be forced to place it in an institution or give it up for adoption."[85] Its staff had understood themselves, first and foremost, to be assisting individual women and their children—any benefit to society writ large was secondary. But in the early twentieth century, this began to change. By the time the SHDMI closed its doors in 1918, its staff described its mission as "helping an unmarried mother to keep her infant in her personal care, *provided her character and mentality made her a suitable guardian for the child*."[86] The SHDMI's staff seem to have decided that their primary responsibility was to safeguard society writ large, over and above the personal well-being of the individual women and children with whom they worked.

Mothers or Menaces

The biggest shift in the SHDMI's language about its work appeared in 1912, following the publication of the Eugenics Record Office's 1911 *Report of the Committee to Study and to Report on the Best Practical Means of Cutting Off the Defective Germ-Plasm in the American Population*. That report argued that the conditions of modern society caused many individuals and family lines which would have died in an earlier age, thanks to "disease, famine, and petty strife," to thrive. Because of the human-caused failure of these "inhuman" means of population control, the committee argued, "it now behooves society in consonance with both humanitarianism and race efficiency to provide more human means for cutting off defectives."[87] This sacrificing of individuals to the supposed good of society, conceived of generally, was "in keeping not only with humanitarianism, but with law and order, and national efficiency."[88]

The 1911 Eugenics Record Office report gave a long list of all those considered "defective," which included anyone with a mental or physical illness or a "criminalistic" tendency—or a racial or family history suggesting a possible proclivity to any of these things. It implied that the number of such individuals was expanding, saying that the committee would continue to "study the facts in reference to the number of and the rate and manner of increase of the socially inadequate."[89] The committee understood part of its mission to be the identification of those "defective" persons "now living who have never been committed to the State's custody," and "those of equally meagre natural endowments and equally anti-social in conduct who, due to the caprice of fortune, have never been taken into custody by the State."[90] Once identified, the committee suggested that these individuals should be institutionalized, for the reproductive period of their lives if not for their whole lives, and likely sterilized.

The SHDMI understood that it could play a significant role in this project. In 1912, its annual report echoed the Eugenics Record Office report in asserting that "there is a large and perhaps increasing class of defectives in the community whose deficiency does not appear upon the surface," and in noting the psychiatric examinations it had sent some of its clients to undergo. The SHMDI realized that it could assist in identifying "the mother who is defective mentally," and work to ensure her institutionalization—thereby separating her from her child, increasing the possibility that it would die and that she would have no other offspring.[91] Its staff didn't pay much attention to physical disorders or deformities; rather, they focused their attention on the "insane," "feeble-minded," and epileptics. They interpreted the first two categories broadly, writing in its final report, "If occasionally a young mother proved stubborn and unmanageable in those [early] days, she was simply considered obstinate or stupid; under our modern methods she would have been given a psychopathic examination by a recognized alienist, and probably would have been adjudged feeble-minded, or at least sub-normal mentally."[92]

Where the Eugenics Record Office's report had suggested that on average 10 percent of Americans were "defectives," the

SHDMI found that among its clients between 1914 and 1918, more than 20 percent were "mentally diseased or defective." Women found to be "insane" had been sent to "appropriate hospitals." Women discovered to be epileptic were put in the care of the State Hospital for Epileptics. For the merely "feeble-minded," the SHDMI had recommended "custodial care for 57 (70.3%) of these patients," though only ten were accepted because of space limitations at the unspecified proposed institutions. Of the total number of women who were its clients in those four years, the SHDMI estimated that half had been separated from their children. And by the end of that period, only 146 of those 512 infants were being cared for by their mothers.[93] In 1914, Ada Sheffield, the SHDMI's president, argued that the institution was "often obliged to make appropriate arrangements for many women who, because of mental or moral defect, might otherwise prove a menace to society."[94] Its final report made the point more clearly: "Just so long as defectives are allowed to multiply, we shall labor under the strain of 'trying to drain the horn whose other end connects with the sea.'"[95] The project of identifying "defectives" was not worth much if it was not complemented by a sterilization schema, or some other method of forcibly preventing such women from becoming mothers and giving birth to children.

By 1915, the SHDMI's apparatus had grown significantly. It acquired an eight-person case committee, a placing-out committee, and an investigator. Two of the three agents were recategorized as "visitors."[96] In Clarke's "Report of the Secretary," she explained the changes made in the SHDMI's workings over the previous years not as a fundamental reorientation on the society's part, but as a necessary adjustment to dramatic changes in society. In the SHDMI's beginnings, she wrote, most of the unmarried mothers she had helped were "well-disposed young women, whose fault was due more to circumstances than to any defect of character or mind." Now, "many of the unmarried mothers who...come to us prove, upon being examined by an alienist, to have the mentality of a child of nine or ten," and ought to be "adequately safeguarded."[97] The SHDMI staff began articulating their task as responsibility for "the social welfare" of the women sent to them, and they aimed "never to drop an applicant until the responsibility is definitely assumed by some other suitable Society, the State, or some competent relative or friend."[98] While the SHDMI's staff still insisted that "each mother is regarded as an individual," they also wrote that "those who are mentally deficient" posed a "great danger" to the community. In 1915, Clarke herself complained that "in many instances the Court has declined to commit a feeble-minded young woman who should be in custodial care" because of the severe overcrowding of state institutions, and that this "question of gravest import to the community" was not being taken seriously enough.[99] In this report, what previously had been introduced as the stories of individual women, or case histories—of both "feeble-minded" and "normal" women—were now termed "Specimen Histories."[100]

The SHDMI Closes Its Doors

The SHDMI remained in operation until the fall of 1918 when, due to financial difficulties coincident with the First World War, it closed its doors.[101] Clarke had resigned less than a year earlier, citing ill health.[102] She was seventy-seven years old, and had devoted the preceding forty-six years of her life to the society. The SHDMI's final report cited fundraising difficulties, the shift in attention to other charities driven by World War I, and changing social conditions as reasons for ending its operations.[103] As opposed to the supposedly simple and easy early days, the SHDMI's president argued, "The picture is a far darker one to-day."[104]

This pessimistic assessment of the times was in no small part due to the society's discovery that, of the women they had served in the preceding few years, supposedly "*one-fifth* proved to be mentally defective or insane," a large portion of whom "though not committable to institutions for the feeble-minded, remained a constant and growing menace to the community, being often the mothers of a succession of illegitimate children, who in their turn were almost certain to inherit and transmit the same mental deficiency."[105] The SHDMI's final report acknowledged that it had made some changes to its operations already, due to the "vital changes that have taken place in social conditions." Yet it concluded that if the SHDMI were to continue, it would have to undergo a major reorganization to better adapt to "this new and widely different situation of the present day"—and there were not funds to accommodate this. In its view, the necessary interventions would have to be made by more than charities. The SHDMI's secretary ended her report on a pessimistic note: "Till . . . the State assumes its responsibilities toward the mentally deficient and morally depraved, conditions will remain much as at present—presenting a hopeless and chaotic front to the appalled social-service worker."[106]

The SHDMI's final report, perhaps slightly disingenuously, lauded Clarke's leadership, vision, and dedication to the society's work: "We recognize with admiration the unflinching courage and firmness with which she has maintained the original standards and the essential idea underlying this work for helping destitute mothers to keep their infants, in days and through years when other workers in this line were far from comprehending the inherent value of the methods employed by this Society and now acknowledged by them all as those most just and effective." While it seems rather that the SHDMI, in its later days, did its best to employ a radically different set of standards and methods than those established by Clarke at its beginning, its staff were nevertheless incapable of ignoring their founder's tenacity and steadfastness.

Clarke herself had provided a summing-up of the SHDMI's work in an article published in the New York magazine *The Outlook* in December 1906, just before the major shift in that work took place. She was then sixty-four and, having been the driving influence behind the society's work for thirty-two years, likely did not expect any significant changes to come in the years ahead—or her own limited participation in those. She assessed the society's work proudly: "In the most important point of all, it has succeeded beyond our fondest hopes."[107] She insisted that the decades had proven the truth of their basic principle—that regardless of the circumstance of a child's birth, "there remains the one saving, purifying influence, the love of the mother for her child, which draws out and educates her whole higher nature."

In many ways, the efforts that Lilian Freeman Clarke undertook in her work for destitute mothers and infants were very different from those taken by other women's rights activists. Yet they complemented those efforts in an extraordinary way. Susan B. Anthony sought to exhibit workingwomen's degradation and suffering with the person of Hester Vaughn, started associations, and instigated unions; Clarke found friends, went with them, almost in secret, to suffering women to assist them in the births of their children, and refused for decades to institutionalize her work. While Anna Densmore lectured crowds, Clarke and her coworkers gave one-on-one advice and counsel. While the Massachusetts Infant Asylum focused on saving the lives of vulnerable infants and thereby assisted their mothers, Clarke's "Invisible Institution" focused on supporting mothers so that their infants would be less vulnerable. Yet these efforts were all of a piece.

The New York women's rights activists had argued that women's degradation meant that their instincts to love their children were obscured, perhaps fully for some women, and could not be restored until the causes of that degradation were remedied. Clarke, while agreeing that these instincts were "either crushed or developed according to [negative] surroundings" in some women, nevertheless believed that they could be rekindled, and enlivened, and made to flourish with friendly, sisterly sympathy and encouragement even while circumstances remained difficult. "It is a wonderful thing to watch the effect of this, as we have done for more than thirty years and in hundreds of cases," Clarke wrote, "and we cannot help feeling that we are working in harmony with a wise Providence by encouraging this instinct."[108] These women all understood that women—especially working-women—were disadvantaged by the sexual double standard; by economic, political, and legal practices; and by the individual circumstances of their lives. They realized that the hard circumstances that women faced often effectively put a mother's well-being and that of her child in conflict. Clarke worked with the mothers she encountered to resolve that conflict, so that they and their children could live better, deeper, richer lives.

Chapter Eight

LOSING SIGHT OF WOMEN AND CHILDREN

What the Society for Helping Destitute Mothers and Infants termed "the vital changes that have taken place in social conditions," Thomas Haskell would later describe as "a division between two different constructions of social reality, two quite different modes of understanding man's nature, his relations in society, and his place in the cosmos."[1] The social scientists and social workers of the early twentieth century inhabited a very different moral universe than the early women's rights advocates, most of whom had been abolitionists. While the early women's rights advocates had been, if anything, overly optimistic about what their work could accomplish, the generation that followed them was anything but sanguine. The gulf that would develop between the "tenderness for the suffering, the weak, the sinful" that characterized the early women doctors' work with vulnerable women, and the horror of the "mentally deficient and morally depraved," which characterized the Society for Helping Destitute Mothers and Infants' (SHDMI) more than thirty years after its founding, starkly illustrates this change.[2] Yet this change did not happen suddenly, or at the same pace in all arenas of society.

There is no little irony in the overlapping of the largely

successful culmination of anti-abortion efforts in the late nineteenth century with the introduction of eugenics into discussions of women's reproductive lives, even within the women's rights press. Advocacy and public consideration preceded law and policy; while Horatio Storer's anti-abortion work had begun in the 1850s, it wasn't until 1900 that every state in the United States listed abortion as a felony. Similarly, while now-disproven theories about heredity appeared in discussions around responsible child-bearing in the pages of *Woodhull & Claflin's Weekly* in the early 1870s, serious public eugenics efforts wouldn't take off until the mid-1900s. Therefore, it should come as no surprise that the *Weekly*'s statements in support of women's rights and against abortion equaled or surpassed *The Revolution*'s in strength and clarity, despite its simultaneous dabbling in eugenics language, which worked against a recognition of individual human dignity.

Abortion Opposition Goes Mainstream

In August 1871, *The New York Times* published a lengthy exposé that is often portrayed as a turning point in the public perception of abortion. It may be seen better as the culmination of a press, pulpit, and medical campaign that had been gathering steam since the end of the Civil War. "The Evil of the Age" asserted that abortion was a "systematic business in wholesale murder conducted by men and women in this City, that is seldom detected, rarely interfered with, and scarcely ever punished by law." It excoriated advertisements and the papers that ran them, especially the *New York Herald*, "a paper which contains strings of disgraceful advertisements" by Madame Restell's husband, "Dr. Mauriceau," who spent "nearly $60,000 per annum" on advertising.[3] The article kicked off a lengthy discussion of abortion in the New York press. The *Times* continued its coverage with an account of an abortionist, "Rosenzweig, Alias Ascher," who had been profiled in the "Evil of the Age" article and was subsequently arrested for the death of a young woman in what came to be known as the "Trunk Murder." He was accused of performing an abortion on Alice Bowlsby, who died, and of stuffing her body into a trunk discovered at a New York railroad station.[4]

The case against Rosenzweig in the court of general sessions provided yet another venue for discussions of abortion. Judge Gunning S. Bedford, speaking to the grand jury in September, depicted Bowlsby as a "sad victim of treachery and deception . . . murdered by an abortionist." Her death illustrated "an atmosphere of abortion," and the judge urged the legislature to declare abortion, unless necessary to save the life of the mother, to be first-degree murder, punishable by death.[5] The law at the time made criminal abortion manslaughter in the second degree, punishable with prison not exceeding seven years.[6] The *New York Herald* vigorously supported the judge's proposal. While "the real cure of the disease must come through a moral revolution among the community," the essay insisted that "in the meantime the scalpel of the law must cut the social cancer out as best it may—and what is more, if needs be we must put a keaner [sic] cutting edge upon that surgical instrument."[7] And not just the New York press was impressed by Bedford. *The Idaho World*, for instance, also published an approving essay that declared that the "great increase in crimes of this character demands an amendment to the criminal laws of not only New York, but of many other States and Territories."[8]

Given the difficulty of securing convictions for abortions, it may be that the desire to make abortion first-degree murder was not simply about retribution but also about naming abortion intentional murder. That is, the law itself was one possible means for reshaping public opinion. Much reporting covered the development of a medico-legal society and the calls of various medical societies for legal reforms that would increase regulation of their profession.[9] These reforms, of course, would also solidify the professional status of those doctors. Abortion restriction and medical professionalization were deeply intertwined. The East River Medical Association, for instance, proposed a bill "To Suppress Criminal Abortions, and to Regulate the Practice of Medicine and Surgery in the State of New York" at its regular meeting in December 1871.[10] The New York press largely cheered them on, though some newspapers objected to proposed penalties for advertisements for abortion.[11] However, it should be pointed out that all the uproar in the press and even the strengthening of anti-abortion legislation did not stamp out the practice. The *Boston Daily Globe* made this point in 1874, when it accused the government of failing to effectively prosecute those few abortionists actually arrested.[12]

The growing importance of the medical profession reworked the abortion narrative. In the language of *The New York Times*'s "Evil of the Age" article, abortion was "medical malpractice": many abortionists lacked medical training and tended to operate under assumed names, though there were educated doctors "who live[d] and thrive[d] by these criminal practices."[13] But where the traditional narrative had a villain or two (seducer and abortionist) and a victim (the woman), the new narrative had a hero as well—the upright doctor. The *New-York Tribune* lauded the city's "two Women's Medical Colleges" because their physicians "offer refuge to unfortunates and honest women alike, the only plea being that they are women, and in need of the tenderest care of their sex." These physicians "while refusing all complicity with cowardly evil...stimulate[d] their patients to be brave, and to endure nature's consequences for the sake of a newer and purer life afterward."[14] Perhaps more characteristically, in "A Medical Martyr," the *Detroit Free Press* described a physician shot in the leg for refusing to perform an abortion on a man's wife. The doctor was clearly the hero, the husband the villain. The woman barely appeared in the story at all.[15]

Woodhull & Claflin Take on Abortion

The women's rights newspapers responded to this uptick in mainstream reporting on abortion by expressing appreciation for some aspects of it and reacting against others. Laura Curtis Bullard's *The Revolution* applauded the fact that "all the vials of editorial wrath have been poured upon the heads of the miscreants [abortionists]—vile panderers to the vilest of crimes."[16] Both the *Women's Journal* and *Woodhull & Claflin's Weekly* criticized the *New-York Tribune* for giving the names and addresses of women arrested in a raid on an abortionist's office, while withholding information about the men arrested with them.[17] Following *The Revolution*'s demise, *Woodhull & Claflin's Weekly* took up where it had left off in integrating public concern for abortion into arguments for women's rights—and took the argument much farther than the former had.

"Society has come to believe it an impertinence in children to be born at all," Sarah F. Norton wrote in an article published in *Woodhull & Claflin's Weekly* in November 1870. The article bore significant similarities to the paper she had presented at the Workingwomen's Association's meeting the previous May following the Hester Vaughn meeting and was one of several she published in the newspaper that year.[18] Disregard for human life, Norton argued in "Tragedy—Social and Domestic," underlaid all of the other more immediate factors driving the increasing abortion rate in New York City. Families with children had difficulty finding housing, and so couples were motivated to remain childless. Husbands pressured their wives to have abortions. Rich women bragged to each other about their abortions in the hearing of their servants, normalizing the practice for both classes simultaneously. Therefore, it was little surprise "that child murderers practice their profession without let or hindrance, and open infant butcheries unquestioned, establishing themselves with an impunity that is not allowed to the slaughterers of cattle."[19]

Norton was pessimistic about the possibility of directly addressing the situation: "Is there no remedy for all this ante-natal child murder? Not any, is the reply to the question so frequently asked. Is there, then, no penalty for the crime? None that can be inflicted."[20] But the *Weekly*'s other contributors were more hopeful, and offered a slew of means for reducing the incidence of abortion. Many were fairly conventional—voluntary motherhood, increasing women's ability to support themselves, increased valuation of motherhood, and physiological education. But other proposals were less expected, including the total abolition of marriage and state support for pregnant women and babies.

Victoria Woodhull had made the newspaper's editorial position on abortion clear earlier, in October 1870, in an article titled "When Is It Not Murder to Take Life?"[21] Her answer was unequivocal: "The truth of the matter is that it is just as much a murder to destroy life in its embryotic [sic] condition, as it is to destroy it after the fully developed form is attained, for it is the self-same life that is taken.... and no amount of sophistry nor excuses can, by one iota, mitigate the enormity of the crime." Another editorial asked, "Is it not equally destroying the would-be future oak, to crush the sprout before it pushes its head above the sod, as it is to cut down the sapling, or to saw down the tree? Is it not equally to destroy life, to crush it in its very germ, and to take it when the germ has evolved to any given point in the life of its development?" Its authors responded simply: "Let those who can see any difference regarding the time when life, once begun, is taken, console themselves that they are not murderers having been abortionists."[22] While this logic was sometimes implicit in *The Revolution*, it was not often spelled out.

Woodhull & Claflin's Weekly doubled down on the physical danger to women posed by abortion, insisting that it risked becoming a murder-suicide, rather than simply a murder. Additionally, the *Weekly*'s editors insisted on "the fact that a woman upon whom abortions are committed soon becomes incapable of bearing a child," and that "a very large portion of womankind" owed their "degenerate sexual condition, their weaknesses, aches and pains" to having undergone abortions.[23] These were not novel explanations for abortion's immorality, but others provided in the pages of *Woodhull & Claflin's Weekly* were.

The Arrival of the Eugenics Argument

Woodhull & Claflin's Weekly's distinctive contribution to discourse on the morality of abortion was a significantly eugenically tinged argument, based on now-outdated ideas about heredity. Woodhull, in acknowledging that some might find her frank treatment of the issue lacking in delicacy, had argued that the importance of issues "upon which the welfare of the human race depends" ought to outweigh any such concerns. The *Weekly*'s editors described children who were born to parents who loved each other, married or not, as "the very choice of the incoming crop of humanity," and their deaths as therefore especially immoral as well as particularly tragic.[24] The newspaper also alleged abortion was bad for society because no pregnant woman could even *think* about aborting her unborn child "without imprinting the thought, the possibility of murder, upon its facile mind."[25] Additionally, they claimed, children born to women who had previously had an abortion were more likely to be "weakly, puling and sickly, perhaps idiotic, or partially idiotic."[26] Thus, Victoria Woodhull could look forward to "the abrogation of forced pregnancy, of ante-natal murder, of undesired children" and "the birth of love children only," as related goals.

A state of affairs in which there would be both no abortion and no "unwanted" children would seem to require either perfectly reliable contraception—which did not exist then, as it still does not entirely in our own day—or that women have sex only when open to the possibility of becoming pregnant. That argument relied on either the ideology of passionlessness or an insistence on self-control, or both. While Woodhull clearly didn't subscribe to the ideology of passionlessness in full—she responded to a woman's claim that she had never experienced sexual desire by exclaiming, "My God, no sexual desires! A sexual idiot then"—she also did propose, as a means of reducing the incidence of abortion, "to so situate woman, that she may never be *obliged* to conceive a life she does not desire shall be continuous."[27] Similarly, the *Weekly*'s editors elsewhere implied that "sexual freedom" would give women "control of their maternal functions" so that they might "thereby be able to bear children only when they desire them, and such as they desire."[28] They implicitly acknowledged that this would require a certain level of self-denial or self-control on even the woman's part, saying that women had a responsibility to undertake "the risk of motherhood only when all the conditions are favorable for a wise parentage and a pure offspring."[29] The weight of motherhood ought not to be taken lightly, the newspaper argued, not only because by becoming a mother a woman contributed to the future of the country, for good or for ill, but because, "for the mother who will permit herself to become the means of giving life to children only to see them drop off, having never come to a realization of what life is—if there is an excuse we have not yet been able to find it."[30]

Woodhull & Claflin's Weekly attributed the fact that the ideal state of affairs outlined above did not actually exist in the United States both to "the rottening of our prevalent state of society" and to the fact that "enlightenment [has become] the rule among the people."[31] While this sounds like a contradiction, it wasn't necessarily. Woodhull adhered to a classical positivist theory in which both societies and individuals could be identified by their place in a "line of evolution" that spanned "from the lower—the evil—to the higher—the good." She laid out this understanding in a speech given at a meeting of the American Association of Spiritualists, to which she gave the title "The Religion of Humanity"—a clear reference to Auguste Comte's philosophy. Woodhull, like Comte, applied her evolutionary theory to both societies and individuals.[32]

While the *Weekly* proffered numerous practical measures that might decrease the incidence of abortion, Woodhull's moral theory seems to have offered little ultimate hope on this topic. While she clearly believed that she could identify good and evil—for in her view, abortion was evil—she believed that individual culpability was difficult, if not impossible, to define. This was not due to humility about knowing an individual's circumstances, personal limitations, or other individualized factors. Rather, she argued, the state of society as a whole worked against the capacity for moral responsibility of all the individuals within it. Her theory relied—to a probably extraordinary extent, given that it did not become widespread until the second half of the twentieth century—on moral relativism. "To a person low down in the scale of development many a thing may be good which, to one further ascended, might be very evil," she argued. Yet the cause of a person's seemingly good or evil actions lay outside that person: "Scarcely a single act of any person can be traced wholly to circumstances within his control; in fact, almost all acts are largely the result of causes over which the actor can have no possible power." It was no surprise, then, that "in spite of all penal and compulsatory laws, society refuses to elevate itself to escape their penalties." If an abortionist's reasons for pursuing his trade did not really stem from his will but rather were a function of the experiences of his childhood and young adulthood, his financial situation, the demand for his services, and so on—and if he understood his work as a good, because he was lower on the "line of evolution" than someone who understood it to be evil—it would be difficult to fault him for his work even if it was obviously evil. Consequently, Woodhull argued, "there is neither merit or demerit in human action."[33]

In Comte's view, "the basic reality is humanity rather than the individual."[34] From the discussions of abortion in *Woodhull & Claflin's Weekly*, it seems clear that, for its editors, the same held true at least in part. While they clearly recognized and named the lack of respect and concern for human life in the United States at that time, when the *Weekly* discussed abortion, it was often to demonstrate something about the state of society at present. "Wives deliberately permit themselves to become pregnant of children, and then, to prevent becoming mothers, as deliberately murder them while yet in their wombs. Can there be a more demoralized condition than this?" the newspaper's editors asked. "It shows a contempt for human life which degrades it to the level of what is necessary for its support and stamps the brand of Cain upon every woman who attempts or is accessory to it."[35] And in an 1873 article titled "Babydom," the newspaper's editors noted that the fact of a human infant's extreme helplessness, which set him apart even from other mammals, "should teach us, collectively as well as individually, our responsibilities toward the little ones."[36] At the same time, the *Weekly* was willing to portray the birth of some infants as a negative thing for society as a whole. "Every infant that is not the fruit of an affectionate union we believe to be more or less of an abortion," its editors wrote, calling such children "monstrosities," and insisting that it was necessary to "reduce the numbers of such forlorn little ones."[37] Correspondingly, they found themselves in the position of excoriating some mothers as "wholly responsible for the degraded, demoralized, half-made-up race of children with which the world is blessed or cursed."[38]

The direction of this logic was indicated, perhaps ironically, in the *Weekly*'s reprinting of a September 1859 *Liberator* article on a speech given by medium Julia Branch. The article, which argued that the institution of marriage was the root cause of many social evils, was presented to show that "in spite of all the efforts of social science reformers, it [the world] does not move very fast." In the article, Branch had observed, "The law allows the rights of marriage to the most depraved and unhealthy, with the knowledge that their children would be equally depraved and unhealthy, if not worse than their parents." More chillingly, she noted, "An unhealthy beast is killed as not capable of reproducing a perfect specimen of its species."[39] The *Weekly* provided no further comment.

While the progression of the anti-abortion argument between *The Revolution* and *Woodhull & Claflin's Weekly* seemed to be one of increasing vehemence and clarity about the immorality of abortion, moral reasoning around abortion began to lose its clarity—and indeed to the modern ear can sound more like arguments for abortion than the reverse. Without a deep awareness of the immorality of abortion—which the newspaper's editors did espouse, but which the moral relativism also made explicit in the newspaper nevertheless worked against—the logic of some of the arguments made in the pages of *Woodhull & Claflin's Weekly* seem to suggest abortion's permissibility. For example, Tennessee Claflin mockingly voiced arguments against attempting to reduce the incidence of abortion, writing that "the shop of the abortionist is a beneficial institution, which protects the virtue and heals the heart sore of a thousand otherwise cursed and unfortunate families." While she clearly took the immorality of abortion as a given, she seemed to view its incidence as inevitable, and she went so far as to argue that there was "no remedy... none, I solemnly believe; none by means of repression and law."[40] Finally, the introduction of eugenically tinged arguments against abortion—such as that which claimed that if a pregnant woman were to even consider abortion, she might thereby induce homicidal tendencies in her child—suggested that society as a whole *might* suffer from the mere existence of some mothers and their children.

Nevertheless, it is not entirely fair to Victoria Woodhull and her associates to suggest that their analyses of abortion and its causes, and their suggestion of possible mitigating factors, are inextricably tied to the broader philosophical framework in which they were presented. The strikingly modern—and wide—variety of ideas proposed in *Woodhull & Claflin's Weekly* for reducing women's demand for abortion demonstrates both intelligence and creativity. And regardless of their understandings of history and sociology, they unequivocally presented abortion as murder and, with extraordinary clarity, argued that the practice was bad for both unborn children and their mothers.

CONCLUSION

In the spring of 1875, just as the nascent Society for Helping Destitute Mothers and Infants was issuing its first formal appeal for support, Susan B. Anthony was in the Midwest debuting a new lecture. In "Social Purity," Anthony drew on her early involvement in the temperance movement—and its increasing popularity—to show how women and their children suffered at the hands of drunken husbands and fathers, and to offer women's suffrage as a necessary precondition for the righting of these wrongs. What can be known of the text of this lecture appears almost a précis of the topics covered by *The Revolution*: "The statutes for marriage and divorce, for adultery, breach of promise, seduction, rape, bigamy, abortion, infanticide—all were made by men. They, alone, decide who are guilty of violating these laws and what shall be their punishment," she insisted.[1] She discussed the precarious economic situations many women found themselves in, the necessity of equal pay for equal work, prostitution, the negative public valuation of motherhood, and the significance of foundling hospitals.

Perhaps most strikingly, Anthony pled for sympathy for and action on behalf of the "thirteen-hundred Rachels weeping for their children because they were not!"[2] The New York women's rights activists—like the women of the New England Hospital for Women and Children (NEHWC), Massachusetts Infant Asylum (MIA), and Society for Helping Destitute Mothers and Infants (SHDMI)—had seen infanticide and infant abandonment as a result of poverty and social norms that restricted the ability of both married and unmarried mothers to financially support their children and other dependents. They fought for respect for women and children against the idea that a woman's worth—and her child's—was a function of her marital status and the context of her sexual experience. At the same time, they had argued, the experience—or expectation—of dependence that reduced women's status in society tended to discourage the growth of virtue in women themselves.

The process of leveling inequalities between men and women meant both holding men to a higher standard of sexual morality, and asking women to rise to their existing and forthcoming civic, social, and economic responsibilities. This meant encouraging "the full development and use of the faculties conferred upon us by our Creator."[3] This concept of individual—and thus social—elevation through the development and practice of virtues and the fulfilling of duties to God, self, and others had its roots in classical republicanism, with its numerous "plausible ways to encourage the good to be more so."[4] It was of a piece with Angelina and Sarah Grimke's significantly earlier "discussion of 'the condition of woman, her duties, and her consequent rights.'"[5] The Bostonian women involved in the NEHWC, MIA, and SHDMI were perhaps especially aware that the responsibility to fulfill these elevating duties and to claim their consequent rights was an obligation that they themselves were under just as much as the less fortunate women they assisted in their philanthropic activities. With this certainty, despite Anna Cabot Lowell's insistence that "we shall make blunders, assuredly, and be blamed for it," and Lilian Freeman Clarke's recognition that "there are a Scylla and Charybdis in all charitable work, and especially in such work as ours," these women devoted their lives to the support of vulnerable women and their children.[6]

Women's rights advocates argued that the sexual double standard should be countered not only by demanding better behavior from men but also by honoring a woman's motherhood regardless of her circumstances. They understood respect for a helpless child's life, and their work against abortion and infanticide, as supporting women whose maternity might have been seen as shameful. Rather, they argued, if a woman's maternity reflected badly on anyone, it should be those who paid hypocritical lip service to Christian sexual morality and laid all the blame for any transgression of that code, consensual or not, entirely on the woman.

Something of the diffusive good that women's rights advocates understood their institutions to do can be seen in Lowell's contribution in the MIA's 1872 annual report. Beyond its immediate clientele of impoverished women, the MIA provided a real benefit for the women who fostered children for the institution. "We help many a deserving woman in her struggle for subsistence; we often aid her morally; a child always brings sunshine to the household," Lowell wrote. "Sometimes it happens that a mother has been bereaved of her own infant, and the baby placed under her care brings new cheerfulness and hope to her heart. It is good for her, too, to see the value we place on the life and comfort of the poorest and most neglected infants."[7] Support for all mothers—married or unmarried, wealthy or impoverished, white or black—would not just improve those individual women's lives, but would also counteract the sexual double standard and contribute to the elevation of all of society.

In addition to working to prevent abortions and infanticide by caring for women who would consider such actions due to a lack of social, familial, or financial assistance, the early women's rights activists showed significant sympathy and compassion for women who had made such choices. Perhaps this can most clearly be seen in *The Revolution*'s early treatment of Hester Vaughn, when its staff argued not that she was guiltless of infanticide but that her culpability was hugely diminished due to the circumstances of her pregnancy and her solitary and impoverished life in New York. In the early women's rights activists' view, to see someone fall short of her potential, whether through her own fault or another's, whether through simple weakness or corruption, had an element of tragedy. In this narrative, Vaughn, like Margaret Garner before her, had committed a horrendous act because her circumstances had inverted her moral vision, making murder appear preferable to life for her child. Regardless of fault, each woman deserved better—her circumstances should be radically changed, and her character elevated, her moral vision restored. It is in this context that Dimock's "tenderness for the suffering, the weak, the sinful" women she saw at the NEHWC and Lozier's "pity for...evil" in the Caroline Fuller case make sense.[8]

Before the Workingwomen's Association's meeting on behalf of Hester Vaughn, Susan B. Anthony counseled Anna Dickinson about her speech, telling her that "these hungry, thirsty souls" in the audience "will draw out from the deep wells of your being the very things they most need."[9] She heartily approved of the title, "A Struggle for Life," adding, "Of course you can't talk of the struggle for woman, without telling how much more terrible are the odds she has to contend with, than are those for men...that she has not an even chance in the start of the struggle...she a helpless, powerless victim of circumstance—he a maker, moulder, controller of not only his own circumstances but those of his sister also."[10] The early women's rights advocates understood that a key part of improving women's lives was increasing their agency, both morally and materially. Thus, they assisted women by improving their earning capacity, bolstering their control over their reproductive lives through physiological education and advocating voluntary motherhood, supporting women in crisis pregnancies, and above all, by offering friendship. When a contributor to *The Revolution* wrote, "Woman has most of the work of her elevation to do herself," she acknowledged the centrality of individual women's agency in this work. This insight characterized the early women's rights movement.

For a brief moment in the aftermath of the Civil War, women's rights advocates, abortion opponents, and early social scientists and social workers all held a common vision of abortion and its intersection with the struggles women faced. In that view, abortion was a self-evident wrong against the unborn children killed by it, a dangerous and suicidal act committed by desperate women who had been wronged by individual men or by society writ large, and a social fact that called for civic, legal, and charitable responses. Suffragists argued for the vote as a remedy against abortion; women's rights advocates more broadly worked to increase women's economic and legal rights; anti-abortion campaigners drew attention to the sexual double standard and called men to greater responsibility; and charitable institutions worked to provide support for desperate women who might otherwise choose abortion.

Yet this moment did not last. By the time Anthony gave her "Social Purity" speech, the narrow moment in time when support for women's suffrage and opposition to abortion were intrinsically connected and publicly allied was fading fast. But the principal insights of this alliance were not quickly abandoned. Women's rights activists still understood that women who saw abortion or infanticide as an unavoidable choice had often been wronged both by specific men and by society at large. And they understood that abortion, as something that caused the death of a living human being, was inherently wrong. But as the women's rights movement was crystallizing its focus on suffrage and abortion was becoming a matter of more general public outrage, these topics were increasingly treated as distinct.

The Revolution had been criticized in the *Woman's Journal*'s first issue—published on the second anniversary of *The Revolution*'s launch—for the breadth of topics it covered. "We protest against loading the good ship 'woman suffrage' with a cargo of irrelevant opinions.... It may be a matter of philanthropic interest whether Hester Vaughan should be executed, but it has nothing to do with the question whether Hester Vaughan should vote," Henry Blackwell wrote.[11] While *The Revolution*'s staff would not grant Blackwell's point, over the next five years, the New York branch of the women's rights movement narrowed its focus around suffrage. As Ellen Carol DuBois has written, "The political conflict of the late 1860s significantly advanced the movement, liberated it from its subservience to abolitionism and propelled it into political independence."[12]

Other changes in American life contributed to the decoupling of arguments about abortion and suffrage. Free-love supporters of women's suffrage increasingly voiced a eugenics-tinged worldview that corrupted the logic of their still-stated opposition to abortion. The first generation of anti-abortion sociomedical investigators died or retired due to ill health. Public attention to the problem of abortion began to shift toward doctors, causing the figures of the woman and child to disappear. And charitable institutions that had focused on the well-being of individual women and their children began to shift their focus to the supposedly distinct well-being of society writ large.

The loss of belief in human agency demonstrated both in *Woodhull & Claflin's Weekly*'s articles related to sociology and in the SHDMI's policies in its later years implied that individual women were less culpable for objectively immoral actions. But unlike in the abolitionist and early women's rights advocates' view, this implied not so much that the woman had suffered moral injury, or that she was in need of elevation, whether moral or material, but rather that her being was defective. If a woman's agency meant primarily that she reacted to differing stimuli, and charitable work with women meant providing kindly stimuli rather than assisting her in developing self-sufficiency and effective self-government, this understanding of her nature also lessened the possibility of her reformation or elevation.

As with trends in newspaper coverage of abortion, the figure of the woman—and of the mother and her child—was lost, as was the edifying concept of personal friendship as her consolation. And the belief in the possibility and benefit of her moral, physical, and intellectual elevation was replaced with an insistence on the elevation of society conceived of as a whole, at the expense of the individuals who composed it. As society broadly lost confidence in the human capacity to act meaningfully within a universe of ever-increasing complexity, the republican emphasis on virtues and freedom lost resonance, and the dignity of the individual human person—unborn or born, female or male—lost significance.

ENDNOTES

Preface

THE MEDICALIZATION OF WOMEN'S REPRODUCTIVE LIVES

1 See, for instance, "Infanticide," *The Boston Medical and Surgical Journal* (Aug. 18, 1864): 66–67. Modern scholars also have made this link: "In both historical and contemporary societies, the problem of children, or potential children, who are unwanted, a strain on resources, or who will bring shame and social ostracism on their parents is one that has been dealt with through infanticide, abandonment, and abortion. There is an enormous overlap between such terms and very difficult problems of definition mean that these words can be deployed and manipulated depending on the circumstances." Sally Crawford, Martin Ingram, Alysa Levene, Heather Montgomery, Kieron Sheehy, and Ellie Lee, "Infanticide, Abandonment and Abortion," in Laurence Brockliss and Heather Montgomery, eds., *Childhood and Violence in the Western Tradition* (Oxford: Oxbow Books, 2010), 58.

2 Susan Pearson dates the beginning of the movement to "change children's status from that of mere chattel" to the 1874 case of Mary Ellen Wilson. Yet the fact that calls to decrease infant mortality using language like Frank Sanborn's (see Chapter 6) predated that landmark case suggests that this trend began somewhat earlier. Susan J. Pearson, *The Rights of the Defenseless: Protecting Animals and Children in Gilded Age America* (Chicago: The University of Chicago Press, 2011), 4.

3 Leslie Reagan shows that in Chicago between 1867 and 1940, "in cases involving abortion, the state prosecuted chiefly abortionists, most often after a woman had died, and prosecutors relied for evidence on dying declarations collected from women near death due to their illegal abortions." She argues, "Although women were not arrested, prosecuted, or incarcerated for having abortions, the state nonetheless punished working-class women for having illegal abortions through official investigations and public exposure of their abortions." Leslie J. Reagan, "'About to Meet Her Maker': Women, Doctors, Dying Declarations, and the State's Investigation of Abortion, Chicago, 1867–1940," *The Journal of American History* 77 (Mar. 1991): 1242, 1243–44.

4 On the ways in which "shifting definitions and registration practices have affected our ability to construct and compare stillbirth rates," see Robert Woods, "Late-Fetal Mortality: Historical Perspectives on Continuing Problems of Estimation and Interpretation," *Population* 63 (Nov. 2008): 610. For a detailed examination of these "shifting definitions and registration practices," see Vincent Gourdon and Catherine Rollet, "Stillbirths in Nineteenth-Century Paris: Social, Legal and Medical Implications of a Statistical Category," *Population* 64 (Oct.–Dec. 2009).

5 Katie Hemphill has shown that in antebellum Baltimore, "poverty was an important factor in nearly every stage of infant death investigations and infanticide prosecutions." She shows, for instance, that inquiries were often launched when an infant's body was found abandoned in a public place, a practice she argues more likely illustrated that a family was "too poor to afford the cost of transporting a body to the periphery of the city or to pay the fee for internment in a potter's field." Similarly, while an infant death in a middle-class home might be treated as a tragic, private matter, a "similar death in the home of a poor or otherwise socially marginal woman might be read as the result of carelessness, neglect, or murder" (Katie M. Hemphill, "'Driven to the Commission of This Crime': Women and Infanticide in Baltimore, 1835–1860," *Journal of the Early Republic* 32 [Fall 2012]: 438, 441–42, 444). On the challenges related to medical evidence in infanticide cases, see Ann R. Higginbotham, "'Sin of the Age': Infanticide and Illegitimacy in Victorian London," *Victorian Studies* 23 (Spring 1989): 330, 336.

6 Elizabeth Potter to Lydia Babcock, Feb. 23, 1864, William Potter Papers, quoted in Anne C. Rose, *Victorian America and the Civil War* (Cambridge, UK: Cambridge University Press, 1994), 157.

INTRODUCTION

1 Susan B. Anthony to Anna Dickinson, July 8, 1868, Box 5, Anna E. Dickinson Papers. Library of Congress.

2 Susan B. Anthony, "What Is American Slavery?," Box 7, Susan B. Anthony Papers: Speeches and Writings, 1848–1895, 1861, Library of Congress Manuscript Division.

3 Garrisonian abolitionists were followers of William Lloyd Garrison, who fully supported women's rights in the midst of his abolitionist advocating.

4 "Public sentiment is more enduring than public opinion; it touches deeper roots in an individual's system of beliefs and values. And it is not purely cognitive and rational; it reflects emotional wellsprings, too. If public sentiment held that slavery was doomed to eventual extinction, that meant something more than acceptance of an abstract proposition. It meant a commitment that sprang from the nexus of religious and ethical conviction, cultural tradition and narrative, and intellectual principle and reason." David Zarefsky, "Public Sentiment Is Everything: Lincoln's View of Political Persuasion," *Journal of the Abraham Lincoln Association* 15, no. 2 (Summer 1994): 38.

5 Ellen Carol DuBois, *The Emergence of an Independent Women's Movement in America, 1848–1869* (Ithaca, NY: Cornell University Press, 1999), 38.

6 Elizabeth Cady Stanton, commenting on "Letter from Frances Power Cobbe," *The Revolution* (New York), Mar. 5, 1868.

7 "First Debate: Ottawa, Illinois." From Mark E. Neely, Jr., *The Abraham Lincoln Encyclopedia* (New York: Da Capo Press, Inc., 1982).

8 Susan J. Pearson, *The Rights of the Defenseless: Protecting Animals and Children in Gilded Age America* (Chicago: The University of Chicago Press, 2011), 7.

For more on the role of moral suasion in mid-nineteenth-century social and political activism, see Lori D. Ginzberg, "'Moral Suason Is Moral Balderdash': Women, Politics, and Social Activism in the 1850s," *The Journal of American History* 15, no. 3 (December 1986). Ginzberg dates women's rights advocates' loss of faith in moral suasion as a means of social transformation to the 1840s and 1850s. Our book demonstrates that, while this shift may have begun prior to the Civil War, it took several decades to permeate fully the women's rights movement.

9 "The Lecture Seasons," *New-York Tribune*, Sept. 27, 1853, quoted in

Angela G. Ray, "What Hath She Wrought? Women's Rights and the Nineteenth-Century Lyceum," *Rhetoric and Public Affairs* 9, no. 2 (2006): 192–93.

10 Horatio Storer, *Criminal Abortion: Its Nature, Its Evidence and Its Law* (Boston: Little, Brown and Company, 1868), 2f. This book was Storer's final book-length discussion of abortion in America.

11 "Sorosis," *New York World*, Jan. 5, 1869, quoted in *The Revolution* (New York), Jan. 21, 1869.

12 Horatio Storer, *On Criminal Abortion in America* (Philadelphia: J. P. Lippincott, 1860), 54–55.

13 "The Pulpit and the Social Evil," *The Woman's Journal* (Boston), Sept. 13, 1871.

14 "Salutatory," *The Revolution* (New York), Jan. 8, 1868.

15 "What the Press Says of Us," *The Revolution* (New York), Mar. 26, 1868.

16 In *The Revolution*'s first issue, the motto was relatively short: "Principle, Not Policy; Justice, Not Favors." In subsequent issues, *The Revolution*'s motto read "Principle, Not Policy; Justice, Not Favors.—Men, Their Rights and Nothing More: Women, Their Rights and Nothing Less."

17 H. B. Stowe and J. B. Hooker to Susan B. Anthony, New York, Dec. 1889, Papers of Susan B. Anthony, Vasser College Library, in Patricia G. Holland and Ann D. Gordon, eds., *Papers of Elizabeth Cady Stanton and Susan B. Anthony* (Wilmington, DE: Scholarly Resources , Inc., 1991), microfilm, series 3.

18 SBA to Isabella Beecher Hooker, New York, Dec. 18, 1869, Isabella Hooker Collection, Stowe-Day Memorial Library and Historical Foundation, Hartford, in Holland and Gordon, *Papers of Elizabeth Cady Stanton and Susan B. Anthony*; SBA to Harriet Beecher Stowe and Isabella Beecher Hooker, Dec. 29, 1869, Isabella Hooker Collection, Stowe-Day Memorial Library and Historical Foundation, Hartford, in Holland and Gordon, *Papers of Elizabeth Cady Stanton and Susan B. Anthony*.

Anthony initially suggested that this line be inserted between *The Revolution*'s title and its motto ("Principle, not Policy . . ."). "How would you like the above explanation line—one of my men helpers—not G.F.T.—suggested putting this line of exposition of the end of The Revolution we seek." SBA to Harriet Beecher Stowe, Isabella Beecher Hooker, Dec. 29, 1869, Isabella Hooker Collection, Stowe-Day Memorial Library and Historical Foundation, Hartford, in Holland and Gordon, *Papers of Elizabeth Cady Stanton and Susan B. Anthony*.

19 Elizabeth Cady Stanton, Susan B. Anthony, and Matilda Joslyn Gage, eds., *History of Woman Suffrage*, Vol. II (New York: National American Woman Suffrage Association, 1922), 85.

20 Col. Charles E. Moss's speech at the first Annual Meeting of the American Equal Rights Association, May 9–10, 1867, quoted in Stanton, Anthony, and Gage, *History of Woman Suffrage*, Vol. II, 154.

21 "Lecture by Lucy Stone on Suffrage for Woman at the Brooklyn Academy, Dec. 26," *The Revolution* (New York), Jan. 8, 1868.

22 Stanton, Anthony, and Gage, *History of Woman Suffrage*, Vol. II, 51.

23 Linda Kerber, "Daughters of Columbia: Educating Women for the Republic, 1787–1805," *Toward an Intellectual History of Women* (Chapel Hill: University of North Carolina Press, 1997). See especially 25–26; Jan Lewis, "The Republican Wife: Virtue and Seduction in the Early Republic," *The William and Mary Quarterly* 44, no. 4 (Oct. 1987): 699, 701.

24 Lewis, "The Republican Wife," 710.

25 Lewis, "The Republican Wife," 721.

26 Kerber, *Toward an Intellectual History of Women*, 283; See also Kerber, "Daughters of Columbia" and "The Republican Mother: Women and the Enlightenment—An American Perspective," in Kerber, *Toward an Intellectual History of Women.*

27 Lucy Stone to Antoinette Brown Blackwell, May 5, 1892, in Carol Lasser and Marlene Deahl Merrill, eds., *Friends and Sisters: Letters Between Lucy Stone and Antoinette Brown Blackwell, 1846–93* (Urbana, IL: University of Illinois Press, 1989), 20; quoted in Mary Kelley, *Learning to Stand and Speak: Women, Education, and Public Life in America's Republic* (Chapel Hill: Omohundro Institute and University of North Carolina Press, 2012), 132.

28 Kelley, *Learning to Stand and Speak*, 277.

29 "The Woman's Rights Convention Held in Albany," *The Una: A Paper Devoted to the Elevation of Woman* (Providence, RI), Mar. 1854.

30 Andrea L. Turpin, "The Ideological Origins of the Women's College: Religion, Class, and Curriculum in the Educational Visions of Catharine Beecher and Mary Lyon," *History of Education Quarterly*, 50, no. 2 (May 2010): 138–39, 142f.

For more on the relationship of republicanism and the women's rights movement, see Rebecca Rix's doctoral dissertation, *Gender and Reconstruction: The Individual and Family Basis of Republican Government Contested, 1868–1925* (Yale University, 2008).

31 Lucy Stone to Antoinette Brown Blackwell, May 5, 1892, quoted in Kelley, *Learning to Stand and Speak*, 132n.

32 Rev. James Freeman Clarke, at the American Woman Suffrage Association convention, May 11–12, 1870, New York City, quoted in Stanton, Anthony, and Gage, *History of Woman Suffrage*, Vol. II, 766.

33 Susan B. Anthony, "Homes of Single Women," October 1877, in Ellen Carol Dubois, ed., *Elizabeth Cady Stanton; Susan B. Anthony: Correspondence, Writings, Speeches* (New York: Shocken Books, 1981), 146–51.

34 Ellen Carol DuBois, *Feminism and Suffrage: The Emergence of an Independence Women's Movement in America, 1848-1869* (Ithaca: Cornell University Press, 1999), 31–40. Kate Clarke Lemay, ed., *Votes for Women* (Washington, D.C.: National Portrait Gallery, 2019), 117.

35 "Pecuniary Independence of Woman," *The Una: A Paper Devoted to the Elevation of Woman* (Providence, RI), December 1853.

The women's rights movement's use of the language of women's "degradation" and "elevation" had its roots in the Grimke sisters' framing. The black female slave was the paradigm of such degradation, followed by the white female prostitute. See Kathryn Kish Sklar, *Women's Rights Emerges Within the Anti-Slavery Movement, 1830–1870* (New York: Palgrave MacMillan, 2000).

36 Sklar, *Women's Rights Emerges Within the Anti-Slavery Movement*, 28.

As Jan Lewis explains, "Because all humans were moral creatures, created free by God to determine their own salvation, no person could rightfully deprive others [of] the freedom to make moral choices" (Jan Lewis, "The Republican Wife," 715).

37 Eleanor Kirk, "What Will Become of the Babies," *The Revolution* (New York), May 28, 1868; Elizabeth Archard in the *Herald of Health*, quoted in "Home Truths," *The Revolution* (New York), Jan. 15, 1868.

38 Elizabeth Cady Stanton, "How Man Legislates for Woman at Albany," *The Revolution* (New York), Mar. 19, 1868.

39 Parker Pillsbury, "The South as It Is," *The Revolution* (New York), Nov. 11, 1869.

40 Infanticide," *The Revolution* (New York), Jan. 29, 1868.

41 Letter from Elizabeth Cady Stanton to the National Woman's Rights Convention, Cooper Institute, 1856, quoted in Elizabeth Cady Stanton, Susan B. Anthony, and Matilda Joslyn Gage, eds., *History of Woman Suffrage*, Vol. I (New York: National American Woman Suffrage Association, 1922), 861.

Madame Restell—otherwise known as Ann Trow Lohman (May 6, 1812–April 1, 1878)—was one of the most notorious abortionists in New York City. She was known for a rather ostentatious lifestyle, and her Fifth Avenue mansion was sometimes referred to as a symbol of the corruption of her life and work.

42 F.E.R., "An Erring Heart," *The Woman's Journal* (Boston), Sept. 9, 1871.

43 F.E.R., "An Erring Heart."

44 "Child Murder," *The Revolution* (New York), Mar. 12, 1868.

45 Caroline Wells Healey Dall, *The College, the Market, and the Court* (Boston: Lee and Shepard, 1867), 48.

46 Mattie H. Brinkerhoff, "Woman and Motherhood," *The Revolution* (New York), Sept. 16, 1869.

47 Ernestine Rose, "To the Editor of the Globe," *The Una: A Paper Devoted to the Elevation of Woman* (Providence, RI), May 1854.

48 Resolution passed at the Quarterly Meeting of the New York Female Moral Reform Society, Jan. 1838, printed in *Advocate* 4, no. 14 (Jan. 15, 1838), quoted in Caroll Smith Rosenberg, "Beauty, the Beast and the Militant Woman: A Case Study in Sex Roles and Social Stress in Jacksonian America," *American Quarterly* 23, no. 4 (Oct. 1971): 572.

49 Linda K. Kerber, *Toward an Intellectual History of Women: Essays* (Chapel Hill: University of North Carolina Press, 1997), 174.

50 The content of women's education formed their approach to women's rights. For example, Lucy Stone's first formal education was at Mary Lyon's Mount Holyoke Female Academy. Before attending a Quaker boarding school, Susan B. Anthony was taught by a graduate of Zilpah Polly Grant's Ipswich Female Seminary. Lyon (who was Grant's student and later colleague) and Catherine Beecher, founder of the Hartford Female Seminary, the American Women's Education Association, and several other educational institutions, are often grouped together with Emma Willard, founder of Troy Female Seminary, as responsible for the introduction of academically rigorous higher education for American women in the 1830s. Beecher believed that women were inherently morally superior to men, and therefore had a greater obligation to serve the public good. However, Grant and Lyon did not believe that either gender was inherently more moral than the other. Unsurprisingly, many early women's rights advocates who would later find themselves opposed to Catherine Beecher's anti-suffrage position received their education from her rivals.

The Seneca Falls Declaration of Sentiments declared that one of man's crimes against woman was the creation of a "false public sentiment giving to the world a different code of morals for men and women."

51 Nancy F. Cott, "Passionlessness: An Interpretation of Victorian Sexual Ideology, 1790–1850," *Signs* 4, no. 2 (1978): 220, 225; Christine Stansell, *City of Women: Sex and Class in New York, 1789–1860* (New York: Alfred Knopf Press, 1986).

52 Cott, "Passionlessness," 235–36.

53 Cott, "Passionlessness," 230.

54 See Wendy Hayden, *Evolutionary Rhetoric: Sex, Science and Free Love in Nineteenth Century Feminism* (Carbondale: Southern Illinois University Press, 2013).

55 Cott, "Passionlessness," 233.

56 "Letter from Mrs. Brinkerhoff," *The Revolution* (New York), Mar. 19, 1868.

57 Martha Brinkerhoff, "Woman and Motherhood," *The Revolution* (New York), Sept. 2, 1869.

58 E.N.A., "Woman's Rights," *The Revolution* (New York), May 7, 1868.

59 Ida Husted Harper, *The Life and Works of Susan B. Anthony*, Vol. 1 (Indianapolis: The Bowen-Merrill Company, 1899), 345–46. The description of Fulton comes from Andrew Hilen, ed., *The Letters of Henry Wadsworth Longfellow* (Cambridge: Belknap Press of Harvard University Press, 1966), 528n.

60 "Female Suffrage: Address of Miss Anthony: Review of Mr. Fulton: True Womanly Education," *Detroit Advertiser and Tribune* (Detroit, MI), Dec. 10, 1869, found in Anthony Scrapbook 3, Susan B. Anthony papers, 1846–1934, Rare Books Division, Library of Congress, in Holland and Gordon, *Papers of Elizabeth Cady Stanton and Susan B. Anthony*.

61 "Female Suffrage: Address of Miss Anthony: Review of Mr. Fulton: True Womanly Education," *Detroit Advertiser and Tribune*, Dec. 10, 1869, in Holland and Gordon, *Papers of Elizabeth Cady Stanton and Susan B. Anthony.*

62 "Woman's Work and Wages," *The Revolution* (New York), July 23, 1868.

Chapter One

ABORTION SHIFTS IN THE PUBLIC IMAGINATION

1 "Seduction, Abortion, and Death," *Chicago Daily Tribune*, Aug. 3,

1857, published in the *Marshall County Republican*, Aug. 13, 1857. Spellings of Swansey's name varied considerably, including "Swanzey," "Swanzy," and "Swanze."

2 Michael Grossberg, *Governing the Hearth: Law and Family in Nineteenth-Century America* (Chapel Hill: University of North Carolina Press, 1988), 183.

As discussed in the introduction, women's victim status was grounded in the ideology of passionlessness, the "Victorian belief that women were unwilling participants in most sexual acts."

3 "The Abortion Case. Disclosures Before the Coroner's Jury," *Chicago Daily Tribune*, Aug. 4, 1857.

4 "Conclusion of the Abortion Case," *Chicago Daily Tribune*, Aug. 7, 1857.

5 The Cook County Recorder's Court had "concurrent jurisdiction within said city with the Circuit Court in all criminal cases, except treason and murder, and of civil cases where the amount in controversy shall not exceed one hundred dollars." Alfred Theodore Andreas, *History of Chicago*, Vol. 1 (Chicago: Arno Press, 1884), 451.

6 "The Abortion Case," *Chicago Daily Tribune*, Aug. 10, 1857.

7 Grossberg, *Governing the Hearth*, 182. This had not always been the case; see Jan Lewis, "The Republican Wife: Virtue and Seduction in the Early Republic," *The William and Mary Quarterly* 11, no. 4 (Oct. 1987).

8 Samuel W. Buell, "Criminal Abortion Revisited," *New York University Law Review* 66 (1991), 1784n; H. Purple, "A Compilation of the Statutes of the State of Illinois of a General Nature," *Force* (Jan. 1, 1857): 365.

9 Purple, "Compilation of the Statutes," 365.

10 "The Abortion Case," *Chicago Daily Tribune*, Aug. 10, 1857; "Recorder's Court," *Chicago Daily Tribune*, Sept. 16, 1857; "Recorder's Court," *Chicago Daily Tribune*, Nov. 10, 1857.

11 "Recorder's Court," *Chicago Daily Tribune*, Sept. 22, 1857.

12 "Recorder's Court," Sept. 22, 1857.

13 "Dr. Swanzy, the Alleged Abortionist," *Bureau County Democrat*, quoted in *Chicago Daily Tribune*, Aug. 17, 1857.

14 "Conclusion of the Abortion Case," *Chicago Daily Tribune*, Aug. 7, 1857; "Swanzy Acquitted," *Chicago Daily Tribune*, Nov. 14, 1857.

A. M. Herrington, one of Swansey's representatives, had been appointed as United States Attorney for the Northern District of

Illinois a few months earlier, in April 1857, and would be removed from his post in March 1858. "Harmonious Democracy," *Chicago Daily Tribune*, Apr. 24, 1857; "U.S. District Attorney," *Islander and Argus* (Rock Island, IL), Mar. 20, 1858.

15 Daniel Brainard, the founder and president of Rush Medical College, argued that "the production of abortion by mechanical means which rupture the membranes was not at all dangerous or injurious to life, if proper care were taken care of the person subsequently." On the contrary, Dr. Nathan Smith Davis, editor of the *Chicago Medical Journal* and founding member of the Chicago and Illinois State Medical Societies, had argued that it was "in the highest degree dangerous, and also as highly injurious to the system in its subsequent effects." "The Abortion Case—The Parties Held to Bail in $10,000 Each," in Zina Pitcher and A. B. Palmer, eds., *The Peninsular Journal of Medicine and the Collateral Sciences* 4 (1856/1857): 215.

16 "Swanzy Acquitted," *Chicago Daily Tribune*, Nov. 14, 1857.

17 "The Abortion Case," *Chicago Daily Tribune*, Nov. 17, 1857.

18 "Seduction, Abortion, and Death," *Chicago Daily Tribune*, Aug. 3, 1857; "Another Horrible Affair," *The Tarborough Southerner* (Tarboro, NC), Aug. 29, 1857.

19 "Seduction, Abortion, and Death," Aug. 3, 1857.

20 "The Abortion Case," *The Alton Weekly Courier* (Alton, IL), Nov. 26, 1857.

21 "The Abortion Case," *The Alton Weekly Courier*, Nov. 26, 1857.

22 James C. Mohr, *Abortion in America: The Origins and Evolution of National Policy, 1800–1900* (New York: Oxford University Press, 1878), 149.

23 Suffolk District Medical Society Committee on Criminal Abortion, *Report*, Apr. 15, 1857.

24 Massachusetts Medical Society, Meeting Minutes (June 3, 1857), Countway Library of Medicine, Harvard University, quoted in Frederick N. Dyer, *Horatio Storer: Champion of Women and the Unborn* (Canton, MA: Science History Publications, 1999), 118.

25 D. Meredith Reese, *Report on Infant Mortality in Large Cities, the Sources of Its Increase, and Means for Its Diminution* (Philadelphia: T. K. and P. G. Collins, 1857), 7.

26 On this point Reese was more correct than he knew. The medical community has learned much in the intervening century and a half. The CDC currently estimates that up to 40 percent of babies born to women with untreated syphilis are stillborn or die as newborns. Con-

genital syphilis also causes miscarriages, usually after the first trimester. "Congenital Syphilis—CDC Fact Sheet," Centers for Disease Control and Prevention. See also Marco De Santis et al., "Syphilis Infection During Pregnancy: Fetal Risks and Clinical Management," *Infectious Diseases in Obstetrics and Gynecology* 2012.

Additionally, the conflation of stillbirths and very early neonatal deaths (referred to as "false stillbirths") in official statistics was common.

27 William Wallace Sanger was no relation to Margaret Sanger. The book would be published the following year, but in an advertisement in printed edition, Sanger acknowledged that the book had been completed in 1857. [William Wallace Sanger, *The History of Prostitution: Its Extent, Causes, and Effects Throughout the World* (New York: Harper and Brothers, 1858), 6.]

28 Sanger, *History of Prostitution*, 482.

29 Horatio R. Storer, "On the Decrease of the Rate of Increase of Population Now Obtaining in Europe and America," *American Journal of Science and Arts* 43, no. 128 (Mar. 1867): 141–55. Given in December 1858, this paper was Storer's first for the AAAS, to which he had been elected as a member six months earlier.

30 Storer, "On the Decrease of the Rate of Increase of Population," 141–55.

31 The Contributions to Obstetric Jurisprudence articles were: "No. I—Is Abortion Ever a Crime?" *North American Medico-Chirurgical Review* (Jan. 1859); "No. II—Its Frequency and the Causes Thereof," *North American Medico-Chirurgical Review* (Mar. 1859); "No. III—Its Victims," *North American Medico-Chirurgical Review* (May 1859); "No. IV—Its Proofs," *North American Medico-Chirurgical Review* (May 1859); "No. V—Its Perpetrators," *North American Medico-Chirurgical Review* (May 1859); "No. VI—Its Innocent Abettors," *North American Medico-Chirurgical Review* (July 1859); "No. VII—Its Obstacles to Conviction," *North American Medico-Chirurgical Review* (Sept. 1859); "No. VIII—Can It Be at All Controlled by Law?" *North American Medico-Chirurgical Review* (Nov. 1859); "No. IX—A Medico-Legal Study of Rape," *New York Medical Journal* (Nov. 1865); and "No. X—The Abetment of Criminal Abortion by Medical Men," *New York Medical Journal* (Sept. 1866).

32 Grossberg puts it well: "Health problems were being redefined as public, not private responsibilities" (Grossberg, *Governing the Hearth*, 175).

For the term "sociomedical investigator" and the place of infant mortality prevention in public health movements, see Richard A. Meckel, *Save the Babies: American Public Health Reform and the Prevention of Infant Mortality 1850–1929* (Baltimore: Johns Hopkins University Press, 1990).

33 Holly Case, "The 'Social Question,' 1820–1920," *Modern Intellectual History* 13, no. 3 (2016).

34 For examples of these advertisements, see Rebecca Onion, "19th-Century Classified Ads for Abortifacients and Contraceptives," *Slate*, Aug. 6, 2014; and Lauren McIvor Thompson, "Women Have Always Had Abortions," *The New York Times*, Dec. 13, 2019.

In 1862, the *New York Herald* published a rant against the election of the cofounder of *The New York Times* as the Speaker of the New York State Assembly that tied newspaper advertisements of abortion to political corruption. Through "these infectious advertisements—more dangerous than the foulest malaria," the *Times* "debauche[d] the ignorant, innocent and unwary" ("The Speaker of the NY Assembly Upon Moral and Morality," *New York Herald*, Jan. 15, 1862). Abortion and political corruption went hand in hand—no matter that the *Herald* ran similar advertisements.

35 Reese, *Infant Mortality*, 9.

The Enlightenment trope of referring to ill-gotten riches as vampirism—perhaps most famously employed in Voltaire's *Encylopédie*—was easily applied to abortion. Voltaire wrote, *"On n'entendait point parler de vampires à Londres, ni meme à Paris. J'avoue que dans ces deux villes il y eut des agioteurs, des traitans, des gens d'affaires qui fucèrent en plein jour le fang du people, mais ils n'étaient point morts quoique corrompus. Ces fuceurs véritables ne demeuraient pas dans des cimetières, mais dans des palais fort agréables."* (Roughly translated: "You didn't hear about vampires in London, or even in Paris. I confess that in these two towns there were stock-brokers, traitors, business people who fled the fang of the people in broad daylight, but they were not dead, although corrupt. These veritable fugitives did not live in cemeteries, but in very pleasant palaces.") Voltaire, "Vampires," *Questions sur L'Encyclopédie par des Amateurs* (Geneva, 1764), 465.

36 "Child Murder," *Liberator*, Apr. 8, 1859.

On Remond, see Sibyl Ventress Brownlee, *Out of the Abundance of the Heart: Sarah Ann Parker Remond's Quest for Freedom*, PhD Diss. University of Massachusetts Amherst, 1997; Sirpa Salenius, *An Abolitionist Abroad: Sarah Parker Remond in Cosmopolitan Europe* (Amherst: University of Massachusetts Press, 2016).

37 "A Nice Anniversary Convention," *The Ashland Union* (Ashland, OH), July 13, 1864.

38 The instinct toward censorship of "obscene" material would eventually become a critical tool in suppressing abortion through the 1873 Comstock Act and similar state-level legislation.

39 Sanger, *History of Prostitution*, 480.

40 Horatio R. Storer, *On Criminal Abortion in America* (Philadelphia: J. B. Lippincott & Co., 1860), 8.

41 Storer, *On Criminal Abortion*, 55.

42 Reese, *Report on Infant Mortality*, 5–6, 10.

43 Reese, for instance, wrote: "The object of the institution of marriage, viz., the birth and nurture of offspring, the sacredness of the family relation, and all the sanctions of virtuous life in the conjugal and parental relation, seem to be ignored in these degenerate days, and need to be revived in the public creed and practice." Reese, *Report on Infant Mortality*, 10.

44 Reese, *Report on Infant Mortality*, 14.

45 Sanger, *History of Prostitution*, 167.

46 Storer, *Criminal Abortion*, 99, 101.

47 Sanger, *History of Prostitution*, 520.

48 Sanger, *History of Prostitution*, 329.

49 For instance: "Notwithstanding the North makes pretensions to all the purity of the land, and essays to look down upon the South in her barbaric practices, yet infanticide the most inexcusable and most disgusting, as well as most horrible of all crimes, is of common occurrence there, while with us it is almost unknown, and when known is confined almost exclusively to the negroes" ("Infanticide at the North," *Vicksburg Weekly Herald*, Feb. 12, 1870).

50 This assertion, however, was frequently restricted to Protestant Christians. Catholics, it was claimed, were highly unlikely to have abortions or to commit infanticide. This claim constitutes one of the few pro-Catholic lines often repeated in the overall still-anti-Catholic American press.

51 Thomas M. Eddy, "Foeticide," *Northwestern Christian Advocate*, March 1867, published in "Foeticide—The Slaughter of the Innocents," *Chicago Tribune*, Mar. 17, 1867.

52 John Todd, "Fashionable Murder," *Orleans Independent Standard* (Irasburgh, VT), May 10, 1867.

53 Eddy, "Foeticide," Mar. 17, 1867.

This was only a moderate exaggeration of the importance of the Methodist churches at this point in time. In 1860, the Methodist Episcopal Church (the main Northern church after the 1845 split over slavery) had some 860,000 full members. The Methodist Episcopal Church, South, had 749,068 full members. It was, according to Mark Noll, "the most pervasive form of Christianity in the United States." Mark Noll, *America's God: From Jonathan Edwards to Abraham Lincoln* (New York: Oxford University Press, 2002), 169.

54 John Todd, "Fashionable Murder," *Orleans Independent Standard* (Vermont), May 10, 1867.

55 Isabella Beecher Hooker, *Womanhood: Its Sanctities and Fidelities* (Boston: Lee and Separd, 1874). According to Hooker, the editor of *The Congregationalist* refused to print her letter, and then went on to publish another article by Todd (Hooker, *Womanhood*, 7–8).

56 Hooker, *Womanhood*, 12.

57 Hooker, *Womanhood*, 26.

58 Hooker, *Womanhood*, 13–14, 16–26, 22–23.

59 The Oneida community was founded in 1848 near Oneida, New York. It was a perfectionist, millennialist community; its members believed that Christ's second coming had already taken place and thus that a perfect human society could exist. While members of the Oneida community practiced "free love," childbearing was heavily regulated; pregnancies were prevented by the practice of "male continence" (coitus reservatus), and prospective parents had to be approved by a committee who would provide them with matches based on characteristics judged to be beneficial for passing on to a younger generations. Children born in this system were raised communally after their infancy, rather than by their parents. This early form of eugenics was referred to as "stirpiculture." For more on the Oneida community, see Louis Kern, *An Ordered Love: Sex Roles and Sexuality in Victorian Utopias—The Shakers (1779–1890), the Mormons (1843–90), and the Oneida Community (1848–69)* (Chapel Hill: University of North Carolina Press, 1981); Spencer Klaw, *Without Sin: The Life and Death of the Oneida Community* (New York: Penguin Books, 1994); George Noyes and Lawrence Foster, *Free Love in Utopia: John Humphrey Noyes and the Origin of the Oneida Community* (Urbana: University of Illinois Press, 2001), among others.

60 "Murder of the Unborn," *The Circular* (Oneida, NY), May 6, 1867.

61 G., "A New Phase of Reform: The Northern Apocalypse," *The Circular* (Oneida, NY), Apr. 15, 1867.

62 G., "New Phase of Reform, Apr. 15, 1867.

63 "Quack Murderers," *New York Herald*, June 14, 1870.

64 "A Word for Women: Who Is Responsible for Foeticide," *Boston Daily Globe*, Sept. 10, 1869.

65 "Crimson Crimes," *Gold Hill Daily News* (Gold Hill, NV), Aug. 26, 1867.

66 Linda Gordon, *Woman's Body, Woman's Right: The History of Birth Control in America* (New York: Penguin Books, 1990), 101, 108; Lana F. Rakow and Cheris Kramarae, eds., *The Revolution in Words: Righting Women, 1868–1871* (New York: Routledge, 2001), 74.

67 "The Social Science Association," *New-York Tribune*, Oct. 12, 1867.

68 "Child Murder," *New-York Tribune*, Jan. 27, 1868; See also "Child Murder," *Harper's Weekly*, Jan. 8, 1868.

69 "State Legislature, Afternoon Session," *The Carson Daily Appeal* (Carson City, NV), Feb. 2, 1869.

70 "The Enemies of Society," *Gold Hill Daily News* (Gold Hill, NV), Sept. 10, 1867.

71 "The Anna Korp Case!" *Marshall County Republican* (Plymouth, IN), Feb. 17, 1870.

Chapter Two

THE REVOLUTION AND 'RESTELLISM'

1 "Various Items," *The Belvidere Standard* (Belvidere, IL), June 16, 1868; Untitled item, *The Muscatine Weekly Journal* (Muscatine, IA), June 12, 1868; "Mail Items," *Leavenworth Daily Commercial* (Leavenworth, KS), June 5, 1868.

2 Excerpt from the *Louisville Journal* published in the *Whig Standard* (Washington, DC), May 1, 1844; "Restellism in Boston," *The Baltimore Sun*, Apr. 3, 1848; "More Restellism," *The New Orleans Crescent*, July 19, 1848.

3 "Restellism the Crime of This Age: Man's Inhumanity to Woman, Makes Countless Infants Die," *The Revolution* (New York), May 7, 1868.

4 "The Great Social Issues; A Batch of Curious Waifs from the 'Revolution,'" *Chicago Tribune*, May 12, 1868; "'Restellism': The Curse of Modern Society," *The Tennessean* (Nashville, TN), May 19, 1868; "Restellism," *Deseret News* (Salt Lake City, UT), June 10, 1868.

5 "Working Woman's Association, Meeting to Protest Conviction of Hester Vaughan," *New York World*, Dec. 2, 1868.

6 Stacey M. Robertson, *Parker Pillsbury: Radical Abolitionist, Male Feminist* (Ithaca, NY: Cornell University Press, 2000), 140; Ellen Carol DuBois, *Feminism and Suffrage: The Emergence of an Independent Women's Movement in America, 1848–1869* (Ithaca, NY: Cornell University Press), 73–74.

7 It is likely that the other editors shared his view on this topic since, as Stacey Robertson notes, "when the editors disagreed, they publicly aired their differences and allowed the readers to decide for themselves" (Robertson, *Parker Pillsbury*, 145).

8 "Salutatory," *The Revolution* (New York), Jan. 6, 1868. For background on *The Revolution* and to further understand its significance, see Lana F. Rakow and Cheris Kramarae, eds., *The Revolution in Words: Righting Women, 1868–1871* (New York: Routledge, 2001).

9 DuBois, *Feminism and Suffrage*, 103.

10 "Salutatory," Jan. 6, 1868.

11 DuBois, *Feminism and Suffrage*, 176

12 "Salutatory," Jan. 6, 1868.

13 Stanton and Pillsbury had previous editorial experience, Stanton with *The Lily*, and Pillsbury with the *Anti-Slavery Standard*.

14 "We now recognize as racist some of the language, reasoning and stereotyping used in editorials by Stanton and Pillsbury.... their racism can be understood in the context of their cultural milieu; along with many others of their day, they believed in a progressive, evolutionary development of the human 'race.' Stanton, for example, sometimes referred to the 'lower orders of mankind,' an indication of her belief that education and 'civilization' were needed to bring groups of people (particularly American Blacks and white working-class immigrants) out of barbarism and to the pinnacle of development" (Rakow and Kramarae, eds., *The Revolution in Words*, 48).

15 E.C.S., "Infanticide and Prostitution," *The Revolution* (New York), Feb. 5, 1868.

16 For more on early women's rights advocates' understanding of the negative effects on women of the sexual double standard, see Aileen S. Kraditor, *Ideas of the Woman's Suffrage Movement* (New York: Columbia University Press, 1965), 112–15.

17 Unsigned editorial note, *The Revolution* (New York), June 18, 1868.

18 Matilda F. Gage, "Is Woman Her Own?" *The Revolution* (New York), Apr. 9, 1868.

19 "Child Murder," *The Revolution* (New York), Mar. 12, 1868.

20 "Child Murder," 1868; Untitled, *The Revolution* (New York), Nov. 19, 1868; "Restellism Rebuked," *The Revolution* (New York), Mar. 18, 1869.

21 For example, an 1859 article from the abolitionist paper *The Liberator* quoted a person discussing "child murder," and then explained "the practice of abortion, which is probably what Mr. R. meant." ("Child Murder," *The Liberator* [Boston], Apr. 8, 1859.) Also see Nicola Beisel and Tamara Kay, "Abortion, Race, and Gender in Nineteenth-Century America," *American Sociological Review* 69, no. 4 (Aug. 2004): 511: "Suffragists agreed with physicians about the moral status of abortion. Lumping abortion with infanticide, they referred to both as 'child murder.'"

22 "Infanticide," *The Revolution* (New York), Jan. 29, 1868.

23 "Child Murder," *New-York Tribune*, Jan. 27, 1868 (emphasis added).

24 "Child Murder," *New-York Tribune*, Jan. 27, 1868.

25 "Child Murder," *Harper's Weekly*, Feb. 8, 1868.

26 Mrs. J. Sumner, "Child Murder," *The Revolution* (New York), Feb. 12, 1868.

27 "Child Murder," *The Revolution* (New York), Mar. 12, 1868.

28 Conspirator, "Child Murder," *The Revolution* (New York), Apr. 9, 1868.

29 Unsigned editorial note, *The Revolution* (New York), May 28, 1868.

30 To this point, Matilda Joslyn Gage (1826–1898) had been moderately involved in the women's rights movement—she spoke at the National Woman's Rights Convention in September 1852—and in anti-slavery efforts. She would go on to help found the National Woman Suffrage Association and the New York State Woman Suffrage Association, and later the Woman's National Liberal Union, and would become an accomplished speaker and writer, as well as an editor of the first three volumes of the *History of Woman Suffrage*. For more on Gage, see Sally Roesch Wagner, *Matilda Joslyn Gage: She Who Holds the Sky* (Aberdeen, SD: Sky Carrier Press, 1998).

31 Matilda Joslyn Gage, "Is Woman Her Own?" *The Revolution* (New York), Apr. 9, 1868.

32 "Child Murder," *The Revolution* (New York), Mar. 12, 1868.

33 Linda Gordon, *Woman's Body, Woman's Right: Birth Control in America* (New York: Penguin Books, 1990), 114.

34 Jan Lewis described the late-eighteenth-century "Edenic vision of marriage": "Like republicanism itself, Edenic republican marriage presented itself as egalitarian. Republican characterizations of marriage echoed with the words *equal*, *mutual*, and *reciprocal*, and marriage was described as a friendship between equals.... Indeed, the mutuality and reciprocity that republicans so prized were in an asymmetrical union—the 'slavery' of so-called barbaric cultures, in which women were thoroughly subordinated to men." Jan Lewis, "The Republican Wife: Virtue and Seduction in the Early Republic," *The William and Mary Quarterly* 44, no. 4 (Oct. 1987): 707–8.

35 "Child Murder," *The Revolution* (New York), Mar. 12, 1868.

36 "Infanticide," *The Revolution* (New York), Jan. 29, 1868.

37 See Rakow and Kramarae, eds., *The Revolution in Words*, 190–92.

38 "What the People Say to Us," *The Revolution* (New York), May 14, 1868.

39 "Child Murder," *The Revolution* (New York), Mar. 12, 1868.

40 Julia Crouch, "Babies," *The Revolution* (New York), Oct. 29, 1868.

41 Parker Pillsbury, "Decision Diabolical!" *The Revolution* (New York), July 29, 1869.

42 "Sorosis," *New York World*, Jan. 5, 1869, published in *The Revolution* (New York), Jan. 21, 1869.

43 Robertson, *Parker Pillsbury*, 149.

44 Excerpt from the *Washington Star*, quoted in *The Revolution* (New York), Sept. 3, 1868. For more on Elizabeth L. Daniels, see Mary H. Blewett, *Men, Women, and Work: Class, Gender, and Protest in the New England Shoe Industry, 1780–1910* (Chicago: University of Illinois Press, 1990), 170.

45 Eleanor Kirk, "What Will Become of the Babies," *The Revolution* (New York), May 28, 1868.

46 For example, see: *The Leavenworth Times* (Leavenworth, KS), Oct. 4, 1864; *The Atchison Daily Free Press* (Atchison, KS), Sept. 5, 1867; "Female Suffrage at Atchison," *The Lawrence Tribune* (Lawrence, KS), Sept. 5, 1867; *The Junction City Weekly Union* (Junction City, KS), Oct. 5, 1867.

47 B. C., "The Social Evil," *The Revolution* (New York), April 16, 1868.

48 Mattie H. Brinkerhoff, "The Social Evil," *The Revolution* (New York), June 4, 1868.

49 A German [pseud.], "What the People Say," *The Revolution* (New York), June 24, 1869.

50 A German [pseud.], "What the People Say," June 24, 1869.

51 A German [pseud.], "What the People Say," June 24, 1869.

52 Editorial note appended to A German [pseud.], "What the People Say," June 24, 1869.

53 Mattie H. Brinkerhoff, "Woman and Motherhood," *The Revolution* (New York), Sept. 2, 1869.

54 Brinkerhoff, "Woman and Motherhood," Sept. 2, 1869.

55 Brinkerhoff, "What the People Say," Sept. 16, 1869.

56 Brinkerhoff, "What the People Say," Sept. 16, 1869.

57 The most significant research on Martha Brinkerhoff to date can be found in Louise R. Noun, *Strong-Minded Women: The Emergence of the Woman-Suffrage Movement in Iowa* (Ames, IA: Iowa State University Press, 1869), but it does not go beyond April 1869.

58 "The Idyl [sic] of Battle Creek: A Woman's Rights Lecturer Leaves Her Husband for an Affinity," *Rutland Weekly Herald* (Rutland, VT), May 13, 1873; *Democrat and Chronicle* (Rochester, NY), May 7, 1873.

"The new departure" was a reference to the suffrage strategy that, based on the Constitution's Fourteenth Amendment and the assumption that the right to vote was inherent in citizenship, argued that women were *already* guaranteed the right to vote. Developed in 1869, this strategy was quashed in 1875 with the Supreme Court's deciding in *Minor v. Happersett* that "the Constitution of the United States does not confer the right of suffrage upon anyone."

59 Brinkerhoff told her audience that "she loved Squiers and intended to marry Squiers, but had committed no immoral act with Squiers," whom she had described as "so infinitely above ordinary individuals, so much more grand, more divine, more appreciative than the mass around him," that no one but herself could fully value him. "The Idyl [sic] of Battle Creek: A Woman's Rights Lecturer Leaves Her Husband for an Affinity," *Rutland Weekly Herald* (Rutland, VT), May 13, 1873.

60 Mary Newbury Adams to Amelia Bloomer, quoted in Noun, *Strong-Minded Women*, 99n.

61 Elizabeth Cady Stanton, Susan B. Anthony, and Matilda Joslyn Gage, eds., *History of Woman Suffrage*, Vol. III (New York: National American Woman Suffrage Association, 1922), 614.

62 "Public opinion, then, flows out of these streams—out of classical literature, history, general reading, and the proverbial wisdom of all lands; out of social conventions, and customs and newspapers."

Caroline Wells Healey Dall, "How Public Opinion Is Made," *The College, the Market, and the Court, Or, Women's Relation to Education, Law, and Labor* (Boston: The Rumford Press, 1914), 51.

63 "The Revolution Will Advocate," *The Revolution* (New York), Jan. 8, 1868.

64 The statement of *The Revolution*'s goals appeared again, with its advertising policy formulated this way, in the following issue. It reappeared again in the newspaper's tenth issue, under the heading "The Revolution Will Discuss." By the beginning of the newspaper's second volume, the lengthy statement was pared down, but the advertising policy was only stripped of its jibe at other publications.

65 Modern scholarship on this question concurs with these explanations of the frequency of abortion advertising; James Mohr writes, "To document fully the pervasiveness of those open and obvious advertisements would probably require the citation of a substantial portion of the mass audience publications circulated in the United States around midcentury" (James C. Mohr, *Abortion in America: The Origins and Evolution of National Policy*, 1800–1900. [New York: Oxford University Press, 1978], 47). Also see Gordon, *Woman's Body, Woman's Right*, 53.

66 Horatio R. Storer, "Contributions to Obstetric Jurisprudence, No. 1, Criminal Abortion," *North American Medico-Chirurgical Review* (Jan. 1859), published in Horatio R. Storer, *On Criminal Abortion in America* (J. B. Lippincott & Co., 1860), 29.

67 "Foeticide—The Slaughter of the Innocents," *Chicago Tribune*, Mar. 17, 1867.

68 "Murder of the Unborn," *The Circular* (Oneida, NY), May 6, 1867.

69 Parker Pillsbury, "Quack Medicines," *The Revolution* (New York), Mar. 26, 1868.

70 Unsigned editorial, *The Revolution* (New York), Nov. 19, 1868.

71 "Address of Dr. E. L. Plympton," *Ashtabula Weekly Telegraph* (Ashtabula, OH), June 29, 1867.

72 Parker Pillsbury, "Quack Medicines," *The Revolution* (New York), Mar. 26, 1868.

73 Pillsbury, "Quack Medicines," Mar. 26, 1868.

74 Susan B. Anthony, "About Me and Mine," *The Revolution* (New York), May 26, 1870.

75 Anthony, "About Me and Mine," May 26, 1870.

76 Bullard was heir to the Mrs. Winslow's Soothing Syrup fortune.

77 See Rakow and Kramarae, eds., *The Revolution in Words*, 11; they agree on the fundamental continuity of *The Revolution*'s content under Anthony and Bullard's proprietorships.

78 "Thug Doctors" *The Revolution* (New York), Mar. 23, 1871; Also see "Social Sacraments," *The Revolution* (New York), Nov. 3, 1870, and "Sister Irene and the Little Foundlings," *The Revolution* (New York), Feb. 23, 1871.

79 "Thug Doctors," Mar. 23, 1871.

80 "Notes About Women," *The Revolution* (New York), Apr. 13, 1871.
"Keno and Faro banks" most likely refers to gambling establishments; Kano and Faro are gambling games. See "faro banks," Merriam-Webster.com.

81 "Thug Doctors," Mar. 23, 1871.

82 "Newspaper Responsibility," *The Revolution* (New York), Sept. 28, 1871.

Chapter Three

WOMEN'S ELEVATION AND THE MEDICAL PROFESSION

1 Helen Deese, ed., *Daughter of Boston: The Extraordinary Diary of a Nineteenth-Century Woman, Caroline Healey Dall* (Boston: Beacon Press, 2005), xxi, xvii.

2 Caroline Wells Healey Dall's journal entry for Feb. 23, 1869, Box 22, Folder 3, Caroline Wells Healey Dall papers, Massachusetts Historical Society, Boston, MA, microfilm, reel 29.

3 Mary Putnam Jacobi, "Woman in Medicine," published in Annie Nathan Meyer, ed., *Woman's Work in America* (New York: Henry Holt and Company, 1891), 182.

4 Horatio Storer, "Female Physicians," *The Boston Medical and Surgical Journal* 75 (1866): 192.

5 Agnes Vietor, ed., *A Woman's Quest: The Life of Marie E. Zakrzewska* (New York: Arno Press, 1972), 67.

6 Vietor, *A Woman's Quest*, 113.

7 Vietor, *A Woman's Quest*, 113.

8 "The Boston Lying-In Hospital," *Boston Medical and Surgical Journal* 54, no. 21 (June 28, 1855), 423–25.

9 Frederick N. Dyer, *Champion of Women and the Unborn: Horatio*

Robinson Storer, M.D. (Canton, MA: Science History Publications, 1999), 80–83.

10 "An Introductory Lecture..." *Boston Medical and Surgical Journal* 53, no. 20 (Dec. 13, 1855), published in J. V. C. Smith, M.D., W. W. Morland, M.D., and Francis Minot, M.D., eds., *The Boston Medical and Surgical Journal*, Vol. 53 (Boston: David Clapp, Publisher and Proprietor, 1856), 410.

11 "The Boston Lying-In Hospital," *Boston Medical and Surgical Journal* 54, no. 2 (Feb. 14, 1856): 46–47.

12 Arleen Marcia Tuchman, *Science Has No Sex: The Life of Marie Zakrzewska, M.D.* (Chapel Hill: The University of North Carolina Press, 2006), 80.

13 Emily Blackwell and Elizabeth Blackwell, *Address on the Medical Education of Women* (New York: Baptist & Taylor, 1864), 5.

14 Vietor, *A Woman's Quest*, 180.

15 Jacobi, "Woman in Medicine," in Myer, ed., 179.

16 Zakrzewska's addendum to this was "I may here remark that after many years of agitation, her infamous business succeeded in placing her and some of her disciples in prison, and, eventually, she killed herself by drowning in the spacious bathtub of the extravagantly luxurious house on Fifth Avenue, where she resided under her real name" (Vietor, *A Woman's Quest*, 180).

17 Elizabeth Blackwell, *Pioneer Work in Opening the Medical Profession to Women* (London: Longmans, Green and Co., 1895), 30.

18 Vietor, *A Woman's Quest*, 206.

19 *An Appeal in Behalf of the Medical Education of Women* (New York: 1856), 5.
Arleen Tuchman sees this document as, in part, positioned against female abortionists: the appeal's "reference to the 'ignorant' and 'unworthy' may have been a veiled criticism of unorthodox physicians.... However, they may also have been attacking female abortionists. Although they do not develop this point in their pamphlet, at other times Zakrzewska described abortionists, like the infamous Madame Restell, as the greatest threat to the reputation of women physicians" (Tuchman, *Science Has No Sex*, 81).

20 Vietor, *A Woman's Quest*, 213.

21 For a list of these articles, see Chapter 1, note 30; H.R.S., Review of W. F. Montgomery, *An Exposition of the Signs and Symptoms of Pregnancy; with Some Other Papers on Subjects Connected with Midwifery*, in *North American Medico-Chirurgical Review* 1, no. 2 (March 1857): 250.

22 *Eleventh Annual Report of the New-England Female Medical College* (Boston: published by the Trustees, 1860), 8.

23 Vietor, *A Woman's Quest*, 242.

24 *Eleventh Annual Report of the New-England Female Medical College*, 4.

25 *Twelfth Annual Report of the New-England Female Medical College* (Boston: published by the Trustees, 1861), 4.

Anita Tyng's grandmother, Sarah Higginson Tyng, and Thomas Wentworth Higginson's father, Stephen Higginson, were siblings, the children of Stephen Higginson (1743–1828), so Higginson was Tyng's first cousin once removed. See Thomas Wentworth Higginson, *Descendants of the Reverend Francis Higginson* (privately printed, 1910), 21–22, 26–29.

26 Tuchman, *Science Has No Sex*, 135.

27 Tuchman, *Science Has No Sex*, 154.

28 Comparison of 1862 and 1863 Annual Reports for the New England Female Medical College: *Fourteenth Annual Catalogue and Report of the New-England Female Medical College* (Boston: published by the Trustees, 1862); *Fifteenth Annual Catalogue and Report of the New-England Female Medical College* (Boston: published by the Trustees, 1863).

29 "An Act to Incorporate the New England Hospital for Women and Children," *Acts and Resolves Passed by the General Court of Massachusetts in the Year 1863* (Boston: Wright & Potter, 1863), 412.

30 "Annual Meeting of the 'Hospital for Women and Children,'" *The Liberator* (Boston), Nov. 14, 1862.

31 "Lecture on Hospitals," *The Liberator* (Boston), Jan. 30, 1863.

32 Vietor, *A Woman's Quest*, 310.

33 "Hospital for Women and Children," *The Liberator* (New York), Nov. 20, 1863.

34 Tuchman, *Science Has No Sex*, 201.

35 In her earlier work, Zakrzewska had found Tyng a "woman of talent" and "splendid in all mechanical work," and had placed her in charge of the New England Hospital after the resident physician resigned and she herself was forced to take time off for her health. (Vietor, ed., *A Woman's Quest*, 253, 309). *History of the New England Hospital for Women and Children* (Boston: George H. Ellis, 1899), 6; Ann Preston, *Valedictory Address to the Graduating Class of the Female Medical College of Pennsylvania at the Twelfth Annual Commencement* (Philadelphia: William S. Young, 1864), 2.

36 Storer, "Female Physicians," 192.

Anita Tyng graduated from the Philadelphia Women's Medical College in 1864. (Preston, *Valedictory Address*, 2.) When Tyng started working at the NEHWC as an Assistant Surgeon, she became the first woman appointed as a surgeon in a hospital in the United States, at the age of twenty-six. [Robert Baker, *Before Bioethics: A History of American Medical Ethics from Colonial Period to the Bioethics Revolution* (New York: Oxford University Press, 2013), 283.]

37 Ednah D. Cheney, "Report," *Annual Report of the New-England Hospital for Women and Children for the Year Ending Nov. 10, 1864* (Boston: Prentiss & Deland, 1865), 3–4.

38 Storer, "Female Physicians," 191.

39 Horatio R. Storer, "The Surgical Treatment of Amenorrhea," *Chicago Medical Examiner* 5, no. 1 (Jan. 1864). Amenorrhea is the "abnormal absence or suppression of menses" ("amenorrhea," Merriam-Webster.com).

40 Storer, "Surgical Treatment of Amenorrhea," 36.

41 Storer, "Surgical Treatment of Amenorrhea," 41. Here, Storer cites his March 1857 review of W. F. Montgomery's *An Exposition of the Signs and Symptoms of Pregnancy.*

42 Storer, "Surgical Treatment of Amenorrhea," 34.

43 "Minutes of the Fifteenth Annual Meeting of the American Medical Association, Held in the City of New York, June 7th, 8th, and 9th, 1864," *Transactions of the American Medical Association* 15 (Philadelphia: 1865): 50.

44 Horatio Robinson Storer, *Why Not? A Book for Every Woman* (Boston: Lee and Shepard, 1866), 71. Note that this did not mean that Storer didn't think they could be performed safely when necessary; cf. Gordon, *Woman's Body, Woman's Rights*, 52.

45 Storer, *Why Not?*, 75, 76.

46 Storer, *Why Not?*, 81.

47 Storer, *Why Not?*, 78.

48 Marie E. Zakrzewska, "Report of the Attending Physician," *Annual Report of the New-England Hospital for Women and Children, No. 14, Warren Street, for the Year Ending November 14, 1865* (Boston: Prentiss & Deland, 1865), 13.

49 M. E. Zakrzewska, "Report of the Attending Physician," *Annual Report of the New-England Hospital for Women and Children, No. 14,*

Warrenton Street, for the Year Ending Nov. 1, 1868 (Boston, Prentiss & Deland, 1868), 10.

50 Horatio Robinson Storer, *Successful Removal of the Uterus and Both Ovaries by Abdominal Section* (Boston: David Clapp & Son, 1866), 17.

51 Storer, *Successful Removal of the Uterus and Both Ovaries by Abdominal Section*, 17, 32.

52 Horatio Robinson Storer, "The Clamp Shield. An Instrument Designed to Lessen Certain Surgical Dangers, More Particularly Those of Extirpation of the Uterus by Abdominal Section," *The Transactions of the American Medical Association* 17 (Philadelphia: printed for the Association, 1866): 204–27.

53 Storer, "Clamp Shield," 204.

54 Horatio Robinson Storer, "A New Operation for Umbilical Hernia, with Remarks upon Exploratory Incisions of the Abdomen," *The Medical Record* 1 (Apr. 2, 1866): 73, 74.

55 "Extract from Records of Society for Medical Improvement," *Boston Medical and Surgical Journal* (July 15, 1858): 481, quoted in Storer, "A New Operation for Umbilical Hernia," 76.

56 "An assistant instructor in the Harvard Medical School, he [Horatio Storer] was dropped from his place in 1866, 'in order to do penance,' the faculty espousing a private quarrel into which he had been forced by three of his fellow-subordinates." "Salutatory by the Publishers," *The Journal of the Gynaecological Society of Boston* 1, no. 1 (July 1869), 9.

57 Lucy E. Sewall, "Report of the Resident Physician," *Annual Report of the New-England Hospital for Women and Children, No. 14, Warren Street, for the Year Ending November 1, 1866* (Boston: Prentiss & Deland, 1866), 14.

58 Ednah D. Cheney, "Report," *Annual Report of the New-England Hospital for Women and Children, No. 14, Warren Street, for the Year Ending November 1, 1866* (Boston: Prentiss & Deland, 1866), 10.

59 Storer, "Female Physicians," 191–92.

60 Storer, "Female Physicians," 191–92.

61 Storer, "Female Physicians," 191–92.

62 Cheney, "Report," 11.

63 In explaining that Storer's position had not yet been filled, Cheney noted that "surgical cases have been treated by the Resident and Attending Physicians and Assistant Surgeon, with the valuable aid of Dr. Samuel Cabot" (Cheney, *Annual Report of the New-England*

Hospital for Women and Children, No. 14, Warren Street, for the Year Ending November 1, 1866, 11).

64 Storer, "Female Physicians," 191.

65 *History and Description of the New-England Hospital for Women and Children* (Boston: 1876), 11.

66 Cheney, *Annual Report of the New-England Hospital for Women and Children, No. 14, Warren Street, for the Year Ending Nov. 1, 1866*, 11.

67 Dall was a founder of the American Social Science Association (ASSA), with Franklin Benjamin Sanborn and others. For more on her role in the ASSA, and the ASSA's relationship to suffrage and other women's rights issues, see Kathryn Wagnild Fuller's doctoral dissertation, *"Cool and Calm Inquiry": Women and the American Social Science Association, 1865–1890* (Indiana University, 2001).

68 Horatio Robinson Storer, *Is It I? A Book for Every Man. A Companion to Why Not? A Book for Every Woman.* (Boston: Lee and Shepard, 1867), 139.

This is not the only time Dall went on the record in favor of Storer, his position on abortion, and *Why Not?* See Caroline Dall, "The Christian Demand and the Public Opinion," *The College, the Market and the Court: Woman's Relation to Education, Labor and Law* (Boston: Lee and Shepard, 1868), 27.

69 "'Why Not? A Book for Every Woman': A Woman's View," *Boston Medical and Surgical Journal* (Nov. 1, 1866), published in Storer, *Is It I?*, 150.

Storer biographer Frederick Dyer suggests that this insistence on anesthesia as a preventive of abortion may indicate that Storer himself, or one of his friends, may have been the author of this letter: "The woman's letter so closely mimicked Horatio's view on use of chloroform during childbirth; the high and increasing frequency of criminal abortion; the agony of childbirth, 'akin to nothing else on earth;' and the unspeakable vice of holding fashion as god that it could have been written by Horatio himself. However, Horatio would later expressly deny any knowledge of who wrote it when he called attention to it in *Is It I?*" (Dyer, *Champion of Women and the Unborn*, 228).

70 Storer, *Is It I?*, 149.

71 Storer, *Is It I?*, 151.

72 Joanna Bourke, "Sexual Violation and Trauma in Historical Perspective," *ARBOR Ciencia, Pensamiento y Cultura* 186, no. 743 (2010), 407–16.

73 Storer, *Is It I?*, 152.

74 Storer, *Is It I?*, 153.

75 Storer, *Is It I?*, 154.

76 Storer, *Is It I?*, 12.

77 Storer, *Is It I?*, 12–13.

78 Storer, *Is It I?*, 89–90.

79 Storer, *Is It I?*, 108.

80 Storer, *Is It I?*, 94–95.

81 Storer, *Is It I?*, 117–18.

82 Henry Knowles Beecher and Mark D. Altchsule, *Medicine at Harvard: The First Three Hundred Years* (Hanover, NH: University Press of New England, 1877), 462.

83 "Matriculation of Women at Harvard Medical School," Harvard University Joint Committee on the Status of Women, n.d. George Cheyne Shattuck was the dean of the Harvard Medical School from 1864 to 1869.

84 Anita E. Tyng to Caroline Wells Healey Dall, June 18, 1870, Box 5, Folder 6, Caroline Wells Healey Dall papers, Massachusetts Historical Society, Boston, MA, microfilm; Anita E. Tyng to Caroline Wells Healey Dall, Oct. 11, 1872, Box 5, Folder 14, Caroline Wells Healey Dall papers, Massachusetts Historical Society, Boston, MA, microfilm.

85 Virginia G. Drachman, *Hospital with a Heart: Women Doctors and the Paradox of Separatism at the New England Hospital, 1862–1969* (Ithaca, NY: Cornell University Press, 1984), 67; Regina Morantz-Sanchez, *Sympathy and Science: Women Physicians in American Medicine* (New York: Oxford University Press, 1985), 148; Caroline Wells Healey Dall to Horatio Robinson Storer, Boston, Sept. 9, 1868, Box 22, Folder 3, Caroline Wells Healey Dall papers, Massachusetts Historical Society, Boston, MA, microfilm, reel 29; Marie E. Zakrzewska, "Report of Resident Physician," *Annual Report of the New-England Hospital for Women and Children, Codman Avenue, Boston Highlands, for the Year Ending September 30, 1875*, 2nd ed. (Boston: Press of W. L. Deland, 1876), 15–16.

86 Caroline Wells Healey Dall to Horatio Robinson Storer, Sept. 9, 1868, Massachusetts Historical Society.

87 Horatio Robinson Storer to Caroline Wells Healey Dall, Sept. 21, 1868, Hotel Pelham, Caroline Wells Healey Dall papers, Massachusetts Historical Society, Boston, MA, microfilm, reel 5.

88 George D. Hersey, "Anita E. Tyng, M.D.—An Appreciation," *The Providence Medical Journal* 17, no. 5 (Sept. 1916), 295.

89 Anita E. Tyng to Caroline Wells Healey Dall, Jan. 13, 1873, Box 5, Folder 15, Caroline Wells Healey Dall papers, Massachusetts Historical Society, Boston, MA, microfilm, reel 6.

90 "Woman's Suffrage," *The New York Times*, Oct. 27, 1870.

91 "Woman's Suffrage," *The New York Times*, Oct. 27, 1870.

92 Anita E. Tyng to Caroline Wells Healey Dall, Providence, Oct. 27, 1870, Box 5, Folder 10, Caroline Wells Healey Dall papers, Massachusetts Historical Society, Boston, MA, microfilm, reel 6.

93 Anita E. Tyng to Caroline Wells Healey Dall, Jan. 13, 1873, Massachusetts Historical Society.

94 Zakrzewska, "Report of Resident Physician," *Annual Report of the New-England Hospital for Women and Children, Codman Avenue, Boston Highlands, for the Year Ending Sept. 30, 1875*, 15–16.

95 Meyer, *Woman's Work in America*, v.

96 Tyng presented a paper on "Eclampsia Puerperalis" to the Society in 1874, a paper to the Alumnae Association of the Women's Medical College of Pennsylvania on "Dysmenorrhoaea" in 1880, and two more, "A Case of Haematocele" and "The Removal of Both Ovaries by Abdominal Section for the Relief of a Fibroid Tumor of the Uterus," to the Alumnae Association in 1881. The last article was published in the *American Journal of Medical Sciences*.

97 Anita E. Tyng, "On Causes of Ill Health Among Women," *Acts and Resolves Passed by the General Assembly of the State of Rhode Island and Providence Plantations at the May Session, 1878, and the Adjournment Thereof in June 1878* (Providence: E. L. Freeman & Co, 1878), 140–41.

98 Tyng, "On Causes of Ill Health," 138–39.

99 Tyng, "On Causes of Ill Health," 138.

100 Caroline Dall, "Diary when in Rhode Island," unspecified date between May 16 and June 14, 1870, Box 22, Folder 4, Caroline Wells Healey Dall papers, Massachusetts Historical Society, Boston, MA, quoted in Dyer, *Champion of Women and the Unborn*, 206.

101 Tyng, "On Causes of Ill Health," 139.

102 Tyng, "On Causes of Ill Health," 139.

103 Tyng, "On Causes of Ill Health," 142.

104 Tyng, "On Causes of Ill Health," 139.

105 Tyng, "On Causes of Ill Health," 138.

106 Tyng, "On Causes of Ill Health," 142.

107 Tyng, "On Causes of Ill Health," 140.

108 Tyng, "On Causes of Ill Health," 142, 140.

The "notion that harming a child's character was as pernicious as harming his or her body" was widely accepted at this time. [Susan J. Pearson, *The Rights of the Defenseless: Protecting Animals and Children in Gilded Age America* (Chicago: The University of Chicago Press, 2011), 95.]

109 Tyng, "On Causes of Ill Health," 139.

110 Tyng, "On Causes of Ill Health," 142, 138.

111 Tyng, "On Causes of Ill Health," 141.

112 Tyng, "On Causes of Ill Health," 142.

113 Tyng, "On Causes of Ill Health," 142.

114 Tyng, "On Causes of Ill Health," 141–42.

115 "Concerning Women," *Oxford Democrat* (Paris, ME), Aug. 8, 1882; *Transactions of the Twenty-Fifth Annual Meeting of the Alumnae Association of the Woman's Medical College of Pennsylvania* (Philadelphia: published by the Association, 1900), 103.

116 Tyng, "On Causes of Ill Health," 126.

117 Hersey, "Anita E. Tyng, M.D," 296.

118 "Pasadena Brevities," *The Los Angeles Times* (Los Angeles, CA), Jan. 13, 1895; Laura Jo Brunson and Kendall Brunson, *Legendary Locals of Jacksonville, Florida* (Charleston, SC: Legendary Locals, 2014), 55.

119 Hersey, "Anita E. Tyng, M.D," 297.

120 Anita E. Tyng to Caroline Wells Healey Dall, January 13, 1873, Massachusetts Historical Society.

Chapter Four

RESHAPING PUBLIC OPINION IN NEW YORK

1 Untitled article, Paulina Wright Davis, *The Revolution* (New York), Jan. 20, 1870.

2 This phrasing comes from a series of resolutions passed by the women's club Sorosis, as published in *The Revolution*, Jan. 14, 1869. If a legitimate child is one whose parents were legally married to each

other, perhaps it makes sense to refer to a "legalized" pregnancy, and conversely, to an "unlegalized" pregnancy in the case of the birth of an illegitimate child.

3 1850 U.S. Census, Suffolk County, Massachusetts, population schedule, Boston Ward 10, page 342b, dwelling 311, family 546, Henry Walmsley; NARA microfilm publication M432, roll 337.

4 Marriages Registered in the City of Boston for the Year 1851, Number 146, *Massachusetts Vital Records, 1911–1915*, New England Historic Genealogical Society, Boston, MA.

5 Deaths Registered in the City of Boston for the year 1854, page 65, number 2899, Clarence S. Densmore, *Massachusetts Vital Records, 1840-1911*, New England Historic Genealogical Society, Boston, MA; 1860 U.S. Census, Worcester County, Massachusetts, population schedule, Northborough, page 957, dwelling 813, family 1007, Daniel Densmore, Family History Library Film: 803528.

6 1860 U.S. Census, Worcester County, Massachusetts, population schedule, Northborough, page 957, dwelling 813, family 1007, Daniel Densmore, Family History Library Film: 803528.

7 *Fourteenth Annual Catalogue and Report of the New England Female Medical College* (Boston: Published by the Trustees, 1862), 7.

8 *Matriculation Book*, 18–19, Records of Women's Medical College of Pennsylvania Medical Students 1850–1981, Women Physicians 1850s–1970s, Drexel University College of Medicine Archives and Special Collections.

9 Clemence Lozier would become Charlotte's mother-in-law.

10 I. M. Ward, M.D., "First Annual Report of the New York Medical College for Women," in *Documents of the Assembly of the State of New York* (Albany: C. Wendell, 1865), 131.

The College's *Prospectus and Announcement* for the year 1863–64 had stated that "It will be wholly unsectarian, and no effort will be spared to earn for it a position of scientific value second to none in the world." (William Harvey King, ed., *History of Homoeopathy and Its Institutions in America*, Volume III (New York: The Lewis Publishing Company, 1905), 129.

11 John S. Haller, Jr., *The History of American Homeopathy: The Academic Years, 1820–1935* (New York: Pharmaceutical Products Press, 2005), 137–38.

12 Densmore graduated on March 1, 1865, and her husband died on April 30, 1865. Her daughter, Florence, was listed as one year old in

the 1860 census, which meant that she turned six in 1865. "Albert M. Densmore," Town and City Clerks of Massachusetts, Massachusetts Vital and Town Records, Provo, UT: Holbrook Research Institute (Jay and Delene Holbrook); Ward, M.D., "First Annual Report of the New York Medical College for Women," in *Documents of the Assembly of the State of New York* (Albany: C. Wendell, 1865), 131; 1860 U.S. Census, Worcester County, Massachusetts, population schedule, Northborough, page 957, dwelling 813, family 1007, Daniel Densmore, Family History Library Film: 803528.

13 "Dr. Densmore has been for some years professor of obstetric medicine to the New York College for Women, and has acquired a private practice that might be envied by the majority of our London physicians" ("American Lady Doctors," *Public Opinion* 12 no. 315 [Oct. 5, 1867], 387); "The Women's Parliament," *Demorest's Monthly Magazine* 7 (January 1870), 23.

14 1850 and 1860 census records list her father's occupation as "farmer." 1850 U.S. Census, Jackson, Michigan, population schedule, Napoleon, page 445a, dwelling 339, family 341, Jacob S. Denman, NARA microfilm publication M432, roll 352; 1860 U.S. Census, Winona, Minnesota, population schedule, Rollingstone, page 719, dwelling 92, family 90, Jacob S. Denman, Family History Library Film: 803576.

15 She was thirteen when her mother died (Cyrus D. Foss, "Memorial Address," *In Memoriam: Mrs. Charlotte Denman Lozier, M.D.* [New York: Wynkoop & Allenbeck, 1870], 7). Her father remarried in 1858, and had at least five more children, the youngest of whom would be born eight months after the birth of Charlotte's youngest ("Minnesota Marriages, 1849–1950," Index, FamilySearch, Salt Lake City, UT, 2009, 2010; Harriet Newell Harris, *Denman Family History: From the Earliest Authentic Records Down to the Present Time* [Glendale, CA: *The Glendale News*, 1913], 66). She attended the Minnesota State Normal School for its first year, and while she didn't graduate—its first graduation took place several years afterward—she participated in its first commencement ceremony in June 1861 (C. O. Ruggles, *Historical Sketch and Notes, Winona State Normal School, 1860–1910* [Winona, MN: Jones & Kroeger Co., 1910], 39).

16 Alida C. Avery, M.D., "A Christian Worker: The Lesson of Her Life, A Lecture Delivered at Vassar College," *In Memoriam*, 24.

17 "Charlotte Irene Denman," Indiana, Marriages, Salt Lake City, UT: FamilySearch, 2013.

18 "Wedded in Mourning," *Star-Gazette* (Elmira, NY), Jan. 16, 1896.

19 James J. Walsh, *History of Medicine in New York: Three Centuries of*

Medical Progress (New York: J. J. Little & Ives Co., 1919), 554.

20 Foss, "Memorial Address," *In Memoriam*, 8.

21 The announcement for its third year (1865–66) made this change clear, stating that the College was "the first and only one in the world where the law of '*similia*' is recognized as the only true guide in the administration of drugs." The New England Female Medical College was founded in Boston in 1848, and the Women's Medical College of Pennsylvania was founded in 1850 (King, *History of Homeopathy*, 129). "Similia Similibus Curentur," meaning "like treats like," is the principle guiding the practice of homeopathy. See Rafaella Aversa et al, "About Homeopathy or 'Similia Similibus Curentur,'" *American Journal of Engineering and Applied Sciences*, 9, no. 4 (2016): 1164–72; John Haller, *The History of American Homeopathy*, 138.

22 Walsh, *History of Medicine in New York*, 555.

23 She earned $209 in August 1866. *Internal Revenue Assessment Lists for Minnesota, 1862–1866*, Series: M774, Roll: 1, NARA, Washington, DC; Harris, *Denman Family History*, 66; Walsh, *History of Medicine in New York*, 554.

24 The Women's Medical College had been founded as a regular school in 1850 by a group of people who had "much zeal, but little knowledge," which led to the Philadelphia County Medical Society's refusal to recognize the college in 1860. But in 1862, when Emeline Horton Cleveland returned from her medical studies in Europe to become its "first adequate teacher," the college began to improve significantly. (Mary Putnam Jacobi, "Woman in Medicine," *Woman's Work in America*, 157–58.)

25 Charlotte Lozier was listed as a physician in the *Trow's New York City Directory* for 1867–1868, at the same street address given for her husband and mother-in-law. *Trow's New York City Directory, 1867–8* (New York: John F. Trow & Co.), 549.

26 Harriet Newell Harris, *Denman Family History*, 66; Walsh, *History of Medicine in New York*, 554; "Memorial Words," *The Woman's Advocate* 3, no. 2 (New York: February 1870).

27 Sarah Furnas Wells, "Women in Medicine and Their Colleges: An Address at the Opening Exercises of the Woman's Medical College of the Pacific Coast" (1885), 29n, Oberlin College Archives, 30/145, Box No. 2, Other Individuals, Dr. A. Clair Siddall, folder 1; King, *History of Homoeopathy*, 1; "Obituary," *New-York Tribune*, Jan. 4, 1870.

28 "Bunyan Hall," *The Revolution* (New York), Jan. 15, 1868.

29 "A Medical Lecture by Dr. Anna Densmore," *The New York Times*, Jan. 12, 1868.

Considering two anecdotal observations recorded by Elizabeth Blackwell and Horatio Storer makes it easier to understand the need for education around sexuality, pregnancy, and childbirth. Storer, in an article on the definition of consent in laws pertaining to rape, told the story of a thirty-year-old woman who was "of weak mind, but not imbecile," who had gone to see a physician. The doctor told her that she had "womb disease," and that it was absolutely necessary that he examine her—at which point he proceeded to rape her. She later testified that she "did not know what he did was anything more than a medical examination. She had no knowledge on the subject, and only became aware of the nature of the act on being confined" (Horatio R. Storer, "Art. III: The Law of Rape," *The Quarterly Journal of Psychological Medicine and Medical Jurisprudence* 2, no. 1 [Jan. 1868]: 51–52). This situation was not necessarily due to the woman's mental capacity; Blackwell reported that a "London lady of great intelligence and high social position" had told her, "You can hardly have an idea of the state of complete ignorance I was in, with regard to everything relating to the body, when I married! I knew there was some mystery connected with the relation into which I was entering, that I regarded with dread, and my distress for some time after marriage was very great. Before my first confinement, I suffered from the same want of knowledge, and looked forward with terror to the birth of my child" ("Speech: 'Anatomy,'" Elizabeth Blackwell Papers, 1836–1946, Box 59, Blackwell Family Papers, 1759–1960, Manuscript Division, Library of Congress, Washington, DC).

30 "A Medical Lecture by Dr. Anna Densmore," *The New York Times*, Jan. 12, 1868.

31 A Teacher, "Lectures of Dr. Anna Densmore," *The Revolution* (New York), Mar. 19, 1868.

32 A Teacher, "Lectures of Dr. Anna Densmore," Mar. 19, 1868.

33 A Teacher, "Lectures of Dr. Anna Densmore," Mar. 19, 1868.

34 A Teacher, "Lectures of Dr. Anna Densmore," Mar. 19, 1868.

35 A Teacher, "Lectures of Dr. Anna Densmore," Mar. 19, 1868.

36 It seems that physiological education was intended to decrease the incidence of abortion in two ways. First, as reported by *The Revolution*, it countered the prevalent notion that "the little being was devoid of life during all the earlier period of gestation," by proving that a fetus was a living, individual being before its existence could be proved with certitude. (A Teacher, "Lectures of Dr. Anna

Densmore," Mar. 19, 1868.) But such lectures by women's rights advocates may also have imparted the current, albeit only partially correct, scientific knowledge about women's relative fertility at different points in their menstrual cycles. This information would tend to allow a woman to choose to have sex at points in her cycle when she would be more or less likely to conceive—and therefore have a morally unproblematic way of delaying conception.

In her "Motherhood" essay in *Womanhood: Its Sanctities and Fidelities*, Isabella Beecher Hooker recommended that "modern science" be a key part of the education women should receive—specifically, the "present well-received theory of generation," that "God has set apart one portion of every month in a woman's life as sacred to motherhood," the fertility of which contrasted to "the comparative sterility of other days" (Hooker, *Womanhood*, 23). Hooker attributed the popularization of this knowledge to M. J. Michelet, despite his providing it "as a Frenchman must." Michelet's *L'Amour*, published in English in the United States in 1859, described this theory in more detail: "Each month the ovum matures, ruptures its envelope, and makes its way from the ovary to the matrix. . . . conception only takes place when the discharge announces the appearance of the ovum; that is to say, that it occurs during the courses, as well as a little before or a little after. Hence there is barrenness during a part of the month" [M. J. Michelet, *Love* (*L'Amour*), ed. J. W. Palmer (New York: Rudd & Carleton, 1859), 339]. While the theory cited by Michelet misidentifies what type of discharge indicates ovulation, further progress was being made on this topic. For example, while it appears that W. Tyler Smith similarly misunderstood menstruation as triggering ovulation, Smith argued that "the time when impregnation is most likely to take place" is "when . . . is cervix uteri is most empty, or when its contents are in the most fluid condition." [W. Tyler Smith, M.D., *Pathology and Treatment of Leucorrhoea* (London: John Churchill, 1860), 37]. This connection of ovulation (and therefore increased odds of conception) with cervical mucus is the basic insight upon which the Billings Ovulation Method of family planning—which debuted almost a hundred years later, in the mid 1950s—is based.

This sort of information had the potential to provide women with an ethical way of delaying pregnancy that did not require recourse to abortion. Of course, its efficacy was limited by the limited science of the time, and depended on the practice of voluntary motherhood. That physiological education had both moral and scientific content is underscored in the partial draft of an anatomy lecture written by Elizabeth Blackwell. In the lecture, Blackwell argued that by learning about the human body (and in particular, the reproductive system), her audience would gain not only a "clear understanding of the functions of these parts" but also insight into "the deep meaning hidden in this arrangement, and the noble life that should spring from it," because such knowledge would "enable us to deduce those rules of action, which will make life happier and holier." ("Speech: 'Anatomy,'" Elizabeth Blackwell Papers, 1836–1946, Box 59, Blackwell Family Papers, 1759–1960, Manuscript Division, Library of Congress, Washington, D.C.)

37 "The Social Evil: Lecture on the Subject by Dr. Charlotte Lozier," *The New York Times*, May 9, 1869.

38 "The Social Evil," May 9, 1869.

39 "The Social Evil," May 9, 1869.

Experts like Reese assumed that some number of stillbirths were the result of induced abortions, an assumption based on the unsophisticated methods used for most abortions at the time. A "criminally concealed" birth meant that a dead infant's body (stillbirth or neonatal death) had been buried or otherwise disposed of without reporting the birth and death to the authorities. It was a lesser charge than infanticide, reflecting the difficulty of securing a conviction for the latter. See "Concealment of Birth or Death," in David S. Garland and Lucius P. McGehee, eds., *The American and English Encyclopaedia of Law*, 2nd ed., Vol. 6 (Long Island: Edward Thompson Company, 1898), 424–30.

40 "The Social Evil," May 9, 1869.

41 "The Social Evil," May 9, 1869.

42 "The Social Evil," May 9, 1869.

43 "The Social Evil," May 9, 1869.

44 "The Social Evil," May 9, 1869.

45 "The Social Evil," May 9, 1869.

46 "Topics of To-Day," *Brooklyn Daily Eagle* (Brooklyn, NY), May 10, 1869.

47 "Without sharing in her anticipations of good from this source [legislators and women-physicians], we join with her in the hope that 'the great tidal wave of immorality which has so deluged the nation with crime is near the point when, like many other publicly recognized evils, its very enormity demands and will secure its abolishment.'" "Infanticide," *New York World*, published in *The Daily Evening Telegraph* (Philadelphia), June 16, 1869.

48 Charlotte Lozier's name was proposed for membership in Sorosis by Cecelia Burleigh, along with seven others, including Matilda Joslyn Gage. The names were voted on, and only two of the seven—excluding Lozier and Gage—were selected for admission. (Sorosis meeting minutes for May 3, May 17, and June 7, 1869, Box 1, Folder 1, Sorosis Records, Sophia Smith Collection, Smith College, Northampton, MA.)

49 For more on Sorosis's relation to the women's rights movement, see Karen J. Blair, *The Clubwoman as Feminist: True Womanhood Redefined, 1868–1914* (New York: Homes and Meier Publishers, 1980) and Anne Firor Scott, *Natural Allies: Women's Associations in American History* (Urbana, IL: University of Illinois Press, 1992).

50 Sorosis meeting minutes for March 31, 1868, Box 1, Folder 1, Sorosis Records, Sophia Smith Collection, Smith College, Northampton, MA.

51 The first meeting of Sorosis took place on March 31, 1868. Before its name was assumed with finality, "The Order of the Pen" was proposed but was criticized as "assuming too much," and "The Blue Stocking" was assumed—a reference to the late 1700s British literary society founded and led by women intellectuals. (Sorosis meeting minutes for March 31, 1868, Sorosis Records, Smith College.) But following objections to that name at the next meeting, Jane Cunningham Croly, the driving force behind the club's beginning, and Charlotte Beebe Wilbour suggested "Sorosis," which they explained meant "A botanical name for an order of fruits, which were produced from many flowers." This proposal eventually won out. (Sorosis meeting minutes for April 6, 1868, Box 1, Folder 1, Sorosis Records, Sophia Smith Collection, Smith College, Northampton, MA.)

52 Sorosis meeting minutes for June 22, 1868, Box 1, Folder 1, Sorosis Records, Sophia Smith Collection, Smith College, Northampton, MA.

53 "Sorosis," *The Revolution* (New York), Jan. 14, 1869.

On the deep relationship between spiritualism and women's rights, see Ann Braude, *Radical Spiritualism and Women's Rights in Nineteenth-Century America*, 2nd ed. (Bloomington: Indiana University Press, 1989, 2001).

54 "Sorosis," Jan. 14, 1869.

55 "Sorosis," Jan. 14, 1869.

56 "Sorosis," Jan. 14, 1869.

57 "Sorosis," Jan. 14, 1869.

58 "Sorosis," Jan. 14, 1869.

59 "Sorosis," Jan. 14, 1869. Charlotte Wilbour and Mary Cheney Greeley were among the committee's members.

60 "Sorosis," Jan. 14, 1869.

61 "The ability of these apparently compassionate people to turn their backs on foundlings, to, in a sense, doubly abandon them, marks them as bearers of a worldview that held that the fate of sinners and the very young was in the hands not of compassionate men and women but of God" [Julie Miller, *Abandoned: Foundlings in Nineteenth-Century New York City* (New York: New York University Press, 2008), 3].

62 Miller, *Abandoned*, 3–5.

63 Miller, *Abandoned*, 44–45.

64 Miller, *Abandoned*, 45.

65 *New York World*, Jan. 5, 1869, quoted in *The Revolution*, "Sorosis," Jan. 21, 1869. According to officialdata.org/us/inflation, $20 and $5 in 1868 dollars are roughly equivalent to $421 and $105 in 2023 dollars. The average weekly wage for unskilled labor in 1869 was $1.91. "The Wages of Unskilled Labor in the United States 1850–1900," *The Journal of Political Economy* 13 (June 1905), 363.

66 *New York World*, Jan. 5, 1869.

67 *New York World*, Jan. 5, 1869.

68 *New York World*, Jan. 5, 1869.

69 *New York World*, Jan. 5, 1869.

70 *New York World*, Jan. 5, 1869. In her report, Densmore described the ignorance that led unmarried pregnant women to seek abortions: "The poor unfortunate candidate for motherhood nearly always grasp[s] eagerly for this supposed immunity from guilt—in her ignorance thanking God that deliverance from tangible proof of her misfortune or sin came without bloodshed, and that she is free to recommence life without the dreaded millstone about her neck."

71 It would be interesting to know how, specifically, the women of Sorosis saw the relationship between these two topics. But aside from indicating that they arose around the same time, Sorosis's meeting minutes are silent on this topic.

72 It appears that Sorosis found a way to encourage philanthropic cooperation with the Workingwomen's Association, without going outside their mission: at the May 3, 1869, Sorosis meeting, "a vote of thanks as passed to Mrs. Phelps for her generous assistance to the cause of woman by aiding the Working Women's Association to procure a

house. The Corresponding Secretary was directed to forward a copy of said vote to Mrs. Phelps" (Sorosis meeting minutes for May 3, 1869, Box 1, Folder 1, Sorosis Records, Sophia Smith Collection, Smith College, Northampton, MA).

73 Sorosis meeting minutes for Feb. 8, 1869, Box 1, Folder 1, Sorosis Records, Sophia Smith Collection, Smith College, Northampton, MA.

74 *New York World*, Jan. 5, 1869.

75 Sorosis meeting minutes for May 17, 1869, Box 1, Folder 1, Sorosis Records, Sophia Smith Collection, Smith College, Northampton, MA.

76 Sorosis meeting minutes for May 17, 1869.

77 "The Social Evil," *The American Spiritualist* (Cleveland, OH), June 19, 1869.

78 "The Social Evil," June 19, 1869.

79 "The Social Evil," June 19, 1869.

80 "The Social Evil," June 19, 1869.

81 "The Social Evil," June 19, 1869.

82 Olive Logan, an actress who lectured on suffrage and contributed to *The Revolution*; Cora Hatch Tappan, a renowned Spiritualist medium; and Matilda Joslyn Gage, the radical abolitionist and women's right advocate, also spoke. (Sorosis meeting minutes for May 17, 1869, Sorosis Records, Smith College.)

83 Sorosis meeting minutes for May 17, 1869, Sorosis Records, Smith College; *Public Ledger* (Memphis, TN), Mar. 4, 1869; *Grass Valley Daily Ledger* (Grass Valley, CA), Mar. 27, 1869. This information was attributed to "Mrs. Dr. Lozier," who would have been either Charlotte Lozier or her mother-in-law.

84 Sorosis meeting minutes for Oct. 4, 1869, Box 1, Folder 1, Sorosis Records, Sophia Smith Collection, Smith College, Northampton, MA.

85 Jane Cunningham Croly, *The History of the Woman's Club Movement in America* (New York: Henry G. Allen & Co., 1898), 26.

On the history of these institutions, see Miller, *Abandoned*, and Maureen Fitzgerald, *Habits of Compassion: Irish Catholic Nuns and the Origins of New York's Welfare System, 1830–1920* (Urbana: University of Illinois Press, 2006).

86 The act incorporating the Association listed "Susan B. Anthony, Elizabeth Smith Miller, Mary Olmstead King, Martha Olmstead Loomis, Charlotte J. Lozier, Hannah Mac L. Shepard, Elizabeth C. Browne, Harriet Brewstre [sic], Eleanor Kirk, Cecilia Burleigh,

Sarah Frances Norton, Susan Johns and Augusta Lewis, and their successors" as incorporators and directors for the its first year. "An Act to Incorporate the Working Women's National Association, Passed April 19, 1869," *Laws of the State of New York Passed at the Ninety-Second Session of the Legislature*, Vol. 1 (Albany: C. Van Benthuysen & Sons, 1869), 462–64.

87 S.F.N., "To the Editors of The Ithacan," *The Ithacan* (New York), Apr. 16, 1869; "The Workingwomen," *New York World*, Oct. 7, 1868 in Patricia G. Holland and Ann D. Gordon, eds., *Papers of Elizabeth Cady Stanton and Susan B. Anthony* (Wilmington, DE: Scholarly Resources, Inc., 1991), microfilm, series 3, reel 13.

88 "Working-Women's Association," *New York World*, June 4, 1869, in Holland and Gordon, *Papers of Elizabeth Cady Stanton and Susan B. Anthony*.

The New York College referred to is probably the City College of New York, founded in 1849. In May 1869, Lozier referred to an opportunity created by the New York College's being without a president; the first president of the City College of New York stepped down during that year. Sydney C. Van Nort, *The City College of New York* (Charleston, SC: Arcadia Publishing, 2007), 12.

89 Alida C. Avery, M.D., "A Christian Worker: The Lesson of Her Life, A Lecture Delivered at Vassar College," *In Memoriam*, 24.

90 "Mrs. Dr. Charlotte Lozier," *New-York Tribune*, Jan. 5, 1870, published in *In Memoriam*, 21; "The Weekly Suffrage Meeting," *The Revolution* (New York), July 29, 1869.

Lozier was later remembered for, in a local campaign, successfully advocating for petition takers to register the names of men as well as women. She argued that "it would add strength to the request, for if distinguished men would sign it, their wives would also add their names and influence" ("The Weekly Suffrage Meeting," *The Revolution* [New York], July 29, 1869). It may be worth noting that while her proposal was well received, it is more characteristic of the Bostonian women's rights movement to suggest that it fully involve both sexes; New York suffrage advocates more often believed it should almost entirely be women for themselves. This, and Lozier's rejection from Sorosis, suggests that she was a bit of an outsider in New York women's rights crowds, despite her enthusiasm for the work. Having grown up in Minnesota and having divided her education between so many different schools probably meant that her approach to these issues wasn't particularly formed by any one group.

91 On Lozier's role in the nascent club's board of directors, see "The

Brooklyn Women's Club," *The Brooklyn Daily Eagle* (Brooklyn, NY), Jan. 7, 1870.

92 "A Peculiar Case," *New York Herald*, Nov. 22, 1869. Caroline's last name is given as Tulle, Tuller, and Fuller in various news reports from that time.

93 "Infanticide and Bribery," *New-York Daily Tribune*, Nov. 26, 1869.

94 "A Peculiar Case," *New York Herald*, Nov. 22, 1869. *The Revolution* later described it as an attempt to "procure an abortion." "Restellism Exposed," *The Revolution* (New York), Dec. 2, 1869; *Springfield Republican* (Springfield, MA), reprinted in *The Revolution* (New York), Dec. 2, 1869.

95 "Restellism Exposed," *The Revolution* (New York), Dec. 2, 1869.

96 "A Peculiar Case," Nov. 22, 1869.

97 "A Peculiar Case," Nov. 22, 1869.

98 "Infanticide and Bribery," *New-York Daily Tribune*, Nov. 26, 1869.

99 Lozier's youngest daughter, Jessie Charlotte Lozier, was born on Jan. 1, 1870. Assuming that Jessie was full-term when she was born, in late November 1869, her mother would have been roughly eight months pregnant. (Harris, *Denman Family History*, 66.)

100 "A Peculiar Case," Nov. 22, 1869.

101 "A Peculiar Case," Nov. 22, 1869.

102 "A Peculiar Case," Nov. 22, 1869.

103 "A Peculiar Case," Nov. 22, 1869.

104 "Infanticide and Bribery," *New-York Daily Tribune*, Nov. 26, 1869; "Restellism Exposed," *The Revolution* (New York), Dec. 2, 1869.

105 *New York World*, quoted in "Restellism Exposed."

106 *New York World*, quoted in "Restellism Exposed."

107 *New York World*, quoted in "Restellism Exposed."

108 "The Foundling Hospital," *New York Herald*, Nov. 23, 1869.

109 Miller, *Abandoned*, 145.

110 "The Foundling Hospital," Nov. 23, 1869.

111 The cause of death was given in the papers as "fever following childbirth"; census data shows her cause of death as peritonitis. "Personal Gossip," *Burlington Free Press* (Burlington, VT), Jan. 14, 1870; "Charlotte Lozier," New York State Education Department, Office of Cultural Education, Albany, New York; U.S. Census Mortality

Schedules, New York, 1850–1880, Archive Roll Number: M7, Census Year: 1870, Census Place: New York, New York.

112 "Resolutions by the Brooklyn Women's Club," *In Memoriam*, 32. The board of trustees and the students of the New York Medical College and Hospital for Women also passed resolutions on her death, as did the National Working Women's Association. "Resolutions: New York Medical College for Women," "Resolutions by the Students of the College," and "Resolutions by the National Working Women's Association," *In Memoriam*, 29–31.

113 Foss, "Memorial Address," *In Memoriam*, 9–10.

114 Frank Russell, "Address," *In Memoriam*, 12, 13.

115 "Whereas: The members of Sorosis hold in grateful remembrance and profound esteem, Dr. Charlotte J. Lozier for what she has done for the women of the nineteenth century; Resolved, That as a body we are deeply sensible of the loss sustained by ourselves and by the community at large, in the early and sudden death of one so gifted and beloved, That we grieve for the ever-widening field of influence which she so graced and honored, from which her loving nature and untiring energy are withdrawn, and for the profession around which her enthusiasm, intuition, and womanly grace throw a lasting halo, and in connection with which her name will long be lovingly remembered. Resolved, That we tender to the bereaved family our condolences and heartfelt sympathy in a sorrow which time alone can soften and God console." Sorosis meeting minutes for Jan. 3, 1870, Box 1, Folder 1, Sorosis Records, Sophia Smith Collection, Smith College, Northampton, MA.

116 Editorial note, *The Revolution* (New York), Jan. 6, 1870.

117 "Death of Mrs. Dr. Lozier," *Chicago Tribune*, Jan. 5, 1870. "This city" referred to New York City.

118 "Death of a Physician," *The Daily Phoenix* (Columbia, SC), Jan. 8, 1870.

119 *Home Journal*, January 12, 1870, published in *In Memoriam*, 17.

120 G., "From New York," *Evening Courier and Republic* (Buffalo, NY), Jan. 12, 1870.

121 Foss, "Memorial Address," *In Memoriam*, 9.

122 "Death of Mrs. Dr. Lozier," *Evening Journal* (Albany, NY), Jan. 5, 1870.

123 Paulina Wright Davis, *The Revolution* (New York), Jan. 20, 1870.

Chapter Five

DEATH OR DISHONOR: WOMEN'S RIGHTS, ECONOMIC INEQUALITY, AND THE SEXUAL DOUBLE STANDARD

1 "Topics of To-Day," *The Brooklyn Daily Eagle* (Brooklyn, NY), Dec. 7, 1868.

2 "Topics of To-Day," Dec. 7 1868.

3 "Hester Vaughan: Workingwomen's Meeting at Cooper Institute: A Plea for Mercy," *New York World*, Dec. 2, 1868, in Patricia G. Holland and Ann D. Gordon, eds., *Papers of Elizabeth Cady Stanton and Susan B. Anthony* (Wilmington, DE: Scholarly Resources, Inc., 1991), microfilm, series 3, reel 13.

4 Caroline Wells Healey Dall, "Death or Dishonor," *The College, the Market, and the Court* (Boston: The Rumford Press, 1914), 135.

5 Dall, "A Preface: To Be Read After the Book," *The College, the Market, and the Court*, xl; Dall, "Death or Dishonor," *The College, the Market, and the Court*, 144.

6 Dall, "Death or Dishonor," 140.

On Duchâtelet, see "A. J. B. Parent-Duchâtelet (1790–1835)," *Nature* 137, no. 732 (1936).

7 Dall, "Death or Dishonor," 134.

The phrase "the perishing classes" comes from a sermon given by Theodore Parker in 1846. Theodore Parker, "A Sermon of the Perishing Classes in Boston—Preached at the Melodeon, on Sunday, August 30, 1846," *Speeches, Addresses and Occasional Sermons*, Vol. 1 (Boston: Horace B. Fuller, 1867), 186–225.

8 Dall, "Death or Dishonor," 142.

9 Dall, "Death or Dishonor," 149.

10 In *The Ideas of the Woman Suffrage Movement*, Aileen Kraditor says that many unwed mothers also faced this choice. Aileen S. Kraditor, *The Ideas of the Woman Suffrage Movement* (New York: W. W. Norton & Company, 1981), 107.

11 Ellen Carol DuBois says that *The Revolution*'s "commitment to and faith in the poor tended to be idealized and romantic." Ellen Carol DuBois, *Feminism and Suffrage: The Emergence of an Independent Women's Movement in America, 1848–1869* (Ithaca, NY: Cornell University Press), 119.

12 "Women living with a man's support were not so adversely affected, but single women and their dependents could suffer terribly. Women's charities and urban writers reacted to this situation by absorbing the figure

of the seamstress into the traditional category of the 'worthy' poor. Like other philanthropic constructions, the sentimental seamstress, solitary, pallid and timid, embodied bourgeois aspirations and prejudices, but there can be no doubt she also represented, however distortedly, real situations." Christine Stansell, *City of Women: Sex and Class in New York, 1789–1860* (New York: Alfred A. Knopf, 1986), 110.

13 Lori Mersin, "Representing the 'Deserving Poor': The 'Sentimental Seamstress' and the Feminization of Poverty in Antebellum America," in *Our Sisters' Keepers: Nineteenth-Century Benevolence Literature by American Women*, ed. Jill Bergman and Debra Bernardi (Tuscaloosa: University of Alabama Press, 2005), 50–52, 60–61. DuBois also discusses the "sexual division of labor" in the labor market. (Dubois, *Feminism and Suffrage*, p. 126–28.)

14 Mersin, "Representing the 'Deserving Poor,'" 59.

15 DuBois, *Feminism and Suffrage*, 136.

16 Mersin, "Representing the 'Deserving Poor,'" 60–69; Stansell, *City of Women*, 68–75.

17 DuBois argues that for suffragists, "the representative working women was the statistically insignificant skilled worker, whose craft opened up to her the possibility of honorable independence and equality with men" (DuBois, *Feminism and Suffrage*, 137). Nevertheless, *The Revolution* did attend to the plight of seamstresses and embroiderers.

18 M.C.B., "Female Compositors," *The Revolution* (New York), Mar. 19, 1868. Compositors arranged type for printing machines in printing shops.

19 Tupto, "The Working Women of New York: Article II," *The Revolution* (New York), Feb. 26, 1868, 4–5. The pseudonym "Tupto" was a Greek verb often used as an example of conjunction in Greek textbooks, meaning "I strike." [For example, see Richard Grant White, "The Grammarless Tongue: A Chapter of 'Words and Their Uses,'" *The Galaxy* 7 no. 3 (Feb. 1869), 268–69.]

To learn more about the store "Tupto" might have been discussing (and more about *The Revolution*'s critiques of the burdens facing workingwomen in New York City), see Deborah S. Gardner, "'A Paradise of Fashion,' A. T. Stewart's Department Store, 1861–1875," in *A Needle, a Bobbin, a Strike*, ed. Joan Jenson and Sue Davidson (Philadelphia: Temple University Press, 1984).

20 Tupto, "The Working Women of New York," 4–5.

21 Tupto, "The Working Women of New York," 4–5.

22 Tupto, "The Working Women of New York," 4–5.

23 Tupto, "The Working Women of New York," 4–5.

24 "The Working Women of New York," *The Revolution* (New York), Feb. 19, 1868.

25 "The Working Women of New York," Feb. 19, 1868.

26 Stansell, *City of Women*, 111.

27 H.M.S., "A Plea," *The Revolution* (New York), Feb. 26, 1868.

28 It may be worth noting that a Hannah Mac L. Shepard was listed among the incorporators of the eventual Working Women's National Association. "An Act to Incorporate the Working Women's National Association, Passed April 19, 1869," *Laws of the State of New York*, 462–64.

29 Miss H. M. Shepard, "Experiences," *The Revolution* (New York), Apr. 23, 1868.

30 Shepard, "Experiences," Apr. 23, 1868.

31 Shepard, "Experiences," Apr. 23, 1868.

32 "Female Compositors," Mar. 19, 1868.

33 L., "Life and Death by the Needle," *The Revolution* (New York), Apr. 9, 1868.

34 Eleanor Kirk, "A Word to Our Sewing Girls," *The Revolution* (New York), June 11, 1868; William Wirt Sikes, "Among the Poor Girls," *Putnam's Magazine* 1, no. 4 (April 1868), 432–43, published in *Putnam's Magazine: Original Papers on Nature, Science, Art, and National Interests*, Vol. 1 (New York: G. P. Putnam & Son, 1868).

Eleanor Kirk was the pen name used by Eleanor Maria Easterbrook Ames (1831–1908). A prolific author near the beginning of her career in 1868, she was motivated by very tangible concerns: "Her first literary work was done in the early sixties, when she was left a widow with children to support. She secured a position as reporter and special writer, paid at space rates, on the old New York Standard.... She covered every sort of assignment, by day and by night, and gained a wide experience which helped her in later years. Her children were entirely dependent upon her and while she had a severe struggle at first, she managed to bring them up and educate them all well by the work of her pen. She soon branched out into magazine work and wrote many stories and poems." "'Eleanor Kirk' Dead at Rhode Island Home," *The Brooklyn Daily Eagle*, June 25, 1908.

35 Sikes, "Among the Poor Girls," 442–43.

36 Sikes, "Among the Poor Girls," 443.

37 Sikes, "Among the Poor Girls," 443.

38 "Table Talk," *Putnam's Magazine* 1, no. 5 (May 1868), 647. Published in *Putnam's Magazine: Original Papers on Nature, Science, Art, and National Interests*, Vol. 1 (New York: G. P. Putnam & Son, 1868).

39 Kirk, "A Word to Our Sewing Girls," June 11, 1868.

These suggestions that seamstresses should enter domestic work, though well intentioned, also unjustly suggested women avoided such work out of misplaced pride. However, the "light exercise" Kirk referred to was likely to be long hours of hard manual labor such as laundry and ironing. Live-in work demanded nearly every moment of a woman's time, not merely being on-call in the middle of night, but very early hours. Employers often resented women asking for time to attend church on Sundays, especially if the church happened to be a Catholic one. Domestics were expected to rearrange their schedule at the whims of their employers and were often not permitted to entertain guests. In short, such employment was not only difficult for anyone not young and in good health, but almost impossible for a woman with dependents, and it deprived even single women of time for socialization or even generally lauded activities such as churchgoing or cultural activities. Finally, domestic work was not free from the failure to pay just wages. On the experience of domestics, see, for example: Faye Dudden, *Serving Women: Household Service in Nineteenth-Century America* (Middletown, CT: Wesleyan University Press, 1983); Stansell, *City of Women* (especially Chapter 8); and Vanessa H. May, *Unprotected Labor: Household Workers, Politics, and Middle-Class Reform in New York, 1870–1940* (Chapel Hill: University of North Carolina Press, 2011.

40 Kirk, "A Word to Our Sewing Girls," June 11, 1868.

41 In November 1863, hundreds of workingwomen had formed the Working Women's Union to advocate for shortened work days and better pay. The men involved in the union's founding, however, had quickly overtaken its leadership and made it clear that there would be no strikes; the union would "'secure legal protection from fraud,' 'appeal respectfully...to employers' for higher wages and shorter hours, and create a registry for unemployed women." By December 1863, the name of the organization changed to the Working Women's Protective Union of the City of New York. While it was effective at its male-defined aims, its paternalistic stature denied women's agency. Felice Batlan, "The Birth of Legal Aid: Gender Ideologies, Women, and the Bar in New York City, 1863–1910," *Law and*

History Review 28, no. 4 (2010): 935–36.

42 "New Yorkisms," *The Evening Telegraph* (Philadelphia, PA), Sept. 19, 1868.

43 "New Yorkisms," Sept. 19, 1868.

44 Kraditor, *The Ideas of the Woman Suffrage Movement*, 260–61.

45 "The Sewing Women," *The Revolution*, Aug. 20, 1868. It appears that Stanton was trying to set up separate "women's suffrage" and "workingwomen's suffrage" associations. On the dominance of suffrage in the women's rights movement in the post-war years, see Lisa Tetrault, *The Myth of Seneca Falls: Memory and the Women's Suffrage Movement, 1848–1898* (Chapel Hill: University of North Carolina Press, 2014).

46 DuBois, *Feminism and Suffrage*, 128.

47 Susan B. Anthony to Friends, Aug. 30, 1869, Papers of Susan B. Anthony, Vassar College Library, Poughkeepsie, in Holland and Gordon, *Papers of Elizabeth Cady Stanton and Susan B. Anthony*.

Aileen Kraditor acknowledges that this was not unusual for the suffrage pioneers; "To Mrs. Stanton, etc.... it [suffrage] was never more than a means toward woman's all-around development or toward social regeneration" (Kraditor, *The Ideas of the Woman Suffrage Movement*, 261).

48 "Workingwomen's Association: From the N.Y. Times," *The Revolution* (New York), Sept. 24, 1868. Also see Anne Firor-Scott, *Natural Allies: Women's Associations in American History* (Urbana, IL: University of Illinois Press, 1993), 4, and DuBois, *Feminism and Suffrage*, 134.

49 "Workingwoman's Association, *New York World*, Sep. 22, 1868, in Holland and Gordon, *Papers of Elizabeth Cady Stanton and Susan B. Anthony.*

In 1978, DuBois wrote, "Almost nothing is known about Emily Peers, who like most nineteenth century women labor leaders briefly rose into prominence and then disappeared into the masses of working women" (DuBois, *Feminism and Suffrage*, 134). Though more than four decades have passed, still little can be discovered about Peers outside of her involvement with the Workingwomen's Association.

50 See, for example, "News of the Day: General," *The New York Times*, Sept. 22, 1868.

51 *New York World*, published in "Workingwomen's Association, No. 2: Meeting at the Workingwomen's Home," *The Revolution* (New York), Oct. 1, 1868.

52 Robert Fitts argues that "literature produced by 19th-century mission-

aries and moral reformers helped myths…[in which] the Five Points symbolized the immorality of urban life and was used to show middle-class readers the importance of their own ideology of domesticity." Robert Fitts, "The Rhetoric of Reform: The Five Points Missions and the Cult of Domesticity," *Historical Archaeology* 35, no. 3 (2001): 115.

53 Henry Julius Cammann and Hugh N. Camp, *The Charities of New York, Brooklyn, and Staten Island* (New York: Hurd and Houghton, 1868), 489.

54 Cammann and Camp, *The Charities of New York, Brooklyn, and Staten Island*, 489. Similar efforts were being made in Boston around the same time; for example, see Firor Scott, *Natural Allies*, 114, on the School of Horticulture.

55 *New York World*, Oct. 1, 1868.

56 DuBois, *Feminism and Suffrage*, 21–22.

57 *New York World*, Oct. 1, 1868.

58 "The Workingwomen," *New York World*, Oct. 7, 1868, in Holland and Gordon, *Papers of Elizabeth Cady Stanton and Susan B. Anthony.*

59 "The Workingwomen," Oct. 7, 1868.

60 An average daily wage of $1 works out to a weekly wage of $7. (These amounts are roughly equivalent to $22 and $154 in 2023 dollars, according to officialdata.org/us/inflation.) For contrast, in 1869, Aurora Phelps estimated that "only about one-fourth of the working women of Boston worked by the week, and that of these only about one-tenth received over $3 a week.…Another speaker, however, said that…the average…[was] $3 a week" (Helen L. Sumner, *Report on Condition of Woman and Child Wage-Earners in the United States*, Vol. 9, *History of Women in Industry in the United States* [Washington, DC: Government Printing Office, 1910], 148–49). $3 in 1869 dollars is roughly equivalent to $66 in 2023 dollars, according to officialdata.org/us/inflation. ("The Workingwomen," Oct. 7, 1868.)

61 "The Workingwomen," Oct. 7, 1868.

62 "The Workingwomen," Oct. 7, 1868.

63 "The Workingwomen," Oct. 7, 1868; "Meeting of the Workingwomen," *New-York Tribune*, Oct. 7, 1868, in Holland and Gordon, *Papers of Elizabeth Cady Stanton and Susan B. Anthony*.

64 "Workingwomen's Association," *The Revolution* (New York), Nov. 5, 1868.

During the previous month, officers of the Workingwomen's association had approached Charlotte Wilbour, one of the founding members of Sorosis and a firm supporter of suffrage, to ask whether "Sorosis would assist in the formation of one consolidated association of Working Women" (Sorosis meeting minutes for Oct. 12, 1868, Box 1, Folder 1, Sorosis Records, Sophia Smith Collection, Smith College, Northampton, MA). While the proposal prompted vigorous discussion "upon the claims of working women and of women who employed them," and a committee was appointed to look into the matter, it was soon decided that "Sorosis could not, as an association, assume the care, or management of the association of Working Women" (Sorosis meeting minutes for Oct. 12 and Nov. 2, 1868, Box 1, Folder 1, Sorosis Records, Sophia Smith Collection, Smith College, Northampton, MA). Nevertheless, Charlotte Wilbour, on her own initiative, attended the meeting called by Anthony, and was elected to a committee to draft a constitution and by-laws. "Workingwomen's Association," *The Revolution* (New York), Nov. 5, 1868.

65 "Workingwomen's Association," Nov. 5, 1868.

66 "Workingwomen's Association," Nov. 5, 1868.

67 "General News," *The Burlington Free Press* (Burlington, VT), Nov. 9, 1868; "Anna E. Dickinson in Cooper Institute," *The Revolution* (New York), Nov. 12, 1868.

This appears to be the first time that Dickinson gave this lecture; she continued giving it around the country. See, for example, "'A Struggle for Life': Miss Anna Dickinson's Lecture Last Night," *The Daily Pantagraph* (Bloomington, IL), Mar. 6, 1869; "Lecture To-Night," *Daily Evening Herald* (Stockton, CA), Aug. 24, 1869.

68 "Hester Vaughan: Workingwomen's Meeting at Cooper Institute: A Plea for Mercy," *New York World*, Dec. 2, 1868, in Holland and Gordon, *Papers of Elizabeth Cady Stanton and Susan B. Anthony*.

69 "Legal Intelligence: Court of Oyer and Terminer—Judges Ludlow and Brewster," *The Philadelphia Inquirer*, July 1, 1868.

The court of oyer and terminer had jurisdiction over criminal cases. ("oyer and terminer," Merriam-Webster.com.)

70 "Legal Intelligence," July 1, 1868.

A post-mortem examination found that Rose Solomon's infant's lungs floated, and this was taken as evidence that the infant had breathed on its own. It should be noted that this test was later discovered to be unreliable, because "postmortem gas formation due to decomposition will keep a piece of lung afloat even if breathing did not occur," and "In certain situations, the live born, breathing neonate will have lungs that do not float." Werner E. Spitz and Daniel J. Spitz, *Spitz and Fisher's Medicolegal Investigation of Death: Guidelines for the Application of Pathology to Crime Investigation*, 4th ed. (Springfield, IL: Charles C Thomas, Publisher, Ltd., 2006), 347.

71 "Legal Intelligence," July 1, 1868.

72 "Legal Intelligence," July 1, 1868.

73 Defendants in criminal cases were not allowed to testify, per the then-unchallenged common law. See Robert Popper, "History and Development of the Accused's Right to Testify," *Washington University Law Review* 1962, no. 4 (Jan.); "Legal Intelligence: Court of Oyer and Terminer—Judges Ludlow and Brewster—Infanticide," *The Philadelphia Inquirer*, July 2, 1868.

74 In Pennsylvania, concealing the death of an infant who, if born alive would have been illegitimate, was a crime punishable by imprisonment of up to three years. See W. Logan McCoy, "The Law of Pennsylvania Relating to Illegitimacy," *Journal of Criminal Law and Criminology* 7, no. 2 (1917): 511. The provision was part of the Act of March 31, 1860, P. L. 397 §§87, 88, 89.

75 "Legal Intelligence," July 2, 1868.

76 "Infanticide," *The Revolution* (New York), August 6, 1868.

77 "Legal Intelligence," July 2, 1868.

78 "Infanticide," August 6, 1868.

79 "Infanticide," August 6, 1868.

80 This description of the *Press* article comes from the "Hester Vaughn" article in *The Revolution*; per the Library of America's *Chronicling America* project, it appears that there are no extant copies of this edition of *The Press* in the United States. See "Libraries That Have It: The Press. [Volume] (Philadelphia [PA]) 1857–1880," *Chronicling America: Historic American Newspapers*.

81 M, "Hester Vaughan," *The Revolution* (New York), Sept. 17, 1868. For more on the analogy of womanhood with slavery, see Ana Stevenson, *The Woman as Slave in Nineteenth Century American Social Movements*, (New York: Palgrave Macmillan, 2019).

82 M, "Hester Vaughan," Sept. 17, 1868.

83 For a discussion of the connections between the Garner case and the Hester Vaughan trial, see Keira V. Williams, "Feminism, Infanticide, and Intersectionality in Victorian America," in *Bad Mothers: Regulations, Representations, and Resistance*, ed. Michelle Hughes Miller, Tamar Hager, and Rebecca Jaremko Bromwich (Ontario, Canada: Demeter Press, 2017).

84 Levi Coffin, *Reminiscences of Levi Coffin* (Cincinnati: Robert Clarke & Company, 1880), 565. See Caroline Winterer, *The Mirror of Antiquity: American Women and the Classical Tradition, 1850–1900* (Ithaca, NY: Cornell University Press, 2007), 186–87, on the abolitionist press's casting of Garner as a classical heroine in the mode of a Roman matron, or Virginius (a Roman man), or Medea.

85 E.C.S., "Hester Vaughan," *The Revolution* (New York), Nov. 19, 1868.

86 E.C.S., "Hester Vaughan," Nov. 19, 1868.

87 E.C.S., "Hester Vaughan," Nov. 19, 1868.

88 "Workingwoman's Association," *The New York Times*, Nov. 24, 1868, in Holland and Gordon, *Papers of Elizabeth Cady Stanton and Susan B. Anthony.*

89 "Hester Vaughan: Workingwomen's Meeting at Cooper Institute: A Plea for Mercy," *New York World*, Dec. 2, 1868, in Holland and Gordon, *Papers of Elizabeth Cady Stanton and Susan B. Anthony*.

This was not the only mass meeting organized by the *Revolution*'s staff—one was organized related to the McFarland trial, and there were others.

90 "The Case of Hester Vaughan," *The Revolution* (New York), Dec. 10, 1868.

91 Since Charlotte Lozier had been identified by her first name in the beginning of this article, and because she was serving as secretary, and none of the other speakers was an officer of the meeting, it seems likely that this refers to Charlotte's mother-in-law. Since both women were involved with the Workingwomen's Association, it makes sense that both of them would be involved in advocacy for Hester Vaughn.

92 Anthony would later say, "If nothing else had been done [by the Workingwomen's Association] besides that of bringing Eleanor Kirk to the surface and developing her powers, they had accomplished a noble and praiseworthy work" ("The Workingwoman's Association," *New-York Tribune* [New York], May 28, 1869, in Holland and Gordon, *Papers of Elizabeth Cady Stanton and Susan B. Anthony*). This episode in particular shows Anthony engaged in the kind of work that Mary Kelley describes in *Learning to Stand and Speak*. While Kelley's book looks earlier, here Anthony is engaged in a similar—and conscious—effort in a very different setting. Mary Kelley, *Learning to Stand and Speak: Women, Education, and Public Life in America's Republic* (Chapel Hill: Omohundro Institute and University of North Carolina Press, 2012.)

93 "Hester Vaughan: Workingwomen's Meeting at Cooper Institute:

A Plea for Mercy," *New York World*, Dec. 2, 1868, in Holland and Gordon, *Papers of Elizabeth Cady Stanton and Susan B. Anthony*.

94 "The Case of Hester Vaughan," *The Revolution* (New York), Dec. 10, 1868.

95 "Hester Vaughan," *New York World*, Dec. 2, 1868.

96 "Hester Vaughan," Dec. 2, 1868.

97 "Hester Vaughan," Dec. 2, 1868.

98 On "seduction" as code for "rape," see Estelle B. Freedman, *Redefining Rape* (Cambridge: Harvard University Press, 2013). Chapter 2 covers the "The Crime of Seduction," and Freedman discusses Vaughn in chapter 3.

99 "Hester Vaughan," Dec. 2, 1868.

100 On puerperal mania, see I. Loudon, "Puerperal Insanity in the 19th Century," *Journal of the Royal Society of Medicine* 81 (Feb. 1988). On postpartum blindness, see Kimberly A. Chambers and Terry Wayne Cain, "Postpartum Blindness: Two Cases," *Annals of Emergency Medicine* 43, no. 2 (Feb. 1, 2004): 243–46.

101 "The Case of Hester Vaughan," *The Revolution* (New York), Dec. 10, 1868.

102 "The Case of Hester Vaughan," Dec. 10, 1868.

103 *New York World*, Dec. 1, 1868, quoted in "Hester Vaughn," *The Evening Telegraph* (Philadelphia, PA), Dec. 2, 1868.

104 "Hester Vaughan: Workingwomen's Meeting at Cooper Institute: A Plea for Mercy," *New York World*, Dec. 2, 1868, in Holland and Gordon, *Papers of Elizabeth Cady Stanton and Susan B. Anthony*.

105 "Hester Vaughan," Dec. 2, 1868.

106 "Hester Vaughan," Dec. 2, 1868.

107 "Workingwomen's Association," *The New York Times*, Dec. 22, 1868, in Holland and Gordon, *Papers of Elizabeth Cady Stanton and Susan B. Anthony*.

108 "Workingwomen's Association," Dec. 22, 1868.

109 "The Workingwoman's Association," *New-York Tribune*, May 28, 1869, in Holland and Gordon, *Papers of Elizabeth Cady Stanton and Susan B. Anthony.*

110 "The Workingwoman's Association," May 28, 1869.

111 E.C.S., "Hester Vaughan," *The Revolution* (New York), Dec. 10, 1868.

112 P.P., "The Hester Vaughan Meeting at Cooper Institute," *The Revolution* (New York), Dec. 10, 1868.

113 "Suffrage: The Movement in Favor of an Extension of the Elective Franchise: Two Conventions Yesterday," *Chicago Times*, Feb. 12, 1869, in Holland and Gordon, *Papers of Elizabeth Cady Stanton and Susan B. Anthony*.

114 "Workingwomen's Association," *New York World*, May 20, 1869, in Holland and Gordon, *Papers of Elizabeth Cady Stanton and Susan B. Anthony.*

Sarah Frances (Rice) Norton (*ca.* 1838–1910) was a writer and novelist. She was introduced as a "new lecturer" in *The Revolution*, but later broke with the suffrage movement—giving a lecture on "the humbug of woman suffrage." Nevertheless she was more radical than the majority of women's rights advocates in speaking and writing against marriage: "The inequality of woman finds its origin in marriage. To make political equality possible to her, social equality of the sexes must precede it; and as marriage is the back-bone of social life as at present constituted, the back-bone of social life must be broken." "A New Lecturer," *The Revolution* (New York), Oct. 22, 1868; "Letter from New York," *San Francisco Examiner*, Nov. 28, 1871; "Sarah Frances Rice Norton," *Find a Grave*, Memorial ID: 170181001; "CPT Norris Randall Norton," *Find a Grave*, Memorial ID: 163165994; Sarah F. Norton quoted in Justitia, "Thoughts on Marriage by Leading Thinkers," *Woodhull & Claflin's Weekly* (New York), Dec. 17, 1870.

115 "The Workingwoman's Association," *The New York Times*, May 20, 1869.

116 "Workingwomen's Association," *New York World*, May 20, 1869, in Holland and Gordon, *Papers of Elizabeth Cady Stanton and Susan B. Anthony.*

117 "Workingwomen's Association," May 20, 1869.

118 "Workingwomen's Association," May 20, 1869.

Chapter Six

THE CREATION OF THE MASSACHUSETTS INFANT ASYLUM

1 F. B. Sanborn to Editors of the *Revolution*, Apr. 11, 1868, in P.P., "Foundling Hospitals Again," *The Revolution* (New York), Apr. 30, 1868.

2 P.P., "Foundling Hospitals," *The Revolution* (New York), Mar. 26, 1868.

3 P.P., "Foundling Hospitals," Mar. 26, 1868.

4 F. B. Sanborn, "First Annual Report of the Secretary of the Board of State Charities," *First Annual Report of the Board of State Charities* (Boston, Wright & Potter, 1865), 264.

5 P.P., "Foundling Hospitals," Mar. 26, 1868.

6 Before becoming the secretary of the MBSC, Sanborn had taught school in Concord for eight years at Ralph Waldo Emerson's behest, written for the *Springfield Republican*, and been editor of the *Boston Commonwealth*. [Thomas L. Haskell, *The Emergence of Professional Social Science: The American Social Science Association and the Nineteenth-Century Crisis of Authority* (Urban, IL: University of Illinois Press, 1977), 52–55.] The other members of the "Secret Six" were Samuel Gridley Howe, Theodore Parker, Thomas Wentworth Higginson, George Luther Stearns, and Gerrit Smith.

7 *First Annual Report of the Directors of the Massachusetts Infant Asylum* (Boston: Alfred Mudge & Son, 1868), 24.

8 *First Annual Report*, 26.

9 "Records of the Public Meetings: First Meeting—Infants Home," Volume 1: 1867–1876, Massachusetts Infant Asylum Records, 201.

10 "Records of the Public Meetings," 201–2.

11 F. B. Sanborn to Editors of the *Revolution*, April 11, 1868, in P.P., "Foundling Hospitals Again," *The Revolution* (New York), Apr. 30, 1868.

12 P.P., "Foundling Hospitals Again," *The Revolution* (New York), Apr. 30, 1868.

13 Ednah Dow Cheney, *Reminiscences of Ednah Dow Cheney* (Boston: Lee & Shepard, 1902), 107–9; "Thomas Austin Goddard," *Find a Grave*, Memorial ID: 90347846.

14 "In Memoriam: Miss Matilda Goddard," *Fifteenth Annual Report of the Kindergarten for the Blind, August 31, 1901* (Boston: Press of George H. Ellis, 1902), 203.

15 "New England School of Design for Women," *The Liberator* (Boston, MA), July 25, 1851; "Indigent Females' Relief Association," *The Boston Globe*, Jan. 10, 1873; "Charities," *Boston Post*, Aug. 16, 1875; "The Home for Aged Women," *The Boston Globe*, Jan. 9, 1880.

16 Cheney, *Reminiscences of Ednah Dow Cheney*, 108; "Matilda Goddard," *Find a Grave*, Memorial ID: 124106948.

17 Cheney, *Reminiscences*, 108.

18 "I was, if possible, even more pleased with Mrs. Matilda Goddard

who for 15 years or more has had an Infant's Home, at first, entirely at her own expense and now, she devotes her means and life to it. She is a small elderly woman, with plain dress, gray hair and face worn with care, but she spoke with energy, clear good sense and tender feeling. She gave some of the results of her own experience. She had sent out for adoption more than 700 children. The mortality had been small compared to that in public institutions. The children had been readily adopted. She had followed up their history after adoption as far as possible, and in far the larger number of cases, the homes had proved good ones. She too had understood to keep up the tie between mother and child where it was possible." Anna Cabot Lowell, Feb. 1, 1868, Diary No. 214, Dec. 1867–Feb. 1868, Anna Cabot Lowell diaries, 1818–1894, Ms. N-1512, Massachusetts Historical Society, Boston.

19 Agnes Vietor, ed., *A Woman's Quest: The Life of Marie E. Zakrzewska, M.D.* (New York: D. Appleton and Company, 1924), 279–80. This effort led her to "one of the greatest philanthropists to these little creatures, namely, Miss Matilda Goddard, who had at that time provided good homes for about eight hundred infants, keeping a record as well as an oversight of them all" (Vietor, 280).

20 Transcript of letter from Marie Zakrzewska to Franklin Sanborn, Feb. 9, 1865, Volume 1: 1867–1876, 227–32, Massachusetts Infant Asylum (Jamaica Plain, Boston, Mass.) Records, Massachusetts Historical Society, Boston.

In 2023 dollars, this is approximately $119. This meant that the weekly cost—for eight infants and three adult staff members—would be more $1,300, and the monthly cost would be over $5,000 in current dollars. The operating costs for nine months would have been more than $47,000 in current dollars.

21 Transcript of letter, Feb. 9, 1865, 227, 231.

22 Transcript of letter, Feb. 9, 1865, 227–32.

23 Transcript of letter, Feb. 9, 1865, 228.

24 Transcript of letter, Feb. 9, 1865, 228–29.

25 Julie Miller, "Transatlantic Anxieties: New York's Nineteenth-Century Foundling Asylums and the London Foundling Hospital," *Annales de Démographie Historique* 2, no. 114 (2007): 41.

26 F. B. Sanborn, "Second Annual Report of the Secretary of the Board of State Charities," *Second Annual Report of the Board of State Charities* (Boston: Wright & Potter, 1866), 150; F. B. Sanborn, "Third Annual Report of the Secretary of the Board of State Charities, 1865–6,"

Third Annual Report of the Board of State Charities of Massachusetts (Boston: Wright & Potter, 1867), 205.

Storer and Sewall, as we have seen, both had a close association at the New England Hospital for Women and Children: Storer had resigned that September, and Sewall was now its resident physician.

27 *Fifth Annual Report of the Board of State Charities of Massachusetts* (Boston: Wright and Potter, 1869), xlvi. Sanborn retired as secretary of the Board of State Charities of Massachusetts effective Oct. 31, 1868.

"Foundlings were seen as the embodiments of illicit sexuality and also, seemingly, were evidence of an explicit rejection of maternal values. For reformers, to whom the sexuality of abandoning mothers loomed larger than their poverty, the foundling was the hidden made visible, and, as such, was both symptom and symbol of the moral, cultural, and physical decay this group of leaders associated with the big cities." Julie Miller, *Abandoned: Foundlings in Nineteenth-Century New York City* (New York: New York University Press, 2008), 10.

28 Miller, "Transatlantic Anxieties," 37–58.

29 *First Annual Report of the Directors of the Massachusetts Infant Asylum*, 30.

30 *First Annual Report*, 17. Another twenty-five children were listed as "otherwise removed" or as having died.

31 "Records of the Public Meetings: First Meeting—Infants Home," Volume 1: 1867–1876, Massachusetts Infant Asylum Records, 200.

32 Sanborn, "Third Annual Report of the Secretary of the Board of State Charities, 1865–6," 206.

33 Sanborn, "Third Annual Report," 206.

It is worth noting that, unlike the anti-cruelty campaigners, those who worked against abortion and other causes of infant mortality with the motivation of protecting young life seem to have done so simply on the basis of shared humanity, rather than with specific references to infants' helplessness. Perhaps this was due to their abolitionist background. See Susan J. Pearson, *The Rights of the Defenseless: Protecting Animals and Children in Gilded Age America* (Chicago: University of Chicago Press, 2011), 23.

34 F. B. Sanborn, "Fifth Annual Report of the Secretary of the Board of State Charities, 1867–8," *Fifth Annual Report of the Board of State Charities of Massachusetts* (Boston: Wright and Potter, 1869), 62–63.

35 Sanborn, "Fifth Annual Report," 63.

36 "Questions in Regard to Foundling and Deserted Infants," Volume 1: 1867–1876, Massachusetts Infant Asylum Records, 209–12.

37 "Records of the Public Meetings: First Meeting—Infants Home," Volume 1: 1867–1876, Massachusetts Infant Asylum Records, 198.

38 Julie Miller, "The Murder of the Innocents: Foundlings in 19th-Century New York City," *Prospects: An Annual of American Cultural Studies* 30 (2005), 275–76.

"Baby farmers" were individuals who supported themselves by taking care of numerous infants for pay. Miller notes that "baby farmers, whether they took in almshouse foundlings or the young children of poor, working mothers, developed an unsavory reputation in both English and American cities by the 1850s. These women were often accused of neglecting the children they were paid to care for, or even of making unwanted infants disappear through underground adoptions or fatal neglect" (Miller, *Abandoned*, 67).

39 "Records of the Public Meetings: First Meeting—Infants Home," Volume 1: 1867–1876, Massachusetts Infant Asylum Records, 201–2.

40 "Records of the Public Meetings: Second Meeting—Infants Home, March 15, 1867," Volume 1: 1867–1876, Massachusetts Infant Asylum Records, 201–2. The committee members listed were Frank Sanborn, Mr. Donahoe (possibly Mr. Donnelly?), Ednah Cheney, Lucy Goddard, and Lucy Sewall.

41 "Records of the Public Meetings: Third Meeting on 'Infants Home,' March 27, 1867," Volume 1: 1867–1876, Massachusetts Infant Asylum Records, 201–2. Mrs. Dr. Bowditch, Mrs. John Phelps Putnam, Miss Anna C. Lowell, Hon. Samuel E. Sewall, Mrs. Augustus Hemmenway [sic], Mr. Charles F. Donnelly, and Rev. John Parkman were chosen as incorporators.

42 Volume 1: 1867–1876, Massachusetts Infant Asylum Records, 212.

43 Morse Stewart, ed., *Memorial of Mrs. Morse Stewart* (privately printed, 1889), 12, 13, 16. Her husband, Dr. Morse Stewart, was also an outspoken opponent of abortion; see, for example, Morse Stewart, "Criminal Abortion," *Detroit Review of Medicine and Pharmacy* 2, no. 1 (January 1867): 1–11.

44 Volume 1: 1867–1876, Massachusetts Infant Asylum Records, 224.

45 Volume 1: 1867–1876, Massachusetts Infant Asylum Records, 212–13.

46 Volume 1: 1867–1876, Massachusetts Infant Asylum Records, 216. These are impressively low numbers for this time period.

47 Susan J. Pearson describes how "anticruelty organizations expanded state power through private means" (Pearson, *Rights of the Defenseless*, 3). While the focus of her book is later than the events covered

in this book, this episode demonstrates a similar dynamic at work in this early public-private partnership.

48 Volume 1: 1867–1876, Massachusetts Infant Asylum Records, 223–24.

49 Miller, *Abandoned*, 3.

50 Volume 1: 1867–1876, Massachusetts Infant Asylum Records, 235.

51 Marie E. Zakrzewska, "Report of the Attending Physician," *Annual Report of the New England Hospital for Women and Children, No. 14, Warren Street, for the Year Ending Nov. 14, 1865* (Boston: Prentiss & Deland, 1865), 13.

52 "Lives have thus been saved which otherwise would have certainly been lost," Zakrzewska wrote in the 1868 NEHWC *Annual Report*, describing the impoverished patients seen by the hospital who might die without the care that they were offered. "Whether the lives of such poor creatures are worth saving, as has been questioned, is not for us to decide; nor ought this to be the spirit of our enlightened age, when, nineteen hundred years ago, not one would come forward to cast the first stone at the unfortunate." She described the issue of caring for unwed mothers similarly: "A woman in labor must be taken care of" [Marie Zakrzewska, "Report of the Attending Physician," *Annual Report of the New England Hospital for Women and Children, No. 14, Warrenton Street, for the Year Ending Nov. 1, 1868* (Boston: Prentiss & Deland, 1868), 11].

53 Marie Zakrzewska, "Report of the Attending Physician," *Annual Report of the New England Hospital for Women and Children, No. 14, Warrenton Street, for the Year Ending Nov. 1, 1868*, 11–12.

54 F. B. Sanborn, "Second Annual Report of the Secretary of the Board of State Charities," *Second Annual Report of the Board of State Charities* (Boston: Wright & Potter, 1866), 150.

55 "Historical Timeline," Massachusetts Society for the Prevention of Cruelty to Animals—Angell Animal Medical Center (Boston, MA); "History," Massachusetts Society for the Prevention of Cruelty to Children (Lexington, MA).

56 James Turner, *Reckoning with the Beast: Animals, Pain, and Humanity in the Victorian Mind* (Baltimore: Johns Hopkins University Press, 1980), 34–35.

57 Turner, *Reckoning with the Beast*, 35.

58 *First Annual Report of the Directors of the Massachusetts Infant Asylum*, 26.

59 Horatio R. Storer and Franklin Fiske Heard, *Criminal Abortion: Its Nature, Its Evidence, and Its Law* (Boston: Little, Brown, and Com-

pany, 1868), 142n. Storer's section of this book contained many of his "Contributions to Obstetric Jurisprudence" articles. In referring to what would become the Massachusetts Infant Asylum, Storer failed to note his involvement in its creation or that he had served as one of the institution's incorporators.

60 "Records of the Public Meetings: First Meeting—Infants Home," Volume 1: 1867–1876, Massachusetts Infant Asylum Records, 201–2.

61 Horatio R. Storer, *On Criminal Abortion in America* (Philadelphia: J. B. Lippincott & Co., 1860), 95.

62 Storer, *On Criminal Abortion in America*, 96.

63 Volume 1: 1867–1876, Massachusetts Infant Asylum Records, 222.

64 Volume 1: 1867–1876, Massachusetts Infant Asylum Records, 235.

65 *Fifth Annual Report of the Board of State Charities of Massachusetts* (Boston: Wright & Potter, 1869), 68–69.

66 "First Monthly Meeting of the Directors," Volume 1: 1867–1876, Massachusetts Infant Asylum Records, 11; Thaddeus J. Butler, *The Catholic Church in America: A Lecture Delivered Before the Literary, Historical, and Aesthetical Society in the Catholic University of Scotland* (Dublin: W. B. Kelly, 1869), 31.

67 Anna Cabot Lowell, Nov. 15, 1867, Anna Cabot Lowell diaries, Diary No. 213, Oct.–Dec. 1867.

68 The Massachusetts State Census for 1865 shows Rebecca A. Lowell, age 70, Anna C. Lowell, 57, and two servants living together in Roxbury, MA. (Massachusetts, 1855–1865 Massachusetts State Census, microform, New England Historic Genealogical Society, Boston.)

69 James Jackson Putnam, *A Memoir of Dr. James Jackson* (Boston: Houghton, Mifflin and Company, 1903), 354–55, 375; Lowell Family Papers (1728–1878), Guide to the Collection, Ms. N-1513, Massachusetts Historical Society, Boston.

70 Lowell, Nov. 15, 1867, Diary No. 213.

71 Lowell, Nov. 15, 1867, Diary No. 213.

72 Lowell, Nov. 16, 1867, Diary No. 213.

73 "Second Monthly Meeting of the Directors," Volume 1: 1867–1876, Massachusetts Infant Asylum Records, 16; "Fifth Monthly Meeting of the Directors," Volume 1: 1867–1876, Massachusetts Infant Asylum Records, 26.

74 "Second Monthly Meeting of the Directors," Volume 1: 1867–1876, Massachusetts Infant Asylum Records, 17.

75 Fanny Hooper was born on Sept. 24, 1844. "Fanny Hudson Chapin," Town and City Clerks of Massachusetts, Massachusetts Vital and Town Records. Provo, UT: Holbrook Research Institute (Jay and Delene Holbrook).

76 Fanny Chapin and Edward Hooper were married on July 6, 1864 by James Freeman Clarke. "Edward W. Hooper and Fanny H. Chapin," No. 1369, Town and City Clerks of Massachusetts. Massachusetts Vital and Town Records, Provo, UT: Holbrook Research Institute (Jay and Delene Holbrook).

77 Fanny Chapin Hooper to Lilian Freeman Clarke, Boston, June 19, 1864; New York, July 30, 1864; New York, Aug. 1864; New York, Oct. 4, 1864; New York, Nov. 10, 1864; New York, Nov. 20, 1864; New York, Jan. 5, 1865, Box 2, Sturgis-Hooper family papers, 1785–1944, bulk: 1820–1909, Ms. N-2411, Massachusetts Historical Society, Boston.

78 Fanny Chapin Hooper to Lilian Freeman Clarke, Brookline, May 14, 1866, Box 2, Sturgis-Hooper family papers.

79 Fanny Chapin Hooper to "Aunt Emma," n.d., Box 2, Sturgis-Hooper family papers.

80 *First Annual Report of the Directors of the Massachusetts Infant Asylum*, 2.

81 "Local Matters," *Boston Daily Advertiser*, Mar. 27, 1867.

82 Hannah Stevenson was an abolitionist, a friend of Theodore Parker, and heavily involved in charitable work in Boston and elsewhere.

83 Anna Cabot Lowell, Jan. 20, 1868, Anna Cabot Lowell diaries, Diary No. 214, Dec. 1867–Feb. 1868.

84 Horatio Storer, "Female Physicians," *The Boston Medical and Surgical Journal*, 75 (1866): 191–92.

85 Lowell, Jan. 20, 1868, Diary No. 214.

86 Lowell, Jan. 20, 1868, Diary No. 214.

87 Lowell, Jan. 20, 1868, Diary No. 214.

88 Aileen Marcia Tuchman, *Science Has No Sex: The Life of Marie Zakrzewska, M.D.* (Chapel Hill: The University of North Carolina Press, 2006), 81.

89 Tuchman, *Science Has No Sex*, 201.

Women's rights advocates were on both sides of the arguments over professionalizing medicine, and it wasn't a central issue to women's rights work, but a serious social issue that they were entangled in on various occasions.

90 Ednah D. Cheney, "Report," *Annual Report of the New England Hospital for Women and Children, No. 14, Warren Street, for the Year Ending Nov. 1, 1867* (Boston: Prentiss & Deland, 1867), 6.

91 Sewall had a particular interest in the success of the MIA; as Sanborn had discovered the previous year, she had personally been paying the board of a baby born and orphaned at the NEHWC. Sanborn, "Third Annual Report of the Secretary of the Board of State Charities, 1865–6," 205.

92 *First Annual Report of the Directors of the Massachusetts Infant Asylum*, 2.

93 Elizabeth Clapp, "Extracts from the Matron's Report to the Directors," *First Annual Report of the Directors of the Massachusetts Infant Asylum*, 33.

At their fifth monthly meeting on Feb. 24, 1868, the MIA's directors had voted that "a competent matron having been appointed by the Board of Directors, to her shall be committed all the duties which naturally belong to the mother of a family; that in the care of the children's health she shall follow the advice of the appointed physicians of the Asylum; that all domestic arrangements shall be intrusted [sic] to her, subject to the sanctions of the Visitor of the Month, and of the Board of Directors at this monthly meeting." Volume 1: 1867–1876, Massachusetts Infant Records, 25.

The MIA's first annual meeting was held just over a month after its opening. Frank Sanborn was commissioned to write the annual report, which resulted in its being more than forty pages long. The report was a hopeful one, stating that the MIA had "secured a convenient location and building, an excellent matron, competent physicians and nurses, and a fund sufficient for present uses." The 82 life members, 204 members (annual subscribers at a rate of $3 or more), 18 "helpers" (subscribers at a rate less than $3), and 208 donors listed in the report had together donated approximately $11,400. *First Annual Report of the Directors of the Massachusetts Infant Asylum.*

94 Elizabeth Clapp, "Extracts from the Matron's Report to the Directors," *First Annual Report of the Directors of the Massachusetts Infant Asylum*, 33.

95 Volume 1: 1867–1876, Massachusetts Infant Asylum Records, 215.

96 Volume 1: 1867–1876, Massachusetts Infant Asylum Records, 232.

97 Volume 1: 1867–1876, Massachusetts Infant Asylum Records, 218, 234.

98 Volume 1: 1867–1876, Massachusetts Infant Asylum Records, 222.

99 Eliza B. Dixwell, "Report of the Directors," *Third Annual Report of the Directors of the Massachusetts Infant Asylum* (Boston: Barker, Cotter, & Co., 1870), 17.

100 Dixwell, "Report of the Directors," 16.

101 *First Annual Report of the Directors of the Massachusetts Infant Asylum*, 32, 30.

102 Lucy E. Sewall, "Report of the Attending Physician," *Third Annual Report of the Directors of the Massachusetts Infant Asylum* (Boston: Barker, Cotter & Co., 1870), 9.

103 Ednah D. Cheney, "Report," *Annual Report of the New England Hospital for Women and Children, No. 14, Warren Street, for the Year Ending Nov. 1, 1867*, 8. These descriptions of the consequences of failed abortion attempts point to the fact that poor women seeking to terminate their pregnancies were not seeking abortions from trained doctors—more likely, they attempted an abortion on their own or sought the services of a "quack."

104 M. E. Zakrzewska, "Report of the Attending Physician," *Annual Report of the New England Hospital for Women and Children, No. 14 Warrenton Street, for the Year Ending Nov. 1, 1868*, 14.

105 *First Annual Report of the Directors of the Massachusetts Infant Asylum*, 25 (emphasis added).

106 Frank Sanborn, "Preservation of Infant Life," *Journal of Social Science: Containing the Transactions of the American Association* 1, no. 1 (Boston: J. H. Eastburn's Press, 1869), 157.

107 M. E. Zakrzewska, "Report of the Attending Physician," *Annual Report of the New England Hospital for Women and Children, No. 14 Warrenton Street, for the Year Ending Nov. 1, 1868*, 10.

108 Lucy E. Sewall, "Report of the Attending Physician," *Third Annual Report of the Directors of the Massachusetts Infant Asylum* (Boston: Barker, Cotter & Co., 1870), 9.

109 Marie E. Zakrzewska, "Report of the Attending Physician," *Annual Report of the New England Hospital for Women and Children, No. 14, Warren Street, for the Year Ending Nov. 14, 1865*, 14–15.

110 L. E. Sewall, "Report of the Resident Physician," *Annual Report of the New England Hospital for Women and Children, No. 14, Warren Street, for the Year Ending Nov. 1, 1866* (Boston: Prentiss & Deland, 1866), 15.

111 Hyperemesis gravidarum is frequently understood as an extreme form of morning sickness. "The condition is defined as uncontrolled vomiting requiring hospitalization, severe dehydration, muscle wasting, electrolyte imbalance, ketonuria, and weight loss of more than 5% of body weight.... If not appropriately treated, it may cause severe adverse effects, including neurologic disturbances, such as Wernicke

encephalopathy, central pontine myelinolysis, and even maternal death." Lindsey J. Wegrzyniak, John T. Repke, and Serdar H. Ural, "Treatment of Hyperemesis Gravidarum," *Reviews in Obstetrics & Gynecology* 5, no. 2 (2012): 78–84.

112 C. A. Buckel, "Report of the Resident Physician," *Annual Report of the New England Hospital for Women and Children, No. 14, Warrenton Street, for the Year Ending Nov. 1, 1870* (Boston: Prentiss & Deland, 1870), 14.

113 Sanborn, "Third Annual Report of the Secretary of the Board of State Charities, 1865–6," 205.

114 Mary R. Parkman, "Directors' Report," *Twenty-Fourth Annual Report of the Directors of the Massachusetts Infant Asylum* (Boston: Thomas Todd, 1891), 9.

115 "Local Matters," *Boston Daily Advertiser*, Mar. 27, 1867.

116 Parkman, "Directors' Report," 9.

117 F. B. Sanborn, "An Experience of Thirty Years," *Massachusetts Infant Asylum: Thirtieth Annual Report of the Directors* (Cambridge, MA: Riverside Press, 1897), 17.

118 Parkman, "Directors' Report," 13.

Chapter Seven

HELPING DESTITUTE MOTHERS AND INFANTS

1 Lillian Freeman Clarke to Jane Addams, Mar. 6, 1912, Jane Addams Collection (DG 001), Swarthmore College Peace Collection, *Jane Addams Digital Edition*.

2 *Report of The Society for Helping Destitute Mothers and Infants for the Year 1912* (Boston: printed for the Society, 1913), 4.

3 The Massachusetts Adoption of Children Act, passed in 1851, is understood to be the first modern adoption law in the United States. Christine Adamec, "Introduction: A Brief History of Adoption," Christine Adamec and Laurie C. Miller, eds., *The Encyclopedia of Adoption*, 3rd ed., (New York: Facts on File, 2007), xxiv.

On the Charles Loring Brace's Children's Aid Society and the orphan train movement, see Stephen O'Connor, *Orphan Trains: The Story of Charles Loring Brace and the Children He Saved and Failed* (Chicago: University of Chicago Press, 2001).

4 Lillian Freeman Clarke to Jane Addams, Mar. 6, 1912.

5 *Report of Aid Given to Destitute Mothers and Infants, Feb. 1, 1875 to Feb. 1, 1876* (privately printed, Apr. 27, 1876), 4.

6 *Report of Aid Given to Destitute Mothers and Infants, Feb. 1, 1875 to Feb. 1, 1876*, 4.

7 *Report of the Society for Helping Destitute Mothers and Infants for the Year 1912*, 3–4.

8 *Report of Aid Given to Destitute Mothers and Infants, Feb. 1, 1875 to Feb. 1, 1876*, 5.

9 Marie E. Zakrzewska, "Report of the Attending Physician," *Annual Report of the New England Hospital for Women and Children, No. 14, Warren Street, for the Year Ending Nov. 14, 1865* (Boston: Prentiss & Deland, 1865), 13.

10 M. E. Zakrzewska, "Report of the Attending Physician," *Annual Report of the New England Hospital for Women and Children, No. 14, Warrenton Street, for the Year Ending Nov. 14, 1868* (Boston: Prentiss & Deland, 1868), 10.

11 C. A. Buckel, "Report of Resident Physician," *Annual Report of the New England Hospital for Women and Children, No. 14 Warrenton Street, for the Year Ending Sept. 30, 1870* (Boston: Deland & Co., 1870), 14.

12 C. A. Buckel, "Report of Resident Physician," *Annual Report of the New England Hospital for Women and Children, No. 14 Warrenton Street, for the Year Ending Sept. 30, 1871* (Boston: Deland & Co., 1871), 9.

13 C. A. Buckel, "Report of Resident Physician," *Annual Report of the New England Hospital for Women and Children, No. 14 Warrenton Street, for the Year Ending Sept. 30, 1871*, 9.

14 C. A. Buckel, "Report of Resident Physician," *Annual Report of the New England Hospital for Women and Children, No. 14 Warrenton Street, for the Year Ending Sept. 30, 1870*, 14.

15 C. A. Buckel, "Report of Resident Physician," *Annual Report of the New England Hospital for Women and Children, No. 14 Warrenton Street, for the Year Ending Sept. 30, 1871*, 9.

16 Ednah D. Cheney, "Report," *Annual Report of the New England Hospital for Women and Children, Codman Avenue, Boston Highlands, for the Year Ending September 30, 1872* (Boston, Press of W. L. Deland, 1873), 8.

17 *Memoir of Susan Dimock: Resident Physician of the New England Hospital for Women and Children* (Cambridge: Press of John Wilson & Son, 1875), 10, 12.

18 *Memoir of Susan Dimock*, 11–14.

19 "Susan Dimock (1847–1875)," University of North Carolina Wilson Library Special Collections.

20 Lilian Freeman Clarke, "The Story of an Invisible Institution," *The Outlook* 84 (Dec. 15, 1906): 933.

21 The first trained nurse in the United States graduated from her program the following year. Michael Reiskind, "Hospital Founded by Women for Women," Jamaica Plain Historical Society (Jamaica Plain, MA).

22 Mary Putnam Jacobi, "Dr. Susan Dimock," *Medical Record*, May 25, 1875, published in *Memoir of Susan Dimock*, 88.

23 Susan Dimock letter to Samuel Cabot, October 9, 1873, Boston, New England Hospital Records, Series II, Personnel: Physicians: Susan Dimock, 1868–73, n.d., Smith College Sophia Smith Collection.

24 Susan Dimock, "Resident Physician's Report," *Annual Report of the New England Hospital for Women and Children, Codman Avenue, Boston Highlands, for the year ending September 30, 1873* (Boston: Press of W. L. Deland, 1874), 11.

25 Susan Dimock, "Resident Physician's Report," 12.

26 Susan Dimock, quoted in *Memoir of Susan Dimock*, 37–38.

27 Clarke, "Story of an Invisible Institution," 933.

28 Clarke, "Story of an Invisible Institution," 933; Susan Dimock, "Report of Resident Physician," *Annual Report of the New England Hospital for Women and Children, Codman Avenue, Boston Highlands, for the year ending September 30, 1874* (Boston: Press of W. L. Deland, 1875), 14.

29 "Perry-Clarke Collection, 1588–1924; bulk: 1761–1923, Guide to the Collection," Ms. N-2155, Massachusetts Historical Society, Boston.

30 Elizabeth Addison, "Families and Friendship," in *The Oxford Handbook of Transcendentalism*, ed. Joel Myerson, Sandra Harbert Petrulionis, and Laura Dassow Walls (New York: Oxford University Press, 2010), 530; *General Catalogue of the Divinity School of Harvard University*, 1898 (Cambridge: published by the University), 26; Charles K. Dillaway, "Education, Past and Present, The Rise of Free Education and Educational Institutions," in *The Memorial History of Boston, Including Suffolk County, Massachusetts, 1630–1880*, Vol. 4, ed. Justin Winsor (Boston: James R. Osgood and Company, 1881), 253.

31 Clarke's uncle was married to Hooper's aunt. "Perry-Clarke Collection, 1588–1924; bulk: 1761–1923, Guide to the Collection," Ms. N-2155, Massachusetts Historical Society, Boston; "First Monthly

Meeting of the Directors," Volume 1: 1867–1876, 11, Massachusetts Infant Asylum (Jamaica Plain, Boston, Mass.) Records, Massachusetts Historical Society, Boston.

32 Ida Husted Harper, ed., *The History of Woman Suffrage*, Vol. 6 (New York: J. J. Little & Ives, 1922), 291n; *Animal Rescue League Ninth Annual Report* (Boston: 1908), 56; "Lilian Freeman Clarke," *The Christian Register* 100, no. 47 (Nov. 24, 1921), 18; Scott W. Alexander, ed., *Salted with Fire: Unitarian Universalist Strategies for Sharing Faith and Growing Congregations* (Boston: Skinner House Books, 1994), 56; "Cheerful Letter Exchange," *Cambridge Tribune* (Cambridge, MA), Apr. 5, 1986.

33 Clarke, "Story of an Invisible Institution," 934.

34 Susan Dimock, "Report of Resident Physician," 14.

35 The appeal is undated, but the expenditure reports it contains are for May 1, 1874–Jan. 1, 1875, and Jan. 1, 1875–Feb. 1, 1875, which suggests that the report was published in or near March 1875.

36 *An Appeal in Behalf of Destitute Mothers and Infants* (privately printed, 1874), 1.

37 *An Appeal*, 3.

38 *An Appeal*, 3.

39 *An Appeal*, 3–4.

40 *An Appeal*, 4.

41 *An Appeal*, 4.

42 *An Appeal*, 3.

43 *An Appeal*, 2.

44 *Report of Aid Given to Destitute Mothers and Infants* (privately printed, 1876), 6.

45 Charles P. Putnam, "Letter from Dr. Putnam," *An Appeal in Behalf of Destitute Mothers and Infants*, 6. Putnam would go on to become a founding member of the American Association for Study and Prevention of Infant Mortality. *Transactions of the First Annual Meeting of the American Association for Study and Prevention of Infant Mortality* (privately printed, 1910), 3.

46 Putnam, "Letter from Dr. Putnam," 6.

47 *Report of Aid*, 7.

48 *An Appeal*, 4–5.

49 *Memoir of Susan Dimock*, 42.

50 Marie E. Zakrzewska, "In Memoriam," *Memoir of Susan Dimock*, 83.

51 "Remarks of James Freeman Clarke at the Services Held at the Church of the Disciples, June 4, in Memory of Dr. Susan Dimock," *Memoir of Susan Dimock*, 96.

52 "Remarks of James Freeman Clarke," 98.

53 *Memoir of Susan Dimock*, 100.

54 *Memoir of Susan Dimock*, 103.

55 Ednah D. Cheney, "Report of the Secretary," *Annual Report of the New-England Hospital for Women and Children, Codman Avenue, Boston Highlands, for the Year Ending Sept. 30, 1875*, Second Edition (Boston: Press of W. L. Deland, 1876), 9.

56 Clarke, "Story of an Invisible Institution," 933.

57 For many years, however, the women involved in this project denied that they were an organization altogether—for instance, the 1894 annual report listed as the first principle of their work, "We are not a society. Our active working force consists of three persons, who give it the larger part of their time." *Report of Aid Given to Destitute Mothers and Infants in 1894* (privately printed, 1894), 3.

58 *Report of Aid Given to Destitute Mothers and Infants, Feb. 1, 1875 to Feb. 1, 1876*, 6.

59 *Report of Aid Given to Destitute Mothers and Infants, May 1, 1874 to Feb. 1, 1875* (privately printed, 1875), 1–2.

60 *Report of Aid, May 1, 1874 to Feb. 1, 1875*, 1–4.

61 *Report of Aid, May 1, 1874 to Feb. 1, 1875*, 4.

62 *Report of Aid, May 1, 1874 to Feb. 1, 1875*, 4.

63 *Report of Aid, May 1, 1874 to Feb. 1, 1875*, 4.

64 *Report of Aid, May 1, 1874 to Feb. 1, 1875*, 5.

65 Clarke, "Story of an Invisible Institution," 935.

66 *Report of Aid, May 1, 1874 to Feb. 1, 1875*, 4.

67 *Report of Aid, May 1, 1874 to Feb. 1, 1875*, 4.

68 *Report of Aid, May 1, 1874 to Feb. 1, 1875*, 5.

69 *Report of Aid Given to Destitute Mothers and Infants in 1882* (privately printed), 12.

70 *Report of Aid, May 1, 1874 to Feb. 1, 1875*, 5. More than a decade later,

the SHDMI began including excerpts of letters from the women it assisted in its annual reports.

71 *Report of Aid Given to Destitute Mothers and Infants in 1904* (privately printed), 2.

72 Margaret C. Magrath, "Report," *Report of the Society for Helping Destitute Mothers and Infants for the Year 1905* (Boston: printed for the Society, 1906), 6.

73 *Report of the Society for Helping Destitute Mothers and Infants for the Year 1908*, 5–6.

74 *Report of the Society for Helping Destitute Mothers and Infants for the Year 1909* (Boston: printed for the Society, 1910), 5.

75 *Report of the Society for Helping Destitute Mothers and Infants for the Year 1909* (Boston: printed for the Society, 1910), 7.

76 Because this process would also benefit the woman's child, the SHDMI insisted, "It is sometimes said that in the interest of the mother we sacrifice the welfare of the child," but that "this is a mistake. The two things must go together." *Report of the Society for Helping Destitute Mothers and Infants for the Year 1910* (Boston: printed for the Society, 1911), 6.

77 Haskell, *The Emergence of Professional Social Science*, 254–55.

78 *Report of the Society for Helping Destitute Mothers and Infants for the Year 1910* (Boston: printed for the Society, 1911), 5.

79 *Report of the Society for Helping Destitute Mothers and Infants for the Year 1911* (Boston: printed for the Society, 1912), 6.

80 *Report of the Society for Helping Destitute Mothers and Infants for the Year 1912* (Boston: printed for the Society, 1913), 6.

81 *Report of the Society for Helping Destitute Mothers and Infants for the Year 1911* (Boston: printed for the Society, 1912), 5, 7, 21.

82 *Report of the Society for Helping Destitute Mothers and Infants for the Year 1912* (Boston: printed for the Society, 1913), 5.

83 *Report of the Society for Helping Destitute Mothers and Infants for the Year 1912* (Boston: printed for the Society, 1913), 6.

84 Haskell, *The Emergence of Professional Social Science*, 225.

85 "Objects and Methods of Our Work," *Report of the Society for Helping Destitute Mothers and Infants for the Year 1908* (Boston: printed for the Society, 1909), 4.

86 E. M. Locke, "Report of the Executive Secretary," *Final Report of the*

Society for Helping Destitute Mothers and Infants, 28. Emphasis added.

87 Harry H. Laughlin, *Eugenics Record Office Bulletin No. 10A: Report of the Committee to Study and to Report on the Best Practical Means of Cutting Off the Defective Germ-Plasm in the American Population. I. The Scope of the Committee's Work* (Cold Spring Harbor, NY: Eugenics Record Office, Feb. 1914), 16.

88 Laughlin, *Eugenics Record Office Bulletin No. 10A*, 16.

89 Laughlin, *Eugenics Record Office Bulletin No. 10A*, 6.

90 Laughlin, *Eugenics Record Office Bulletin No. 10A*, 15.

91 *Report of the Society for Helping Destitute Mothers and Infants for the Year Ending 1913* (Boston, printed for the Society, 1914), 9.

92 Louisa Dresel, "Report of the Secretary," *Final Report of the Society for Helping Destitute Mothers and Infants*, 5.

93 Of the remaining 366 children, 74 were known to have died, 49 had become "public dependents," 43 were "in the care of child-helping agencies," 29 had been adopted, 4 were in "free homes," 68 were known to be in other states or countries but little else was known about then, and the fate of the remaining 99 was unknown. (E. M. Locke, "Report of the Executive Secretary," *Final Report of the Society for Helping Destitute Mothers and Infants*, 19, 20, 32.)

94 Ada E. Sheffield, fundraising insert, *Report of the Society for Helping Destitute Mothers and Infants for the Year 1914–15* (Boston: printed for the Society, 1916).

95 E. M. Locke, "Report of the Executive Secretary," *Final Report of the Society for Helping Destitute Mothers and Infants*, 32.

96 *Report of the Society for Helping Destitute Mothers and Infants for the Year 1914–15*, 4.

97 Lilian Freeman Clarke, "Report of the Secretary," *Report of the Society for Helping Destitute Mothers and Infants for the Year 1914–15*, 7.
An "alienist" is a psychiatrist. ("alienist," *Merriam-Webster.com*.)

98 E. M. Locke, "Report of the Agent," *Report of the Society for Helping Destitute Mothers and Infants for the Year 1914–15*, 10–11.

99 Lilian Freeman Clarke, "Report of the Secretary," *Report of the Society for Helping Destitute Mothers and Infants for the Year 1914–15*, 8–9.

100 Locke, "Report of the Agent, 13.

101 *Report of Aid Given to Destitute Mothers and Infants, May 1, 1874 to Feb. 1, 1875*, 6.

102 *Report of the Society for Helping Destitute Mothers and Infants for the Year 1916–17* (Boston: printed for the Society, 1918), 5.

103 *Final Report of the Society for Helping Destitute Mothers and Infants*, 3–4.

104 *Final Report of the Society*, 6.

105 *Final Report of the Society*, 7.

106 *Final Report of the Society*, 8.

107 Clarke, "Story of an Invisible Institution," 935.

108 Clarke, "Story of an Invisible Institution," 935.

Chapter Eight

LOSING SIGHT OF WOMEN AND CHILDREN

1 Thomas L. Haskell, *The Emergence of Professional Social Science: The American Social Science Association and the Nineteenth-Century Crisis of Authority* (Urban, IL: University of Illinois Press, 1977), 1.

2 Lilian Freeman Clarke, "The Story of an Invisible Institution," *The Outlook* 84 (Dec. 15, 1906): 933; *Final Report of the Society for Helping Destitute Mothers and Infants, Including a Study of the Records of the Society of Five Hundred Cases and Annual Report for the Year 1917–18* (Boston: printed for the Society, 1919), 8.

3 "The Evil of the Age," *The New York Times*, Aug. 23, 1871.

4 "Sketch of the Prisoner Rosenzweig, Alias Ascher," *The New York Times*, Aug. 29, 1871.

5 "Judge Bedford, of New York, on Abortion," *Evening Star* (Washington, DC), Sept. 6, 1871. It isn't clear in the text of this article who, in Bedford's proposal, could be convicted of the crime of abortion. Yet the broader context of this case would suggest that practitioners of abortion, not the women who sought them out, were the intended targets of the proposed law.

6 "Judge Bedford, of New York, on Abortion," *Evening Star* (Washington, DC), Sept. 6, 1871.

7 "The Malpractice Murders—Judge Bedford's Charge," *New York Herald*, Sept. 7, 1871.

8 "The Abortionists," *The Idaho World*, Sept. 21, 1871.

9 "Remodeling the Medical Law," *New-York Tribune*, Nov. 13, 1871.

10 "Criminal Abortions: Another Medical Society Appealing to the

Legislature for Reform," *New-York Tribune*, Jan. 4, 1871.

11 "A Social Reform," *The New York Times*, Jan. 12, 1872.

12 "Unpunished Boston Criminals: The Nefarious Practice of Abortion Unchecked," *Boston Daily Globe*, Aug. 31, 1874.

13 "Evil of the Age," Aug. 23, 1871.

14 "Medical Murders: No Need of Risking a Trunk Murder," *New-York Tribune*, Sept. 7, 1871.

15 *Detroit Free Press*, published in "A Medical Martyr: A Michigan Physician Shot for Refusing to Commit an Abortion," *New Orleans Republican*, Aug. 18, 1872.

16 "Newspaper Responsibility," *The Revolution* (New York), Sept. 28, 1871.

17 "The Pulpit and the Social Evil," *The Woman's Journal* (Boston), Sept. 13, 1871; Mariana, "Good Society," *Woodhull & Claflin's Weekly*, Sept. 23, 1871.

A key difference between abortion coverage in *The Revolution* and *Women's Journal* can be seen in an 1872 editorial by the latter which argued that "there is no more dangerous enemy of public morals than a man who grossly exaggerates social crimes and misfortunes, for the purpose of creating a sensation." "A Defamer of Women," *The Woman's Journal* (Boston), Nov. 23, 1872.

18 Sarah F. Norton, "Tragedy—Social and Domestic," *Woodhull & Claflin's Weekly* (New York), Nov. 19, 1870.

19 Norton, "Tragedy," Nov. 19, 1870.

20 Norton, "Tragedy," Nov. 19, 1870.

21 Woodhull referred to this article in the December 2, 1871, issue of the *Weekly*, stating that "whoever has read the WEEKLY knows I hold abortion (except to save the life of the mother) to be just as much murder as the killing of a person after birth is murder. This was made the subject of a special editorial in the number of date August 8, 1870, entitled 'When Is It Not Murder to Take Life?'" "Letter from Victoria C. Woodhull," *Woodhull & Claflin's Weekly* (New York), Dec. 2, 1871.

22 "The Slaughter of the Innocents," *Woodhull & Claflin's Weekly* (New York), June 20, 1874.

23 "What Will Become of the Children," *Woodhull & Claflin's Weekly* (New York), Jan. 24, 1874; "The Slaughter of the Innocents," *Woodhull & Claflin's Weekly* (New York), June 20, 1874.

24 Sada Bailey, "A Reply to Warren Harris," *Woodhull & Claflin's Weekly* (New York), May 31, 1873; "Babydom," *Woodhull & Claflin's Weekly* (New York), Oct. 11, 1873.

25 "The Slaughter of the Innocents," *Woodhull & Claflin's Weekly* (New York), June 20, 1874.

26 Tennie Claflin, "My Word on Abortion, and Other Things," *Woodhull & Claflin's Weekly* (New York), Sept. 23, 1871.

27 "When Is It Not Murder to Take Life?" *Woodhull & Claflin's Weekly* (New York), Oct. 8, 1870; "Victoria C. Woodhull in the West: Extracts from the Local Press," *Woodhull & Claflin's Weekly* (New York), Mar. 7, 1874. Emphasis added.

28 "Slaughter of the Innocents," June 20, 1874.

29 "To Lovers of Purity Everywhere," *Woodhull & Claflin's Weekly* (New York), Apr. 26, 1873.

30 "Slaughter of the Innocents," *Woodhull & Claflin's Weekly* (New York), June 20, 1874.

This argument bears certain similarities to the civically oriented ideal of Republican motherhood, but that worldview depended on the idea that conscious moral formation was possible.

31 Tennie Claflin, "My Word on Abortion, and Other Things," *Woodhull & Claflin's Weekly* (New York), Sept. 23, 1871; "Slaughter of the Innocents," *Woodhull & Claflin's Weekly* (New York), June 20, 1874.

32 Comte's "line of evolution" began with a theological stage, which was followed by a metaphysical stage, and culminated in a positivist stage. He categorized enlightenment philosophy and rights theory as part of the metaphysical stage which would be superseded by sociology in the more advanced age. Frederick Copleston, S.J., "Ch. 5: Auguste Comte," *A History of Philosophy, Vol. 9, Maine de Biran to Sartre, Part I, The Revolution to Henry Bergson* (New York: Doubleday, 1977).

33 Victoria C. Woodhull, "The Religion of Humanity: A Speech Delivered Before the American Association of Spiritualists in Boston, Wednesday Evening, Sept. 11, 1872," *Woodhull & Claflin's Weekly* (New York), Nov. 2, 1872.

34 Copleston, *A History of Philosophy*, 114.

35 "Slaughter of the Innocents," June 20, 1874.

36 "Babydom," *Woodhull & Claflin's Weekly* (New York), Oct. 11, 1873.

37 "'Harper's Bazar' on Stirpiculture," *Woodhull & Claflin's Weekly* (New York), Oct. 10, 1874.

38 "Slaughter of the Innocents," June 20, 1874.

39 "A Backward Glance," *Woodhull & Claflin's Weekly* (New York), Feb. 7, 1874.

40 Tennie Claflin, "My Word on Abortion, and Other Things," *Woodhull & Claflin's Weekly* (New York), Sept. 23, 1871.

CONCLUSION

1 Susan B. Anthony, "'Social Purity' (United States, 1875)," in *The Essential Feminist Reader*, ed. Estelle B. Freedman (New York: The Modern Library, 2007), 90.

2 Anthony, "'Social Purity,'" 87. On Anthony's presentation of this lecture in the Midwest, see, for example: "Announcements," *Chicago Tribune* (Chicago, IL), Mar. 10, 1875; "Our Wickedness," *The Daily Commonwealth* (Topeka, KS), Mar. 18, 1875; "Social Purity: Miss Susan B. Anthony's Lecture Last Night at Mercantile Library Hall," *The St. Louis Republican* (St. Louis, MO), Apr. 13, 1875.

Anthony was referring to the thirteen hundred women who reportedly had given their infants to New York's Catholic Foundling Hospital in its first six months. But the reference to the Old Testament figure of Rachel carried at least two valences. In Genesis, Rachel dies in childbirth, making the ultimate sacrifice for her child. Later, she appears in a prophecy in Jeremiah, which was understood to pertain to the Israelites' captivity in Babylon: "Thus says the LORD: 'A voice is heard in Ramah, lamentation and bitter weeping. Rachel is weeping for her children; she refuses to be comforted for her children, because they are not'" (Jeremiah 31:15). This verse is cited in the New Testament in relation to the event referred to as "the murder of the innocents": "Then Herod, when he saw that he had been tricked by the wise men, was in a furious rage, and he sent and killed all the male children in Bethlehem and in all that region who were two years old or under, according to the time which he had ascertained from the wise men. Then was fulfilled what was spoken by the prophet Jeremiah: 'A voice was heard in Ramah, wailing and loud lamentation, Rachel weeping for her children; she refused to be consoled, because they were no more'" (Matthew 2:16-18). Thus, references to the person of Rachel could either refer to the maternal self-sacrifice demonstrated by women forced to abandon their children for lack of familial or social support, or the "murder of the innocents"—infant mortality due to baby farming or other forms of neglect, abortion, and infanticide. Foundling hospitals—the topic that led Anthony to cite Rachel—

linked these two meanings, not by preventing an infant's being lost to its mother, who sacrificed her active motherhood in giving the child away, but by hopefully preventing its untimely death.

3 Alice Carey, Opening speech at first Sorosis meeting, quoted in "Sorosis," *The Revolution* (New York), May 14, 1868.

4 Jan Lewis, "The Republican Wife," 715.

5 Kathryn Kish Sklar, *Women's Rights Emerges Within the Anti-Slavery Movement*, 1830–1870 (London: Palgrave MacMillan, 2000), 30.

6 Anna Cabot Lowell, Nov. 15, 1867, Anna Cabot Lowell diaries, Diary No. 213, Oct.–Dec. 1867; Clarke, "The Story of an Invisible Institution," *The Outlook* 84 (Dec. 15, 1906), 934.

7 Anna Cabot Lowell, Massachusetts Infant Asylum Annual Report, 1872, 9.

8 Lilian Freeman Clarke, "The Story of an Invisible Institution," 933; "Address by the Rev. Frank Russell, of Park Congregational Church, Brooklyn," *In Memoriam: Mrs. Charlotte Denman Lozier, M.D.* (New York: Wynkoop & Allenbeck, 1870), 13.

9 Susan B. Anthony to Anna Dickinson, Oct. 19, 1868, Anna E. Dickinson Papers: General Correspondence, 1859–1911, Anthony, Susan B., 1864–1895, undated, Library of Congress.

10 Anthony to Dickinson, Oct. 19, 1868.

11 H.B.B., "Political Organization," *The Woman's Journal* (Boston, MA), Jan. 8, 1870.

The Woman's Journal didn't wholly avoid questions around abortion and infanticide, but it pointedly treated the issue as a distraction from its mission rather than a support for it. A letter published in the *Journal* criticized another publication for implying that decreasing family sizes were due to abortion: "Every conscientious wife would shrink with horror from so wicked an act, and ought not to suffer for the wrong of her less scrupulous sisters; but all such indiscriminate accusations are little less criminal than the act condemned, since it casts a suspicion upon so many fair reputations." Hester, "Ante-Natal Murder," *The Woman's Journal* (Boston, MA), May 13, 1871.

12 Ellen Carol DuBois, *Feminism and Suffrage: The Emergence of an Independent Women's Movement in America, 1848–1869* (Ithaca, NY: Cornell University Press), 200–1.

INDEX

[illegible]
ptist the 6 teachers, & to leave 25 co
ost as requested. I met Mrs Cheney &
. The former spoke of the Infant Asylu
ne of the Corporators, but had expressly
take any office in it) from Mrs Cheney
one of the directors. I said I did not
aintance now with the subject, or exp
said none had, we must be learn
I thought it was better not to have
ague. She said the Institution w
oxbury: they were now treating for
edar St. They hoped the Roxbury ladies
ted in it. They did not mean to
Directors at present, but only some
felt sure. They have asked Mrs Sar
Ellis from Roxbury, Lilian Clarke,
Ed. Hooper Brookline. Mrs Cheney is
eason did not consent to be a respons
will help by advice &c. I still decli
been thinking since whether I ough
it is to be so needed when I could a
time. It is a sort of thing I dread.
many nice moral & prudential qu
e women whose babies are taken in
t I to shrink from taking my sha
ficulties? We shall make blunders
blamed for it, but we must buy our